HOW WE WERE MADE

Second Edition

HOW WE WERE MADE

A BOOK OF REVELATIONS

William Neil

Oracle Books

This edition published in Great Britain in 2007 by

Oracle Books
PO Box 2467
Reading England RG4 7WU

email oraclebooks@onetel.com

First edition published 2003 (0-9545957-0-X)

Copyright © William Neil 2003

The moral right of the author has been asserted

All rights reserved. No parts of this publication may be reproduced, stored in a retrieval system, or transmitted at any time or by any means electronic, mechanical, photocopying, recording or otherwise, without the prior permission
of the publisher.

British Library Cataloguing-in-Publication Data
A catalogue record for this book is available
from the British Library

Second edition published 2007 ISBN 978-0-9545957-1-5

Original images drawn by the author

Printed and bound in Great Britain by
Antony Rowe Ltd
Bumper's Farm, Chippenham, Wiltshire

To Helen

For listening

CONTENTS

I   JUST A PERFECT NUMBER   1

II   IN THE BEGINNING   11

III   COMING FROM OBSCURITY   25

IV   THE MIGRATION   35

V   DIVINE MEASURES   53

VI   SPECIFICATION EARTH   85

VII   BUILDING AND PLACING THE MOON   121

VIII   AD ASTRA   141

IX   JOURNEYS INTO SPACE   165

X   THE PENTAGON   175

XI   CONSTANTS   189

XII   CONCORDANCE   213

ADDENDUM   243

REFERENCES   245

List of Illustrations

The Model Year of the Ancients	19
The Coded Year	21
The Year is a Right Angle	23
Stonehenge and Earth	42
Woodhenge – Another Model of the Solar System	45
Stonehenge – the locality	46
The Paradigm Human Male (PHM)	59
More PHM Numbers Predicated on 6	60
The Hands and Feet of the PHM	61
Jack in the Box	66
The Ark of Utnapishtim	67
"The Iron Yard of our Lord the King"	70
The Eye of Horus	77
Lord of the Artifact of Life & DNA	82,83,84
The Earth Today	87
And as it Once Was	92
Angle of North Face of Great Pyramid	97
Cross Section of Great Pyramid – Φ	100
Egypt Designed	105
Egypt's Modern & Ancient Border	107
Earth Numbers	114,115
The Earth as a Tetrahedron	119

Statute & Nautical Miles on Earth & Moon	125
The Moon – Pi in the Sky	127
The Hollow Moon	130
The Moon's One Rotation	134
The Partners Dance the Pavan	138
The Coded Twins	139
More of the Coded Twins	140
The Cones of Time	145
The Zodiac	146
Saturn's Mile	167
Earth's Furlong	168
Sun and Stars	169
Kepler's Geometric Solar System	174
The Dodecahedron	177
Triangular Connections	181,182
Acropolis	183
Circular Ratios	187
The Wheels of Time	188
Carbon 60	191
Barometer & Thermometer	194
Quartz and Ice	197
A Typical Snowflake	200
Secrets of the Snowflake	201
Quartz – as an Electrical Component	204
Stonehenge and 666	244

Preface

As a boy, my toys were Meccano, trains sets, old watches, indeed anything mechanical; I even used to take the back off the radio set when my parents were out -- with it switched on! I took several electrical shocks, but my guardian angel was watching over me. My nearest playground was the railway goods yard and I can still hear the clang of shunting wagons and the puffing of steam trains. There was also nearby a radio re-transmission station and the maintenance man would let some of us boys inside while he did his work. The place had a hum to it and a terrific smell of hot valves - heady stuff for a young lad. And indeed I grew up to become a Chartered Engineer (electrical). Engineers are creators and inventors; everything we have in life that makes our existence more comfortable has been made by engineers. Without the Industrial Revolution, which started in 1750 in England, we would still be tilling the soil with horses, and be living in hovels. Engineers have questioning minds, and I'm no exception; consequently my thoughts are nearly always about 'how does that work' or 'how did they make that'. I finally got around to asking myself this question about life itself. Did it just happen, or did the gods (engineers from another planet) create the whole thing? I came up with some startling answers.

Briefly, my findings are that man, time, Earth, moon, planets and some of the stars have been constructed, or placed, according to a set of numbers relating back to the Sumerian base of 60. In fact, an engineering specification. This is *not* numerology, but simply an observation of a collection of facts which, when put together, present a rather startling picture of uniformity. Many of the things around us appear to have been designed to a strict rule of size. I have taken this 60 base and developed it to show that its application goes far beyond Sumer, even to the stars, including the enigmatic number 666 which is the key to unlocking the solution.

This book is not about my opinions, or views, it is quite simply a statement of facts which do not seem to have been noticed before and which indicate a creationist past, not an evolutionary one. This was completely contrary to my long held beliefs when I began this investigation.

The book also discusses the properties of certain physical materials; for example that quartz, which controls everything on Earth that requires timing (eg your wrist watch), is also encoded with the hidden numbers, and how man is similarly timed. It will show that the Earth and moon are related very precisely with the same numbers that encode humans. These same measures are also reflected in the precession of the equinoxes (the zodiac), and out to the planets themselves, and the Sun. These are not guesses or approximations but standard measures available in any atlas of space, or reference book, and as such I merely took the measures from those books.

The correlation between all of these supposedly unconnected bodies, and time itself, is staggering. It also answers a lot of questions about enigmatic numbers from the ancient past in Sumer, India, Egypt, China, the Yucatan and England. A certain amount of ancient numbers were not only huge, but also had very special names attached to them, and as to why they should has always been a puzzle, but not any longer for the answers are here.

I also show that, in addition to the already well known special siting of the Great Pyramid at Giza, that its slope angle is tied very tightly to the Precession of the Equinoxes. and that the land of Egypt itself has been designed according to 666.

As you will see, there are, naturally, a lot of numbers contained here, but none of the arithmetic is beyond what a young person should know. Some of the observations which I put forward here are discoveries in themselves.

I do hope you enjoy looking through it, and that you become as intrigued as I have, at these most astonishing findings.

William Neil
London, 2007

I
JUST A PERFECT NUMBER

Once upon a time, long ago, when only a chosen few could read and write, knowledge was sacred, and was kept hidden from the masses, unlike today where it is shared amongst all. Not only was it concealed but it was further encrypted to prevent its accidental discovery. The information contained data on the cosmos, the solar system and indeed our own origins. The methods used to encode the data included what we now call megalithic ancient monuments, the pyramids, and for some peoples – words. In the case of words each and every one had a numerical code assigned to it and which held its true meaning, but even seeing the numbers of that word was not enough to understand, for that number was only a clue to further meaning. So it was with the ancient Greeks and Hebrews whose priests set the secrets in a hidden language made up entirely of words deliberately constructed to carry the message. So important was this system that it was written into the bible "in the beginning there was the word".

This particular process is called "gematria" and was investigated by William Stirling in his 1897 book "The Canon – An Exposition of the Pagan Mystery Perpetuated in the Cabala as the Rule of All the Arts" (Ref 20); a canon being the law, or rule, or standard by which everything is measured. As late as the ancient Greeks the names of their gods were built by individual letters, so as to contain numbers which were values, or measures, of the sacred knowledge which defined geometrical constructions of the planet, solar system and so on; but only a few were entitled to know this methodology, and that exclusion therefore, eventually led to its total loss. It is this gematrical encoding system that makes much of the bible, and the Greek tales of the exploits of their gods and heroes so inexplicable – the writings only have meaning if the reader knows how to decode them. For example they would create a series of encoded words which held certain data, but these words, on their own, would be impossible to remember, and so they were woven into some fantastic story which would be more easily

HOW WE WERE MADE

recalled. To modern eyes they are simply very odd 'myths'. Stirling attempted to unravel some of these, but the process was and is very complicated.

We do not have their encryption methods anymore, they were lost a long time ago, and so are unable to decipher what the ancients wrote. In this book I will show that the measurements are still there for us to see, without having to try to decode esoteric gematria.

Jumping forward in time, in a well known science fiction comedy, an answer is sought to the question of 'What is the meaning of life, the universe and everything?' A huge computer is constructed to provide an answer, and the solution takes thousands of years to accomplish. The answer turns out to be '42'. And we all laughed. The joke works because we all felt that the answer to such a question would fill a very large book on philosophy, and when, instead, we get '42', it shocks us with its outrageous simplicity, so that we laugh at it.

Incidentally, the number 42 did actually have a meaning in the distant past, and it may have been the case that the writer knew of its ancient lineage. For the Egyptians, 42 was the key to a successful transition to the afterlife with the gods, with whom they would dwell forever.

However, I believe the author could have chosen a more accurate answer to the same question, which is 43.2 - but we'll come to that later. The important thing to note about that fundamental query (which we've all surely asked in great seriousness at some point in our lives), is that the answer may not be a philosophical hypothesis, but a number. It may be that we should be looking at the structure of everything (yes, and life and the universe), via arithmetic and physical measure, rather than pondering the 'why' of existence. There is no philosophy involved in the construction of a triangle; the brutal fact is that it obeys a set of strict equations, and knowing some of the parameters in those equations helps us to seek out and find the remainder. We are already familiar with other numbers which run through the Universe such as pi or 'e', and indeed, a whole list of other number constants that apply in science, and which touch our lives without us ever knowing or caring about them.

I will demonstrate here that there appears to be another coded number system at work, which is inherent in space, time and man. As Stirling says (Ref 20 p. 27) "The first measures are said to have been derived from the body of man", and they apply to almost everything else too.

The observations put forward here are not 'opinions', they are just that - observations, facts. Some have been known for a long time, and the only difference is that I have brought them together, and in doing so, present a picture which should cause any thinking person to stop and wonder. All of the measurements I will show are freely available in any number of publications, and, where appropriate, I have listed these in the reference section.

It will become apparent that the numbers involved are not all modern; some have been known for thousands of years in the ancient civilisations of Sumeria, Egypt, India, China and the Yucatan. A few writers have pointed to some of those 'coincidences'. Modern science has also been able to carry out other measurements that appear to have central consistency with the ancient numbers, but this is not apparent unless one makes a conscious effort to look for pattern. In this way Kepler and Bode sought, and found, a system of mechanics that governs the placing and movement of the bodies in the solar system.

I do appreciate that for a large group of people the mere mention of numbers can be an instant turn-off. So, to make the comparisons a little easier to comprehend, I have kept the arithmetic to an absolute minimum. In this way everything is shown to comply with a guiding code - designed by 'them'. Let me hasten to add that I am not discussing Number Theory, which is a branch of heavy mathematics; nor numerology, which is an offshoot of astrology, nor, as I said above – gematria. The coding used by 'them' is quite straightforward, and involves no more than repeated numbers, and some multiplication, over and over again, the sort of arithmetic we knew by the age of 9.

HOW WE WERE MADE

Coding by numbers is a very old technique for passing messages in cypher so that the enemy does not know what is being conveyed, it only requires that the sender and the receiver know what the key is so that the message may be unlocked at the receiving end. Here is a simple example: supposing the letters of the alphabet are numbered quite easily as; 1 for A, 2 for B, 3 for C, etc. We might send each letter encrypted as a four digit code, which introduces a lot of redundancy to fool anyone who does not know the key. Further, we can stipulate that the four digits must be read in a particular fashion in order to get to the real number, such as adding up all of the digits. Thus, sending 1214, 1211, 4332, 1528, actually might be meant to say $1 + 2 + 1 + 4 = 8$, and so on, to be read as 8,5,12,16, which spells out HELP. But to someone not in on the code the intercepted message looks like a string of random digits - 1214121143321528. A fairly modern example of coding is the now famous WW2 German encryption machine called Enigma. This machine was captured, along with its code book, by the British, and once the key was known it became possible to put it into the machine which then typed out the correct answers to intercepted German communications. The key proved to be a set of numbers which spelled out the correct settings for the machine for a specific period of time.

With the encryption method discussed here the essential rule is that we pay absolutely no attention to the decimal point; the important message being in the actual number string itself, no matter where it occurs. For example, the string of numbers - 2468, may be encoded as 0.0002468, 24,680, 24,680,000, etc. However, they must always be seen as the same number. Additionally, they may also be multiples of themselves such as $2468 \times 2 = 4936$, or $0.02468/2 = 0.01234$; or even a multiplying out of all the digits in the string, as in $2 \times 4 \times 6 \times 8 = 384$. It is that elegant and that basic, all we have to do is look and check. A similar secreting of the real number might, for example, be found in changing miles per hour into feet per second; a speed given to us as 454.1 miles per hour means nothing at all, but when this is tested and translated we see 666 feet per second. These are what I have in mind as hidden codes, and it is these three rules which I have used in my search for the veiled roots of our inscrutable past.

Similarly, in the physical world, a particular crystal will have the same shape whether it is broken down into a small grain, or in a large grown form. Both shapes are identical; it is only the magnitude that differs. A grain of quartz that is fitted into a wristwatch has the same structure as a lump of quartz several inches across.

Another example of repetition is the 'fractal'; a word coined by Benoit Mandelbrot. A fractal is a geometrical shape of identical parts that are in turn identical to the overall pattern. The outline of the complete pattern can be found repeated in miniature within the general pattern itself; and within the miniature version a smaller copy of the pattern can also be found. It is hard to determine the area of a fractal since it dwells within itself on many diverse scales: but, the underlying repeating entity may be determined. This is precisely the same process as the number strings which I described above.

Again, geometry provides further examples of repeatability on different scales; a marble has the same shape, and obeys the same universal constants, as the Earth itself. Gravity is still a mystery however; Sir Isaac Newton who discovered the Law of Universal Gravitation and published it in his book of 1713, the *Principia*, said "I have not been able to discover the cause of those properties of gravity from phenomena, and I frame no hypotheses – to us it is enough that gravity really does exist". And we are no further forward. Likewise, similar triangles, whether they be one inch or one mile across, have identical laws and shapes.

An additional demonstration of numbers retaining their string pattern on different scales, can be seen in logarithms. Take the number string 24.68; the log (short for logarithm) of this number is 1.39236; while the log of 24,680 is 3.39236. The first bit of these logs varies and is called the 'characteristic', here it is 1 and 3, and this indicates the scale or size of the original number. But the decimal part of the log - the 'mantissa' (here it is 0.39236) - never changes, no matter where the decimal point is, in the original number. This is why I can say, as I did above, that 0.0002468 is the same as 24,680,000, but simply on a different scale. Both can also be presented as 2.468×10^{-4} and 2.468×10^{7} respectively.

HOW WE WERE MADE

It can be seen then, that the idea of repeating number patterns, has equivalents in other fields too.

Once I became aware of the consistency of number harmony I began researching areas of the past, which involved numbers and measure, to try to ascertain where they might have cropped up before, and also to examine any connections between different cultures which could reflect this same use of identical systems of number strings. By different cultures I mean not only those separated by geography, but also those distanced by time, such as the modern world compared to ancient Sumer. In addition, I decided to attempt a small study of certain elements of life today, which might hold hidden number strings which could otherwise not actually be immediately visible, and which we never see or ask further about. I was soon to discover much more than I had initially ever dreamed of, and was consistently surprised by coming across what are, in fact, discoveries, unknown, as far as I am aware, until now.

Some, but very few, authors have addressed 'numbers' as fair game for rational discussion and research, in a way that is totally ignored by 'academic' historians and archaeologists who have little choice of breaking out of a rut to follow a not-yet-approved path of research. The 'academics' usually disapprove of alternative opinions, presumably due to the not-invented-here syndrome, which seems to be a rampant virus in their ivory towers. In a way this is understandable, for if their view of the world is proven to be skewed, then all of their learning, all of their teaching, all of their writings and books, are nothing. Such a development would be soul destroying; witness the books by Graham Hancock. These have been met with universal disdain by the establishment, because he talks about subjects such as astronomy, about which archaeologists and historians know nothing. He then discusses their pet subjects from a perspective which they have never dreamed existed. He brings these subjects together and dares to suggest that there is a global uniformity in it all. This is not what academia wants to hear. My own contribution is small in quantity, but it does contain a number of fundamental observations and discoveries of great interest.

There is an exception in the world of 'alternative' writers, resident in the world of academia, and that is the book by Professors De Santillana and Von Dechend, 'Hamlet's Mill', Ref 1. In it, they dare to see evidence of myths and numbers which re-occur time and again across the globe, from the ancient past. Myths, which they argue, contain information from an earlier time concerning cataclysmic events which touched the lives of everyone on Earth, but which are now so heavily degraded by time and message-corruption, as to be almost incomprehensible to modern man - a sort of 'Chinese whispers' record. They also rail against other academics for failing to see what is evident to themselves, for not having the courage to stand up and challenge the status quo, and to ask extreme questions. But these occasions, the 'dare to be radical', usually only occur at the end of an academic career when a reputation is no longer important. Another academic author who has challenged accepted chronology, but on a less revolutionary scale, is D M Rohl in his book 'Legend, The Genesis of Civilisation', Ref 2. In it he explores the chronology of Sumer and Egypt, including the origins of the Egyptians, with some wonderful photographs of rock art in the eastern desert (of Egypt), of what are clearly Viking long boats! In Vol 2 page 134, he writes " I myself have first hand experience of how orthodox scholars treat revolutionary new ideas..... Starve it of the oxygen of publicity.... That way the minimum intellectual energy is expended and nobody puts themselves in the front line..... But enough polemic"!

By its very nature this book seeks to examine an area, which, as far as I am aware, has not been looked at before - the encoding of a multitude of fundamental entities. At the root of this search for hidden codes, is the number and numbers which have been encrypted, and this is the number which first started me on this investigation - the number 6 and its multipliers. This number 6, as you will see from what follows, seems to be everywhere. From ancient Sumer, through to systems of measurements we still use today, it is there.

I should point out that in the world of mathematics, 6 is called a Perfect Number. Until recently there were only 12 such numbers known to exist, but, with the aid of computers, 30 are now known. The first four of these were known to the ancient Greeks. Not only is it perfect, but it is also the first in the Perfect Number series. A Perfect Number is one where the sum of

HOW WE WERE MADE

its divisors is equal to itself (including 1 but not the actual number), so, 1 + 2 + 3 = 6. All Perfect Numbers have the property that the sum of their divisors (including themselves), expressed as fractions, always equals 2, no matter how large the number; for 6 the sum is 1/1 + 1/2 + 1/3 + 1/6 = 2. The Greeks also referred to 6 as one of the 'triangular' numbers, in that 6 dots can be arranged in the shape of an equilateral triangle, whose angles are 60, 60, 60.

I had also long been intrigued by the mysterious number of 666 which is quoted in the bible, twice, and the invitation there to reckon it – (Revelations 13.17) ".... that is, the name of the beast or the number of its name. This calls for wisdom: let him who has understanding reckon the number of the beast, for it is a human number, its number is six hundred and sixty six" The beast has risen from the sea and anyone who accepts its 'number' on the hand or forehead will invoke the wrath of God. The number also appears in 1 Kings 10:14 "Now the weight of gold that came to Solomon in one year was six hundred and sixty-six talents of gold". In the same chapter he also made shields containing 600 shekels of gold, and a throne with 6 steps with 12 lions to guard it, along with 12,000 horsemen.

Now, reckon is another way of saying 'calculate', but how can a number be calculated, what does 'calculate 666' mean? I added the three 6's together and got 18 – nothing there. Multiplied it by various numbers and divided it by more of them – nothing. Then I noticed that the three sixes were together and that if I put full-stops between them, to give 6.6.6, this formulation in maths does have a definite meaning, it means multiplication (for example, in school algebra abc means a x b x c) and, in carrying out this operation, a very ordinary looking number is produced.

In fact, William Stirling (Ref 20 p. 57), quoting from Francis Potter's treatise of 1647 AD, notes:
....that the number 666 is not only the number of the Beast's name, but also the number of God, that is, it is a number which God hath pleased to name and reveal to men, *that by counting of this number,* **we might find that other number**, *which it pleased not God expressly to name in this place, but rather mystically to conceal.* My italics.

However, Potter did not find that other number, nor did Stirling, but here it shall be revealed.

I did not realise it at the time but it was this number that was to start me on a journey of discovery that took three years to unravel.

So, having laid the foundation for this trail of investigation, let us proceed along the way.

HOW WE WERE MADE

II
IN THE BEGINNING

Let us assume that the mechanics of our world, the solar system, and man, were designed; that way it will be easier to observe, and describe, what the designers have done Some may assume, alternatively, that all the numbers are pure coincidences, which happened by chance. The more adventurous however, may count them too numerous to be accidental. A coincidence occurs when two things happen together, which one would otherwise believe should not. When three things occur simultaneously this becomes more than a coincidence, but when, say, four, or even more take place, then the situation becomes odd; either that, or those instances are not coincidental at all, but have been caused to happen. So let me start this investigation on the premise that everything has been designed, not by 'God', but by 'them' whom we may call gods, since anyone who can do something on this scale would surely be considered thus by us. If it helps, let us theorise, in a light hearted way, say, that 'gods' is an acronym for the Galactic Ordering and Delivery System, which engineers call up when installing a new solar system. As far as I can see this is the only scenario with which I can work that will explain the facts of these bizarre numbers cropping up all over the place for no apparent reason – unless they were put there. I realise that what I am suggesting here is a view of the past as creationist, as opposed to the Darwin idea (and that's all it is) of gradualism – a completely unproven theory. This idea of "evolution" has been bought lock stock and barrel by the academic gang, who view any challenge to this hypothesis in the same way that the catholic church used to view ideas about the stars, best to burn the heretics at the stake (after some serious torture). In fact, the similarity between modern day academia and the catholic church of 1500 is rather worrying; any dissension from the 'papal bull' of the received wisdom of those who have a job (I nearly said 'work') in the hallowed halls of college, brings down a rain of scorn, whose synchronisation confirms its coordination, upon

HOW WE WERE MADE

any who dare to offer something which does not fit their view of the universe of knowledge.

As Santillana and Dechend say, Ref 1, p 68:

> The simple idea of evolution, which it is no longer thought necessary to explain, spreads like a tent over all those ages that lead from primitivism into civilisation. Gradually, we are told, step by step, men produced the arts and crafts, this and that, until they emerged into light and history. Those soporific words "gradually" and "step by step", repeated incessantly, are aimed at covering an ignorance which is both vast and surprising. One should like to inquire: which steps? But then one is lulled, overwhelmed and stupefied by the gradualness of it all, which is at best a platitude, only good for pacifying the mind, *since no one is willing to imagine that civilisation appeared in a thunderclap.* My italics.

The process of instilling a belief system on this scale, without proof, and by repetition, is very similar to the philosophy expressed by Lewis Carroll in *The Hunting of the Snark, Fit 1. The Landing*, "What I tell you three times, is true"; (although I had known of this quotation for some time, my thanks to Frank Brown for tracing its origin). In fact, the evolutionists are now in exactly the same position that their arch enemies, the creationists, have always been in; believing in something without any proof whatsoever of its existence. The evolutionists however, now occupy the high ground - of academia, with its implication of 'science', and, as no one outside of science understands science, they are in an unassailable position, as they can simply tell the unbelievers that they are ignorant of science. It is a circular argument, which academe cannot lose.

'They' came, 'they' made, 'they' went. As the authors of Ref 1, p 348 go on to say:

> There is nothing left of the ancient knowledge except the

relics, fragments and allusions that have survived the steep attrition of the ages...... the system as a whole may lie beyond all conjecture, *because the creating, ordering minds that made it have vanished forever.* My italics.

Well they certainly have, for they have gone back to whence they came. To quote a verse from Sumer, their departure is actually documented, "Even the gods were terror-stricken at the deluge. They fled and *ascended to the heaven* of Anu [the chief god]. The gods cowered like dogs and crouched in distress. Ishtar cried out ...... The Anunnaki gods cried with her. The gods sat bowed and weeping". My italics again, but just to emphasise that they went up in the air, to heaven, to space, gone.

Be that as it may. For myself, one of the most abiding points of curiosity over a long period of time was how we got to have 90^0 in a right angle. It always seemed to me that it would have been more rational to have had 100^0, thus giving a circle of 400^0 instead of 360^0. Which then led me to observe that 360^0 wasn't all that different from the number of days in the year. Both of these values have been known for at least 5000 years. Since we have 10 fingers and 10 toes, my alternative reasoning of 100^0 seemed even more sensible, so the choice of 90 did appear rather odd. These thoughts had haunted me for years and the more I thought about 360^0 the odder it seemed to get.

Let us surmise that it all started when 'they' first spun the Earth into its orbit around the Sun. Along with the orbit and its daily axial spin, they also gave it a tilt called 'the obliquity of the ecliptic'. Over time the tilted axis itself also rotates in a small circle, thus providing a phenomenon known as the 'Precession of the Equinoxes'. We will come back to this later; I mention it here because it is this tilt which provides the seasons of the year, and was furnished in order to make our existence here a little more interesting while they observe us. The Precessional mechanism presents us with a giant clock in the night sky, whose numerals are the signs of the zodiac.

HOW WE WERE MADE

However, coming back to the orbiting of the Earth around the Sun, I had at first assumed that a mistake had been made in making it take 365 1/4 days to complete a year, because a much 'cleaner' number is 360. 36 is a number (this is an instance of my considering 360 and 36 to be the same number string) which is highly manipulable, having a large number of factors, namely 2, 3, 4, 6, 9, 12, 18 and an integer square root - 6. 36 is the only two digit number to have these two characteristics. It is therefore able to be rendered, by easy divisibility, into sub units. This 'feeling' about 360 is shared by Robert Temple, in his book The Crystal Sun, Ref 3, he says; " I began to become fixated with the duration of the earth's year and its closeness to the number of degrees in a circle, which I hope everyone knows is 360^0 ", and again "My feeling was that an 'ideal' year would be 360 days". He then shows a calculation which changed my original idea, about 365 1/4 being an error on 'their' part, into an astonished acceptance that, for some as yet unknown reason, it was after all a deliberate choice. Quoting Temple again "I divided the duration of the earth's year, which is 365.242392 days, by 360... and wondered what the relationship between the two numbers could be. I was very surprised when I saw that the result was 1.014562, for I instantly recognised that it was the same as the Comma of Pythagoras to the third decimal place". Let me hasten to add, that, until I had read his book, I had been in blissful ignorance of the 'Comma'. Those who wish to learn more about this number, which has a function within music, are referred to his book; but one more quote about it is of special interest; "this important universal constant .... turns out to be 'the greatest secret of ancient Egypt' ". The above quotations come from pages 351/352 of Ref 3.

In a further chapter I shall demonstrate another connection between 360 and 365.25 which is related to the circumference of the Earth.

We two are not the only ones to become intrigued by the two year numbers of 365+ versus 360, for, at least 5300 years ago, 'they' too were busy. So that mankind could properly order his affairs he first needed Time, and a way of measuring it was one of the early gifts of civilisation which was provided to man. The gods, realising that the 365+ days that it takes to orbit the Sun, would be a rather clumsy number for Neolithic man to both remember and manipulate, and anyway is a number that cannot be divided into integers, decided both to tidy it up, and at the same time make it fit into their own 6 based culture. They started by giving the Egyptians and Sumerians a calendar that was not only neat and easy, but which would also have the same numbering systems as other concepts involving time, geometry, geography and astronomy. This way there would not be a host of different numbering bases, and their similarity to each other would help to ensure their continuity through time and vicissitudes. Cyril Aldred, Egyptologist and late Keeper at the Royal Scottish Museum, Edinburgh, said in his book 'The Egyptians', Ref 4, p 92, "It was some unknown genius during the Archaic Period who devised a schematic year of 365 days and fixed its inception upon the rising of Sirius", and "The resulting calendar.... the only intelligent calendar which has EVER existed in human history". (My caps. Archaic Period is that period before 3100 BC in Egypt). The British Museum, Ref 5, p 58 says "This was an admirably simple system, compared with the modern European calendar of unequal months, and it was briefly revived in France at the time of the revolution". In other words, the earliest calendar ever created was also the most perfect, and it became worse the further away in time it got from its commencement. Of course it was perfect - the gods established it - and when man took it over he ruined it, and we are still living with the mess today.

So, in order to make the ugly reality of 365+ days into a more user-friendly piece of computation, they arranged the working year as an elegant and symmetrical number system which would be easy to operate and follow. The number of working days was reduced to 360, with the remaining 5 days to be taken at year's end as a major holiday, in the same way that Christmas and new year are now running into a one year-end celebration, in the west. These 5 days were made very special so that they would not be easily forgotten, and were called The Days of the Gods, each one being named after the 5 most important gods in the Osirian cycle. They were also called The Days Upon the Year. The other quarter day was added on, just as we do, every 4 years. The remaining 11.25 minutes of the 365+ day year, counted up to one add-on year every 1,460 years; that is, every 1,460 years the Egyptians would add on another year to keep the passage of time absolutely accurate. They were shown how to do this by being given a knowledge of

HOW WE WERE MADE

the movement of Sirius, which tracks along the horizon at Sunrise for 730 years, rising at a minuscule distance further away each year. After this, it tracks back again to the original starting point, and, when it reached it, they added on a year. Not bad for a supposedly hunter-gatherer Neolithic man. The only people who could know this cycle had either seen it before, and thus knew how to measure it, or had the mathematical ability to carry out three dimensional calculations based on the Earth's Precessional movement. Whatever, this knowledge is quite remarkable. The later Greeks had been informed of this (by the Egyptians, of whom they were in awe), and gave it the name Sothic Cycle after Sothis, their name for Sirius (Egyptian Sept). A quick calculation shows that for only two of these add-on years to have been so added on, would have taken 2,920 years on Earth to pass.

That is the same length of time, say, from modern-day England, with nuclear power stations, back to a 1000 BC pre-Celtic land not even called England, and inhabited by an unknown people. These are the time spans 'they' planned, and, for reasons we do not know, they aimed to make sure that man faithfully, and accurately, recorded them. 1,460 years represents approximately 850 human generations, taking 25 years per generation; and, therefore, two cycles would require double this at 1700 generations! Putting this into modern context, the time from now back to William the Bastard in 1066, would total 38 generations. Going only up the same male name line we could get our father and his father etc., up to the 38th, into one classroom, and yet this short span of time is almost incomprehensibly long to us today. Zecharia Sitchin, Ref 6, p 200 says "this 1,460 year period coincided with the cycle of the heliacal rising of the star Sirius at the time of the Nile's annual flooding which in turn takes place at about the summer solstice (in the northern hemisphere)", and "Edward Meyer... concluded that when this Egyptian calendar was introduced, such a convergence of the heliacal rising of Sirius and of the Nile's inundation had occurred on July 19. Based on that Kurt Sethe..... calculated that this could have happened in either 4240 BC or 2780 BC". That represents one cycle, but why should this not also have taken place on the previous one too, starting at 5700 BC? And even cycles before that?

In actuality, before the start of Egyptian history in 3100 BC, it was ruled over (according to the priest Manetho 3 C BC) by a series of god dynasties beginning with Ra and ending with a dynasty of 30 demigods who ruled for 3650 years (please note well the numbers here), the total length of all coming to 17,520 years. Sitchin, Ref 6, p 202 says "Karl R Lepsius noted that this time span represented exactly 12 (and note this one too) Sothic cycles of 1,460 years".

The fact that they had an extremely accurate year does not explain away the choice made of reducing the working year to 360 days. Why could they not have plumped for a rounder figure of, say, 350 or even 300? The answer lies in 36, for, in addition to 36 having a large number of factors, its root of 6 x 6 was also of great importance, as 6 was the base of their number system, which was itself related to the place from whence they came.

Not only were the ancients given a beautiful annual calendar, but the year itself was divided up with equal exactitude. The 360 day year, which I call the Model Year, was made up of 12 months, after the 12 lunar cycles. Each month consisted of 3 weeks, and every week contained 10 days, called a Decan. This produces 30 days each and every month, thus there were 36 Decans per year. How neat, 36 Decans in a 360 day year. Each Decan had associated with it a particular star, which, again rather remarkably, rose with the Sun for 10 days, after which a new Decan star would arise. The moon itself was actually placed where it is in order to make it provide 12 encirclements of the Earth, thereby furnishing an easily observable phenomenon by which to further mark the passage of time. The moon as a body will be discussed again further on.

There were 3 seasons of four 30 day months, resulting in 120 days per season. It follows that there were 360 daylight hours per month and 360 night hours per month.

So, here is a system composed of days, up through weeks, months and seasons all measured on a base whose ultimate number is 6, or 6 squared. 24 is also 0.666% of 36.

But they did not stop there, for in portioning the day they used the same

HOW WE WERE MADE

methodology. This was split into 12 hours for daylight and 12 hours for the night. Each hour was divided into 60 minutes and each minute into 60 seconds. There are then 3600 seconds in the hour. See illustration.

The plan is clear, their measurement is a function of 6. 6 times 2 for 12 hours and 12 months; 6 times 4 for 24 hours; 6 times 5 for 30 day month; 6 times 6 for 36 Decans, 360 hours per day and night month, and 3600 seconds per hour; and 6 times 10 for 60 minutes and 60 seconds. We will come to the relevance of 6 cubed (6.6.6) and 6 quadrupled (6.6.6.6) later. In a Model Year there are 8640 hours, this number is 6 x 6 x 6 (x 4) and is exactly one third of the Precessional Cycle (25,920 years), which we shall also come to; there are also 86,400 seconds in a day. The Model Year contains 518,000 minutes (360 x 24 x 60), which is precisely twenty Precessional Cycles, and it also features in the creation of the world, which, again, is covered further on.

These calculations are identical to the Sumerian system of arithmetic, called the sexagesimal base. However the Egyptians used the strictly decimal base of 10, and so their coincidental use of 6 is, for the marking of time, remarkable.

While I was toying with these numbers, and in particular remembering that 6 was the root of 36, I decided to multiply out the number 666; that is, 6 x 6 x 6. At the time the result of 216 meant absolutely nothing to me, just an uninteresting number with no apparent relevance to anything. However, I tucked it away in the back of my mind, as a niggling distant memory, buried almost beyond recall, seemed to be trying to remind me that I had seen it somewhere before. Many months after that, and still occasionally tossing the number around, while out walking, the solution 'popped' into my head. I made the astonishing discovery about 216 and its connection with the 360 day year. And it is this - 21.6 is the middle of the year. The 21st of June is 21.6, Midsummer Day, the Summer Solstice. The coding of the year around 6 squared, and now the marking of the halfway point by 6 cubed was a truly arresting revelation, and a recognition of the precision planning that had gone into the placing of this planet. Furthermore, the Winter Solstice is on the 21st and this is 6 months after the summer. The two equinoxes also

THE MODEL YEAR OF THE ANCIENTS

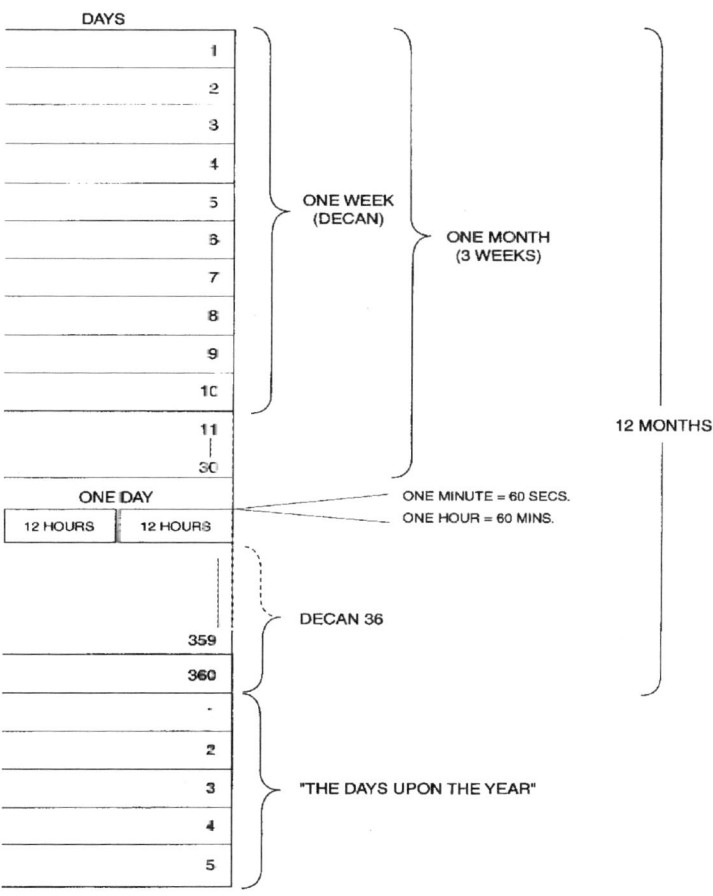

HOW WE WERE MADE

fall on the 21st and they are also 6 months apart - see illustration. The integrity of the number string of 2 and 1 and 6 is thereby maintained.

I made another astonishing find of a connection between 6.6.6 and 36(0), for if all of the numbers between, and including, 1 to 36 are added together (1+ 2+ 3........ 34+35+36), the result is, guess what? Yes, 666 (or 216 in my method). The ratio of 216 to 360 is 10 to 6, man's digital number system against the number of the gods. While 6^2 is 36(0) and 6^3 is 216. We will also see further on that the cosine of 216 is the same as the cosine of 36. These three, 666, 216, and 360 are clearly locked together.

No one has any idea when, or why, the days of the week changed from 10 to 7, although the calendar used today was adopted by Julius Caesar, circa 50 BC, from the Egyptian one, and somehow came with 7 days. Presumably it emerged from the Old Testament when God took 6 days to make the earth (note the 6 here) and rested on the seventh. Although the Romans were certainly not Jews, nor was Christianity a religion then. This was an inaccurate calender, which was modified by Pope Gregory in 1582. It is the one that is still in operation to the present day.

That the Sumerians also worked to an identical calendar is certain. In fact Temple, Ref 8, p 172 points out that the gods of Sumer also assigned 36 constellations to match the 36 Decans. But the archaeological record from Mesopotamia is rather meagre when compared to that from Egypt, even though that country's remains have been successively mined and robbed for the past two hundred years. Had Sumer been blessed with hard building stone such as is present in Egypt, their remains would have been much more numerous. This is why their ziggurats (a Sumerian pyramid) were built of baked clay bricks, whereas the Egyptians built in stone. Such writing, in cuneiform, that has been recovered from Sumer is in the form of clay tablets and cylinder seals, and what they tell us is that they were quite as advanced as the Egyptians, and indeed were awarded their gifts of civilisation before Egypt.

THE CODED YEAR

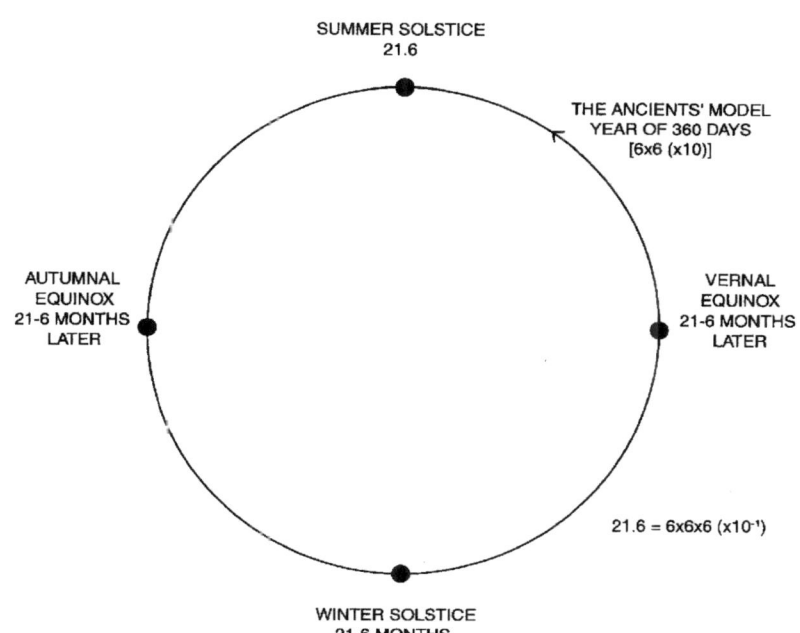

HOW WE WERE MADE

The circle was therefore destined to reflect the Model Year of 360 days, since the year itself is indeed cyclical, that is, it goes around back to the beginning just as in a circle. Drawing the year as a circle and then placing on it the four points, which mark out the year as the equinoxes and solstices, and connecting them together, produces four right angles, or quadrants. The distance in time between each equinox and solstice is therefore 90 days, and the division of 360^0 into four quadrants also yields 90^0. The year is thus coded as a series of right angles comprising 90 days per quadrant; that is, there are 90 days between the equinoxes and the solstices, see illustration.

The geometric circle measured in degrees is the reflection of the chronological Model Year measured in days, with each quadrant mirroring the 90^0 right angle. This is a another quite remarkable observation. In fact this discovery brings me 'full circle' back to the thoughts which I outlined at the beginning of this chapter about the origins of the 90^0 right angle.

Furthermore, we could never have had a circle of 365 1/4 degrees, for the simple reason that that number is unworkable in terms of dividing it up into neat parts, and, as I explained earlier, 36, and hence 360, has a very large number of factors.

The key to discovering exactly how the year and the circle are connected, was only possible because I had cast aside constraints which held me to believe that the 365 day year was sacrosanct, and also the incorrect belief that the ancients were not as clever as we like to think we are. In other words to accept that there might have been ulterior motives to their knowledge, or that those who gave it to them knew (or know) more than we do today.

I decided to take another bold step, to throw off another small stricture of modern science, and to see if there were any other 'Perfect' numbers, the key to which might open up the door to further secrets. Remember, that the ancients knew full well the correct length of the year, but clearly chose, or were given, a Model Year of 360 days, fitting the missing days in at year's end. I knew from earlier readings that the ancients had also used an

THE YEAR IS A RIGHT ANGLE

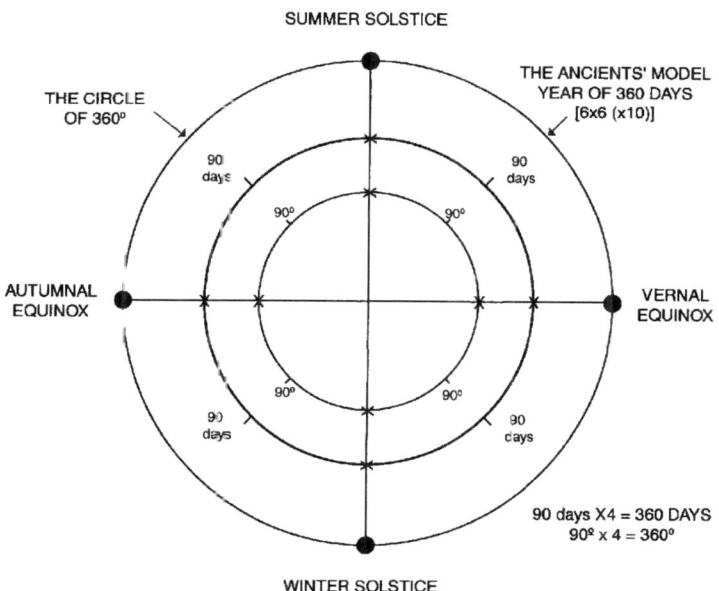

HOW WE WERE MADE

'incorrect' number - which, in a modern, rather arrogant way - I had always assumed was due to ignorance on their part. This number we know as 'pi', a Greek letter. Today, people write whole articles, and even books, about pi, since it is a number without end. As a decimal it is normally given as 3.142, but the decimal part has been shown to be very very long. The 'incorrect' pi in the distant past was taken as 3, which I had long believed to be a reflection of primitive science, but I now find that when pi is used with this value of 3 everything changes, and becomes clear. Just as with the year and the circle, the numbers come tumbling out. I call 3, 'Perfect Pi', like the Model Year of 360 days. It is as if the real value of pi has been used as a 'tease' to throw us off the real scent in this detective work, for in using it in equations, nothing makes sense, all is messy and untidy, no whole numbers, none tying into other parameters such as time, degrees, etc. It is as if real pi is a broken key which will not fit the lock, but which is close enough to the real key of 3 to blind us to the solution. Because the real value of pi is a never ending number, it follows that any calculation using that number can never be accurate, for example if we use 2 x pi x r to find the circumference of a circle, then this will only ever be an approximation.

The great Greek scientists led by Pythagoras underwent a traumatic awakening when they discovered that pi was not actually 3. They sought, and indeed did, try to keep it secret as it upset all of their beautiful calculations, and their understanding that the Universe was built to a system composed of numbers.

We shall return to Perfect Pi later, but it seemed logical to bring it up here, as I was discussing the Model Year and the circle. We have providence to thank that the circle of 360 degrees has not been tampered with, although I would not be surprised to learn that the revolting French (in that they were in revolt) in the 1790's may have had a go at it.

III
COMING FROM OBSCURITY

The Sumerians seem to come from nowhere, fully formed, at the very beginning of time, and they arrive with an amazing number system. It is quite easy to follow and I will keep the explanation simple and succinct. I have to introduce this number base as it is crucial to everything discussed here, and it appears to be the source of all the number strings with which we are concerned. Additionally, the ancient Mayan and Hindu cultures produced similar complex number strings which, as several authors have opined, appear to be rather ridiculous; but, we shall see as we go along, that the very opposite is the case. The Egyptians, somewhat boringly, used our base 10, so there is nothing further to add about their system here.

A comprehensive description of the Sumerian system of maths, and their base, is contained in Georges Ifrah's book The Universal History of Numbers, Ref 7. Chapter 9 of his book is actually entitled 'The Enigma of the Sexagesimal Base', which he starts by saying "In all human history the Sumerians alone invented and made use of a Sexagesimal system - that is to say, a system of numbers using 60 as a base ... *one of the greatest unresolved enigmas in the history of arithmetic ... we do not know the reason which led the Sumerians to choose such a high base*" [my italics]. Although he feels it is "...plausible... to think that the base 60 commended itself to the mystic minds of Sumerians because of their cult of the 'Upper God' Anu, whose number it was". Sitchin, Ref 6 discusses Anu in great detail; it was he who was leader of the 'gods' who took up residence upon the Earth. Later it was also to be the number of the Greek goddess Athena.

Although it is called a sixty based system the Sumerians also used 10, and indeed all the numbers from 1 to 9, for which they had individual names.

HOW WE WERE MADE

Furthermore they had names for all the multiples of 10 below sixty (as we have today e.g. thirty), and so their system was not wholly a 60 one. In fact, from 1 to 60 it was the standard decimal system.

But, above 60 the numbers were obtained by multiplying 60 by the numbers 1 to 10. There were thus ten of these from 60 to 600.

Above 600 another level was created by multiplying it by 1, 2, 3, 4, 5, and 6. The highest number here is therefore 3600.

Above 3600 another level was created by multiplying it by the numbers 1 to 10, giving the highest number of 36,000.

Above 36,000 another level was created by multiplying it by the numbers 1, 2, 3, 4, 5, and 6. The highest number here then becomes 216,000.

All of the numbers mentioned here had a special name, in this last case 216,000 was called a 'sargal', which means 'big 3600', since 3600 is a sar.

Above 216,000 another level was created by multiplying it by the numbers 1 to 10, giving the highest number of 2,160,000.

Finally, above 2,160,000 the last level was created by multiplying it by the numbers 1, 2, 3, 4, 5, and 6. This results in their highest number of all - 12,960,000, which is called sargal-su-nu-tag, "Unit greater than big sar".

Why would such an ancient people want, or even need, numbers of such magnitude, and all created by a very precise 'stepping' arithmetic, and why would they give such incomprehensibly long strings the reverence of a special and individual name? We will see that these vast numbers crop up in other geographical locations far removed from Sumer, and that they are also present in our modern day experience, but only through the use of the sacred system of measures (ie feet and inches etc) which, thankfully, are still with us – just. In fact these numbers are ancient records of essential measurements regarding the Earth, the moon, the solar system and the sun; and man, geometry, time, the stars, and more. Although the numbers would have had meaning attached to them when they were given to us by the 'gods', the knowledge of what they originally stood for has been lost in the mists of time, and now, when they are read by modern man they simply appear to be somewhat silly flights of fancy by the equally ignorant ancestors who liked long strings of numbers. I am afraid the laugh is on us, the old folk knew very well what they were writing down – under instruction of course – they were writing down the structure of everything.

Some of the above outlined numbers are of special interest, and follow the repeating number string which I mentioned earlier, and they all had their own distinctive names, due to their being of individual significance to the Sumerians. These are:

6	as	36	es u as (my construct)
60	ges	360	ges as
600	ges u	3600	sar
		36000	sar u

10,800   sar es (3600x3) 21,600   sar as (3600x6)
108,000 sar-u-es (36,000x3) 216,000 sargal (36,000x6)
1,080,000 sargal-ia (216,000x5) 2,160,000 sargal-u (216,000x10)
10,800,000 sargal-u-ia (2,160,000x5)

432,000 sargal-min (216,000x2)   1,296,000 sargal-as (216,000x6)
4,320, 000 sargal-u-min (2,160,000x2)   12,960,000 sargal-su-nu-tag
                                                (2,160,000x6)

Every number described above has 6 and 10 as their ultimate derivation, but two number strings are prevalent, 36 and 216 (add some naughts on to both of them to create some more numbers). The string 216 is the encoded 666, as is 108, 432, and 1296.

It is interesting to note in passing that there are 1,296,000 seconds in the 360 degree circle and 21,600 minutes. There are 43,200 seconds in a 12 hour day, and 3,600 seconds in an hour. Obviously there are also 1,296,000 seconds of longitude arc around the Earth.

HOW WE WERE MADE

At first sight, it may be thought that it would be difficult to represent physical qualities with this very odd number base, in fact it's quite simple. Using combinations of the four basic symbols for the numbers 1, 6, 10, 60, smallish things, such as, say, 266 sheep would be (60 x IIII) + (10 x II) + 6.

When the quantities became larger they would then bring the bigger numbers, named above, into use. They not only had the four basic arithmetical operations, but also 'powers' - square and cube.

In a bizarre coincidence, shortly after writing this, an advertisement appeared on the History Channel on 21 February 2002, for Virgin Holidays, which said, et al, "Childhood lasts approximately 4320 days" - and it does, for 12 years!

Civilisation in Sumer has been estimated to have begun before 3200 BC, although the named King lists do not start historically until around 2300 BC. While over in Egypt the first dynasty originates in 3100 BC, which is the historical date given to us by a priest called Manetho writing in 250 BC.

Far across the world in the Yucatan peninsular, which is now part of southern Mexico, the ancient Maya also had an extraordinarily accurate understanding of the length of the year, which they measured as 365.242 days, Ref 7, p 297, but which they too operated as a 360 day year. We have a very precise dating of the beginning of their world - "......rather amazing way of calculating the passage of time on their stelae. This 'Long Count'...... began at zero at the date of 13 baktun, 4 ahau, 8 cumku, corresponding quite precisely, according to J E Thompson (1935), to 12 August 3113 BC in the Gregorian calendar", Ref 7, p 316. This date is uncannily close to nascence in both Sumer and Egypt. And the Jews calculate that time began in 3760 BC, as, in the year 1996 of the Common Era, the Jewish calendar counts the year 5758. In fact the much maligned Archbishop of Armagh, James Ussher, who, in 1650, calculated that the world was created on Sunday 23 October 4002 BC, was not that far off if the word 'world' is replaced by the word 'civilisation'. Unfortunately for him discoveries made after his time in the new science of geology claimed that the world was many millions of years old, and he was laughed out of court. Darwin put the final nail in his coffin by claiming that all creatures had evolved over a similar period of time. Now, the old Archbishop is quoted frequently by archaeology lecturers who mention him, and then snigger at the thought of how anyone could be so stupid. In fact it is they who are wrong, as civilisation was created around this time, and, for mankind, his 'world' did start then; with Time, cities, farming, metallurgy, alcohol, and the wheel, et al. In fact, until the coming of the Industrial Revolution, which the English started, the ancients had almost everything, and more, than the western world had until two hundred years ago.

Moving now to the Mayan method, Ifrah gives a very comprehensive description of the Mayan arithmetic and their counting system, which was based on 20 (vigesimal), instead of sixty, but observe that twenty is one third of sixty. The days, and years were calculated as follows, Ref 7, p 116:

```
1 kin                         = 1 = 1 day
1 uinal       = 20 kin        = 20 = 20 days
1 tun         = 18 uinal      = 18 x 20 = 360 days
1 katun       = 20 tun        = 20 x 18 x 20 = 7,200 days
1 baktun      = 20 katun      = 20 x 20 x 18 x 20 = 144,000 days
1 pictun      = 20 baktun     = 20 x 20 x 20 x 18 x 20 = 2,880,000 days
1 calabtun    = 20 pictun     = 20 x 20 x 20 x 20 x 18 x 20 = 57,600,000 days
1 kinchilton  = 20 calabtun   = 20 x 20 x 20 x 20 x 20 x 18 x 20
                                                  = 1,152,000,000 days
1 alautun     = 20 kinchiltun = 20 x 20 x 20 x 20 x 20 x 20 x 18 x 20
                                                  = 23,040,000,000 days
```

Two key numbers multiplied together produce a rather interesting Mayan number string, for 666 x 216.216 216 is equal to 1 baktun of 144,000 days. Similarly, 666 x 4320 (this latter number is $1/6^{th}$ of the Precessional Cycle) makes 1 pictun of 2,880,000 days. Further, 6 baktuns of 144,000 days is the same as 864,000 which is $1/3^{rd}$ of 100 Precessional Cycles. While 6 pictuns of 2,880,000 becomes 17,280,000 which is 2/3 (or 0.666) of 1000 Precessional Cycles.

HOW WE WERE MADE

Like the Sumerian system which is 'mainly' 60 based, the Mayan system also had an irregularity, which makes the method cease to be a wholly 20 based one; that is, they introduced 18 in order to 'force' a year of 360 days. I have not come across any explanation of how they managed the remaining 5.242 days, which were 'left over', and which they knew about, in the same way that the Egyptians had - but in their case an historical record provides the answer. The point being that they did have knowledge of the actual length of the year, but 'chose', or more likely were instructed, to reduce it to 360. Why they needed numbers to represent thousands of millions of days is yet another puzzle which the ancients have left us; however, they did need to be able to measure in millions of days as we shall see below. I can only assume that the requirement for thousands of millions of days was set up to allow for time measurements which would provide the Maya with a calendar until the end of time itself, for 1 alautun (see above) is well-nigh 63 million years. This is a figure of such magnitude as to be incomprehensible, unless it refers to events on a solar or galactic scale. And yet they had it. It is also around that number of years since the dinosaurs were, in the main, wiped out by the 'gods', as otherwise the planet would have remained uninhabitable to intelligent life.

The Maya used the scale listed above, and of course the whole range of other individual named numbers (e.g. 13 is ahua) to name a particular date in a similar way to the notation we use today. When we name a date we are stating the number of years which have elapsed since year zero, and then we name the month and day within that year. The Maya had a more elegant system; in their case they listed down the number of days which had elapsed from their year zero - the beginning of time. Examples show that the dates are given in the form of so many baktuns, katuns, tuns, uinals and kins. Oddly, the largest unit, the baktun, was frequently multiplied by 9 to produce a sufficiently long measure, back to year zero, and 9 x 144,000 = 1,296,000 days, a key number string. The other requisite numbers of units are then added to this to count forward from year zero. This is also a named number from Sumer, the Sargal-as, which itself also multiplies by ten to produce the Sargal-su-nu-tag - 12,960, 000 (see above). It is a number which can also be gotten from 6 x 6 x 6 x 6 (x 10^4). Another calculation which crops up on the Mayan stelae is 3 tuns (3 x 360) to give 1080 days, this is one half of 6 x 6 x 6 (x 10). It follows that 6 tuns, note the 6, (6 x 360) is 2,160 = 6 x 6 x 6 (x 10).

Is it not a remarkable situation to find two cultures on opposite sides of the Earth, coming up with such huge and strange and identical, numbers? I was not aware that we still used them today, but continuing research showed me that indeed we do still have them. We shall find them, and other harmonising numbers, elsewhere. In Ref 1, p 7 the authors say that "when one finds numbers like 108 .... reappearing under several multiples in the Vedas, in the temples of Angkor, in Babylon, in Heraclitus' dark utterances, and also in the Norse Valhalla, it is not an accident". Nor a coincidence!

In India, the country from which we get our so-called 'Arabic numerals', that is 0, 1, 2 etc., Hindu mathematicians were also at work thousands of years ago. Their main sphere of interest was in the field of astronomy, and in measuring vast periods of time connected to astronomical events. Once again, here is an ancient people whose efforts were dedicated to mapping time, both backwards and forwards, on a scale which is, to modern ears, incomprehensible. The root word used to describe the periods, or cycles, of time, was the Yuga, cosmic cycles were Yugas; thus Yuga does not itself have a numerical value.

The word Yuga is still with us today in English, it is yoke (see the Concise Oxford Dictionary of English Etymology, Ed T F Hoad: yoke - from Sanskrit - yuga). Try pronouncing the e in yoke as 'eh' and it can be seen how little it has changed over the millennia, all the way from Sanskrit, through the Teutonic languages, to the modern world; it is still here. Another related Sanskrit word is yoga, which is still used today, and means 'union' (with the divine spirit). My dictionary defines yoke as that which joins together, or a stretch of work, or a bond of union; in this way we are bonded together with the cycles of time which the yuga seeks to define, and which rules our lives through the risings and settings of the Sun, and the changing of the seasons. We are yoked into time.

The prime period is the mahayuga; maha - great, thus great-cycle. This period is made up of 4,320,000 human years. As we saw above, this number

HOW WE WERE MADE

can also come from twice 6 x 6 x 6 (x 10,000). 6 of these mahayuga time periods (note the 6) mark the passings of 1000 Precessional Cycles of 25,920 years.

The Hindus spoke of both 'human years' and 'god years'; and here again we see a significant code unrolling, for one god year was equal to 360 human years - 6 x 6 (x 10).

In this system whole eras are measured, and they start and finish at calculated times, in exactly the same fashion as those other civilisations we have already glimpsed. The mahayuga of 4 million odd years was split into four other yugas, the following description of which comes from Ifrah, Ref 7, p 507 who, in turn, takes it from 'Friedrichs, etc (1989), Dictionniare de la sagesse orientale'.

1 The first of the four yugas was the kritayuga of 4,800 god years, which is therefore equal to 1,728,000 human years. [This number may also be arrived at from eight times the familiar 6 x 6 x 6 (x 1000). The number string 1,728 is still in use today, for it is the number of cubic inches in one cubic foot, and it is also the number of cubic stadia in the Holy City – see later]. This is the golden age in which humans enjoy extremely long lives and everything is perfect. Where virtue, wisdom and spirituality reign supreme, and there is a total absence of vice. Hatred, jealousy, pain, fear and menace are unknown. There is only one god, one law, and everyone fulfills their duties with the utmost selflessness.

2 The tretayuga lasted 3,600 divine years [6 x 6 (x 1000)], or 1,296,000 human years [we've already met that one in Sumer and the Yucatan]. At this point humans' lives are reduced to only three quarters. They are now marked by vice, there are the beginnings of laxity in their behaviour and the first ritual sacrifices are carried out. Self interest increases and rectitude diminishes by one quarter.

3 The dvaparayuga stretched for 2,400 divine years, or 864,000 human years. [Note that this number is half of the first one above, and is consequently four times the triple 6 (216) (x 1000)]. The forces of Evil now

equal those of Good, and where honest behaviour, virtue and spirituality are reduced by half. Illnesses have made their appearance and humans now only live half their lives.

4 Lastly, the kaliyuga, or "iron age", is the one we are living in now. Its time is 1,200 divine years or 432,000 human years. [This is half that above and is twice the triple 6 (216) (x 1000)]. This age began on the 18 February 3,101 BC (Gregorian calendar), according to Brahmagupta writing in 628 AD [and "coincides" precisely with the start dates for Egypt, Sumer and Yucatan]. True virtue has now all but disappeared and conflicts, irreligion and vice have increased manifold. Illnesses, exhaustion, anger, hunger, fear, and despair reign supreme. Living things only live for a quarter of their existence and the forces of Evil triumph over Good. Only a quarter of the original rectitude remains. [I'm sorry, but this sounds horribly like the modern world]. It will end with destruction by fire and water, after which a new cycle, or chaturyuga, will begin again.

Adding the numbers of the human years in all four above ages produces a total of one mahayuga - 4,320,000 human years. Note also that this number is 10 times the kaliyuga above. The total number of divine years comes to 12,000 - twice 6 (x 1000).

Ifrah observes (p. 506) that according to Censorinus, Heraclitus's 'great year' was 10,800 years long, while the Babylonian astronomer Berossus mentions another 'great year' of 432,000 years. They sound like faint echoes of India.

There is a longer period than this, the kalpa, which is 1,000 times a mahayuga, giving a length of 4,320,000,000 human years. This is a familiar length of time to students of geology, for it is approximately the alleged age of the Earth.

Lastly, the largest number of all is the mahakalpa, or great kalpa, which is 20 times a kalpa, 86,400,000,000 human years. This vast period of time may represent the formation of our galaxy, although present day theorists guess that it was formed about 20 billion years ago rather than 86.4 billion.

HOW WE WERE MADE

Perhaps the Hindus are the accurate ones, having been given the information first hand, by the gods themselves.

Look at how 6 x 6 x 6, or 216, produces other fundamental constants (which will be described in due course) when it is divided or multiplied:

$$
\begin{aligned}
216 / 2 &= 108 \\
216 / 3 &= 72 \\
216 / 4 &= 54 \\
216 / 5 &= 43.2 \\
216 / 6 &= 36 \\
216 / 9 &= 24 \\
216 \times 2 &= 432 \\
216 \times 3 &= 648 \\
216 \times 4 &= 864 \\
216 \times 5 &= 1080 \\
216 \times 6 &= 1296 \\
216 \times 8 &= 1728 \\
216 \times 12 &= 2592
\end{aligned}
$$

It is hard to get across how exciting this discovery was, for all of these numbers, every one of them, over and over again, measure various aspects of time and distance on planet Earth, and in the stars, as we shall see further on; and we will do so by adding naughts to these basic strings. Their re-occurrence, time after time, in all areas of our existences, is quite astonishing, as we shall discover, although we have already met most of them as number strings from the ancient mathematicians.

IV
THE MIGRATION

The Chinese were also interested in some of these replicating numbers. Temple, Ref 8 devotes a couple of pages to explaining their knowledge of some remarkable celestial cycles, and he quotes (p. 573) from an article by Dr Robert Chatley "... After the Sun and Moon the most regular.... are the motions of Jupiter and Saturn and the mutual conjunctions of these two great planets. Jupiter moves round the 'ecliptic' (the path of the Sun) once in twelve years.... And Saturn once in thirty years... They thus come into conjunction, as seen from the Sun, every twenty years... And in sixty years (actually 59.5779 is the mean value) they meet again in almost the same place in the sky. The times seen from the Earth are approximately the same 60 years. In 3535 years [this is very close to 3600] the motions of Jupiter and Saturn are repeated with remarkable accuracy." The 60 year conjunction is arrived at from five times the 12 year Jupiter revolution, coinciding with 2 of the 30 year Saturn revolution; 60 therefore being the LCM (lowest common multiple). Once again here is a people who have somehow gotten hold of chronological celestial data which spans millennia, and how could they possibly observe with the naked eye such remote events, and why would they want to? Archaeosociologists will immediately point to worship, mysticism, ritual, divination etc, and dismiss it as a usual piece of uninteresting manic obsessive behaviour of the ancients. The Chinese, like the others we have discussed, were given this information, either directly by the 'gods', or by an intermediary culture such as the Sumerians, and indeed it has been conclusively shown that the earliest Chinese writing was based on the pictographs, from which cuneiform derived, of the Sumerians. A journey from Sumeria to China could also take in northern India, thereby dropping off similar arcane knowledge on the way.

The Sumerians not only migrated to the east, but also to the north (only a

HOW WE WERE MADE

massive catastrophe could initiate such a diaspora). Sitchin, Ref 6, p. 374 tells how the unusual language of the state of Georgia shows affinity to Sumerian, and how they established a capital city called Samara (now Kuybichev), before moving north to the Baltic and west to Hungary. Further to the east in Uzbekistan is one of the world's oldest cities with a similar name - Samarkand. It is a fact that Finland and Hungary share the same linguistic root source, and many believe that both unusual tongues ultimately derive from Sumerian. The language group to which they belong is called Finno-Ugric; Finnish, Estonian and Lapp are Finnish tongues, while Hungarian, or Magyar, is Ugric. There is also a link between Finno-Ugric and the Turkish language. As a matter of fact one of the largest cities in Finland is Turku (pop. 780,000). Staggeringly, the Finnish name for Finland is Suomi (i.e. Sumer).

De Santillana and von Dechend dwell at great length on Finland in Hamlet's Mill, including language, myth, identical numbers and the commonality of these to other cultures. They say that Finland, Estonia and Lapland are a cultural island related to the Hungarians, Turks and other faraway peoples in Siberia. Their language is as unrelated to German as is Basque, and until recently were segregated from the Scandinavian environment. All of this points to there being a common area of culture in the distant past which, probably through some driving force such as calamity, caused the Sumerians to flee in various directions, and in the case of the Finns and Siberians, to the ends of the Earth, for Finland is indeed at the end of the Earth to the north. Their great myth poem Son of Kaleva is examined in some depth in Ref 1, and some "startling parallels were found with Norse and Celtic myth, which must go back before recorded history". The ancient Celtic town (that is, pre-Roman) in Berkshire was called, up until the Romans left England, Calleva Atrebatum. Atrebates being the name of the Belgic Celts who had settled there and named it, circa 300 BC, and which was their civitas capital. The Atrebates ruled over an area covering the location of modern Berkshire. The site today is called Silchester, and is described as the most complete Roman town north of the Alps (the foundations that is, there is nothing above ground except the huge protective Roman boundary walls). The incoming Anglo-Saxons (circa 500 AD) had a formula for renaming places in England, which usually caused the initial syllable to be retained, and, if it was a fortified place, the word cester or chester - old name for castle - would be added to the end; hence Calleva - Calchester - Cilchester - Silchester. So, Calleva is still with us, but hidden. The name Kaleva/Calleva cannot be a coincidence, lining up as it does on three syllables, and anyway, K and C are interchangeable; and both names were of considerable importance to both Finns and Celts, because one gives it as the name of their hero while the other applies it to their capital. I mention these movements of peoples to illustrate that the Sumerians most probably did export their knowledge and beliefs, through the medium of mass migration, of which some traces remain today. Sitchin informs us that the Sumerians recorded the names of their gods, chief of whom was ANU and his wife ANTU, both of whom visited Earth to meet the other gods who were already living here. It is then curious to find a pair of small hills in Ireland, near Killarney, called The Paps of Anu (a pap is a woman's nipple, from Norse; it also means soft baby food) which are shown in a photograph in Ref 9, p 37. While the ancient Egyptian city of Heliopolis (given that by the Greeks) was previously called Annu. Similarly, all across a huge area stretching from India to Britain we find the name Dan or Danu (note the anu in Danu) in river names, even to the name of a people - the Danes. Are we surprised to learn that the Sanskrit word for water is *danu*? We have, for example:- the two English rivers called the Don, which come from Danu (and hence Boldon and Doncaster), the Russian Don, the continental Danube, the French Rodanus (now the Rhone), and the Indian river Don. Clearly there is a common thread here. From Hamlet's Mill (pages 277 & 348) we learn of a sea pilot called Thamus (in the nineteenth year of Tiberius), while Plato (writing some four hundred years earlier) speaks of the god Thamus, "king of all Egypt". The connection with water is reflected in the ancient English river name Thames, which, upstream of Oxford, is called the Isis, one of the major Egyptian goddesses. Readers will appreciate my astonishment at coming across the following gem in The Crystal Sun, Ref 3, p 390 (it refers to the inscription on Cleopatra's Needle by the River Thames, whose twin is in Central Park, New York) "He (the Pharaoh) set up a pair of great obelisks ...., the pyramidions ...., at his third time of the Set Festival, through the greatness of his love of Father Tem". The river by which it now stands is also referred to as Old Father Thames (pronounced Tems)! I came across another reference to this strange name in

HOW WE WERE MADE

G Ashe's Mythology of the British Isles, Ref 9, p. 195. He says that continental documents show that a man described as King of the Britons took an army to central Gaul (France) in the last turmoil of the Western Empire in 468, where he was defeated by the Visigothic King Euric, after which he withdrew the remnants of his army to Burgundy. He is mentioned twice, as Riothamus. Now Rio, still exists as a word today, in Spanish it means River, as in Rio Tinto, or Rio Grande. It would appear therefore that we have a man called River Thamus. My own family name of Neil is pronounced Nile in Germany and the Nordic countries. This name, in all its variants, e.g. Nielsen, is common throughout Britain and northern Europe as a peek into the telephone directories of towns and cities will confirm. The similarities of ancient names with modern ones across these areas is a study in itself, and I mention a few here simply to demonstrate the principle of the dispersal of knowledge and names, similar to the naming of places, say, in the USA, Canada, Australia and New Zealand etc, with names from England.

While in the north, there is a distant echo of some of these divine numbers which is spelled out in the story of Asgard, land of the gods and the home of Valhalla (Valiant hall). That this is concerned with Time as well as other concepts, is made clear by the presence of the three mysterious mighty maidens, Past, Present, and Future, through whose cold fingers run the Golden Threads of Time. They sit at the fount of Urda, above Bifrost the Rainbow Bridge whose entrance is called the Golden Gate, and their seat is called Doomstead. They play with Time, plucking it from each other, and eventually wrapping it around the great roller, Oblivion, which grows heavier and thicker forever. They never reach the end of the Golden Threads of Time, nor do they ever grow weary of their work. On the last day - Ragnarok - the valiant dead would rise up to fight with the gods against monsters and evil. Five hundred gates and forty more (540) - are in the mighty building of Valhalla - eight hundred 'Einherie' [the valiant dead] come out of each one gate - on the time they go out on defence against the wolf. This gives a total of 432,000 Einherie, a number we have met many times already. In the stories of the heroes of Asgard, further numbers come out of Skirnir's journey to Jotunheim. When he reached the home of Gymir he rode around it 9 times; but though there were 20 doors, he could find no entrance; for fierce three-headed dogs guarded every doorway. He was therefore confronted by 60 heads, and looked at 180 doors. Importantly, in both cases, there is a tacit invitation to multiply out the given numbers to arrive at their significant product. Prof. Gwyn Jones in Ref 10, p 240 (this is on the slaying of the Viking King Eric Bloodaxe at the battle of Stainmore (i.e. stone-moor) in County Durham, England, in 954 AD) mentions another, "Odinn had always had high hopes of him, and he died gallantly. Valhalla stood open to receive him, and it was the Volsung heroes Sigmund and Sinfjotli who bade him enter. What heroes, they asked, attend you from the roar of the battle? 'There are five kings,' said Eric, 'I will make known to you the names of all. I am the 6th myself'. Jones comments "With these meaningless permutations......". We see immediately of course the number 6, and also that 5 times 6 is 30. The authors of Hamlet's Mill on p. 141, display a similar incredulity in these ancient numbers "..... betrays the Indian predilection for huge and unrealistic numbers and periods". Digging deeper and looking for hidden meaning however, reveals the guiding hands, as we are discovering.

There is another ancient connection in England with 6, and 60, and that is at the monuments of Stonehenge, and its neighbours Woodhenge and Durrington Walls. The numbers I will bring out have been known about for quite some time, although of no apparent interest to the establishment. As can be seen from the illustration Stonehenge is based on a circle, and the numbers of holes and stones encodes numbers that have already been discussed. Not included in the diagram are the banks and ditches, the four station stones and the slaughter and heel stones, in order that the clock face may be more readily apparent. The outer ring of holes, known as the Aubrey Holes (John Aubrey b. 1626, called them X Holes, but they were re-named in his honour) contains, almost certainly, 60 of these, but only 56 have been discovered. A close examination of highly detailed archaeological drawings (not included here) of these holes reveals several large gaps in this circle, for instance between holes 39 to 41, 51 to 53, and 53 to 55, which is where such missing holes probably fitted. They may well have been destroyed by unknown hands in the distant past - Stonehenge is a much abused ruin, and has been "excavated", or dug out to speak the ugly truth, at least seven times. Each digging destroys context, and the missing holes will now never

HOW WE WERE MADE

be confirmed. "Archaeology" is, by the very nature of what it does, a destructive exercise; once the ground is dug up then that ruins the site forever. The eminent archaeologist, Aubrey Burl, in The Stone Circles of the British Isles, Ref 11, p 303 puts it rather movingly, "....... this ravaged colossus rests like a cage of sand-scoured ribs on the edge of eternity, its flesh forever lost. Stonehenge grudges its secrets. Each one explained - the date, the source of the stones, the builders - leads to greater amazements, a spiralling complexity that even now eludes our understanding......".

The 60 holes laid out in a circle reminds us that there are 60 minutes in the circle of the watch face on our wrists, and of course, the number base of the Sumerians.

The next two circles, the Y and Z Holes (after Aubrey's X Holes), each contain 30 holes, and these recall the 30 days in the original month of the Model Year of the ancients, which has already been raised. In fact these 30 holes confirm the probability of the outer 60 hole circle, as it would be churlish of us to believe that the masters of symmetry who built it would not also have matched all of the circles to a common harmony. None of the Y or Z holes are visible on the surface.

The next ring inwards consists of the famous trilithons, the Sarsen Circle, of 30 upright sarsen stones joined at the top by lintels, and kept together by carved mortise-and-tenon joints, each lintel curved front and back to follow the circle. Only a few still stand and some of these were re-erected in modern times. Their correct placing on being raised up again was assured by their massive weight keeping them from bouncing, or being moved again once they were pushed over and on the ground, that is, they lay precisely where they fell. Furthermore, their footprint in the ground was still clearly visible when excavated, and so it was a 'simple' job of popping them back into their sockets in the ground. All was confirmed when the overhead lintels were placed on top and the stone joints fitted exactly. Again, we see the number 30.

Next in is the Bluestone Circle. This is a slightly different stone from the sarsen stone, but both are extremely hard, being types of sandstone (i.e. composed of quartz, which is a hard mineral; it is 7 on the 1-to-10 Mohs Hardness Scale; talc is 1 and diamond is 10. I will be coming back to quartz further on). This circle was also comprised of 60 stones and is further confirmation of the X hole number.

Next in is another set of five sarsen Trilithons, 10 uprights with lintels on top, forming a horseshoe. 10 is the number of digits we possess and is also the base of our (and the Egyptians) number system.

Last in the arrangement is another horseshoe of 19 Bluestones plus one at the centre, giving a total of 20 stones, one third of 60 - the Sumerian number base.

The total number of rings is 7, which is the number of the position of the Earth as it is approached from outside the solar system, i.e. it is the 7th orbit in. The Altar Stone at the very centre could therefore be the Earth itself. With that hypothesis the rings can then be named after the planets, as shown in the illustration.

On a scale drawing of the Stonehenge rings (which this one isn't), the ratio of the rings to each other, bears a crude relationship to the ratio of the planets' distances from the Sun, to each other. For example the ratio Mars to Earth is 142 million to 93.2 million, or 1.5. While their analogues in Stonehenge, i.e. the Trilithons to the Bluestones, is 1.4. But the ratios are only very approximate. The Avenue, which approaches the open horseshoe very accurately, is like a pointer, showing the way into the destination - the Altar Stone - or Earth. I am not saying that this is a beacon, nor that anything would want to land there, but that this is, perhaps, a memorial. The very large number of mounds, some of which are 20-odd feet in height, and long barrows, in the environs of Stonehenge, appear on the Ordnance Survey maps to look like points on a massive star chart. Yes, burials have taken place in them, but that does not mean they were built as mausoleums. The burials could just as well be, what are called in archaeological circles, 'intrusions'. For instance Anglo-Saxon burials have been found in stone age mounds

HOW WE WERE MADE

***STONEHENGE AND EARTH -
THE 7th PLANET IN THE SOLAR SYSTEM***

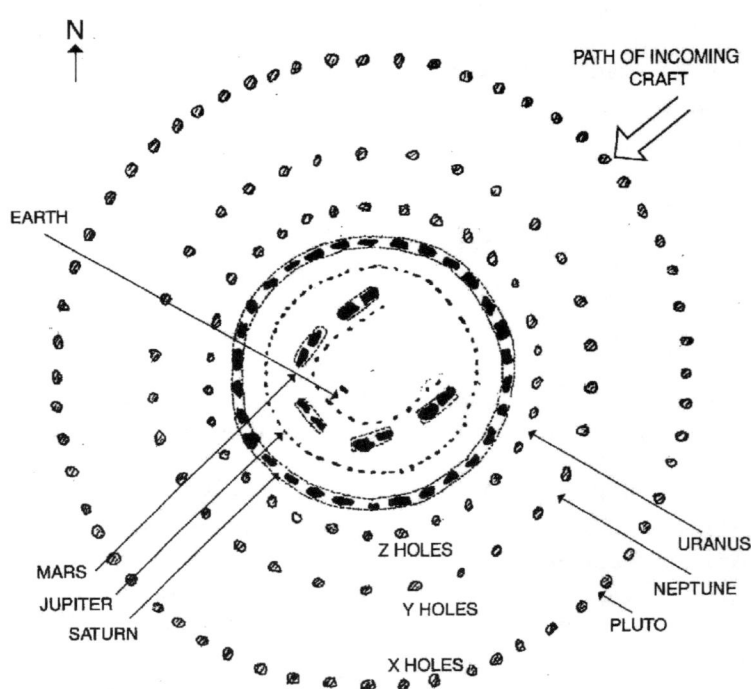

The monument also predicts the risings and settings of the summer and winter sun at the solstices, giving four markers in all. This marking may be carried out with the aid of five sticks in a field, by placing a stick in the ground on sunrise on the 21 June and then putting the other stick between the sun and the stick to form a straight line. On the same day the procedure is repeated at sunset. The whole exercise is done again at the winter solstice, and on removing the centre stick there will be four sticks in the earth forming a square. This square can be imagined stretching to the horizon, and gives rise to the concept of 'the four corners of the Earth'. These four corners are paralleled by the four corners of the year, which are the two solstices and the two equinoxes, although the equinoxes do not form part of the Earth's corners. Burl, in Ref 11, p 306, notes that the siting of Stonehenge, that is, placing it where it is, is also unique; "It was Newham (*Yorkshire Post, 16 March 1963*) who pointed out that the latitude here is virtually unique in that the extreme northern and southern risings and settings of the sun and moon are at right angles to one another......." Clearly, here is a people with an intimate knowledge of a very complex system of planetary motions, and who must have had to carry out the necessary observations over a long period of time bearing in mind the moon's eighteen year cycle. They would have needed to know beforehand that this spot was unique in the northern hemisphere, and was the only place from which they could observe both sun and moon movements. How many books are there today which could explain how to even understand these phenomena, let alone how to seek out a location and chart their movements? They could not have 'accidentally' been living in a unique place, but must have calculated the location and then gone to it to build the thing.

The circumference of Stonehenge is 365.24 (x10) inches, and thus encodes the number of days in the year, which also ties into the Great Pyramid as we shall see later.

Further to the north of Stonehenge are the Rollright Stones in Oxfordshire; this is also a stone circle about 100 feet in diameter, with outriders; the ring originally contained 60 upright stones. Although the integrity of the ring is intact, the stones themselves are much battered, both

HOW WE WERE MADE

by time and the hand of man.

A couple of miles to the north-east of Stonehenge are the remains of a structure now called Woodhenge which were discovered in the 1920's. Several are now known and are properly called treehenges. Since then it has been excavated, 'cleaned up', and concrete pillars inserted where once the wooden posts stood. This site is simply an arrangement of 6 concentric rings of wooden posts as shown in the illustration, surrounded by bank and ditch, which are not included here. Size wise, the diameter of the outer wooden ring is over 100 feet, while the whole circle including bank and ditch is some 240 feet. The post holes did not hold simple poles hammered into the ground, but the trunks of whole trees; Burl says, in Ref 11, (for Ring C) that each post was a five ton oak trunk! Also, the rings were not true circles, nor even true ellipses, but in fact 'ovates', or egg shaped. Drawing a circle is easy, one simply needs a rope and a stick: even an ellipse is simple - once the method is known; two sticks serve as the foci, while a circle of loose rope is strung around both, the rope is then stretched out and an ellipse marked out on the ground. I have never seen a method, nor heard of one, of how to draw out an ovate (clearly, such a one exists); but this arcane geometry was obviously known, and important, to those who built Woodhenge. Oblate rings are few in number in Britain. They are not ellipses gone wrong either, since the ellipse is so easy to create, and people who had the ability to build something like this did not make crude fundamental mistakes. The outer circle - Ring A - contained precisely 60 wooden post holes, the same (probable) number as in the outer circle at Stonehenge. B has 32, C 16, D 18, E 18, and F has 12. In my opinion there are four missed holes in B which would make that 36, similarly I think that there are two missed holes in both D and E. These corrections would then bring it into line with Stonehenge, which is spelling out a number code. 6 rings, with 60 posts in the first ring, is a deliberate act, a calculation, a message to those who understood the medium. This is another model of the solar system.

Literally across the country lane from Woodhenge, to the north, is the mighty Durrington Walls. This is another treehenge, but on a scale which dwarfs Woodhenge's 240 feet diameter; it being 1440 feet, including bank and ditch. Once again, there are 6 concentric rings of large tree post holes.

WOODHENGE - ANOTHER MODEL OF THE SOLAR SYSTEM WITH EARTH AS THE 7th PLANET

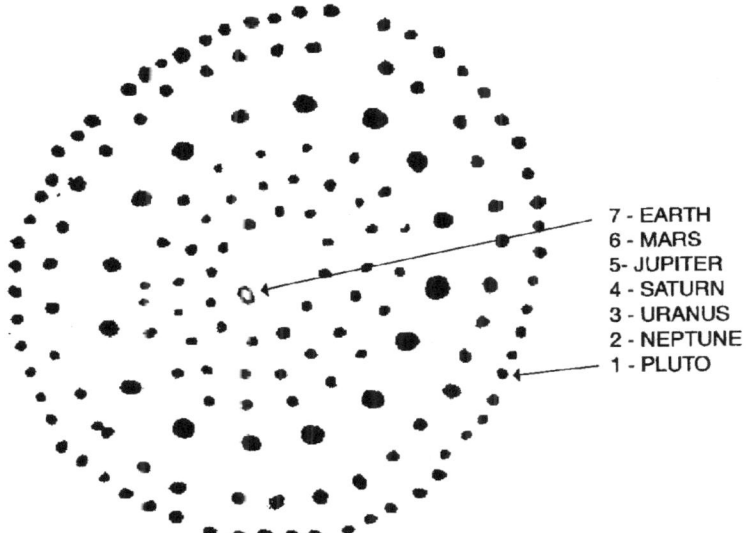

7 - EARTH
6 - MARS
5 - JUPITER
4 - SATURN
3 - URANUS
2 - NEPTUNE
1 - PLUTO

HOW WE WERE MADE

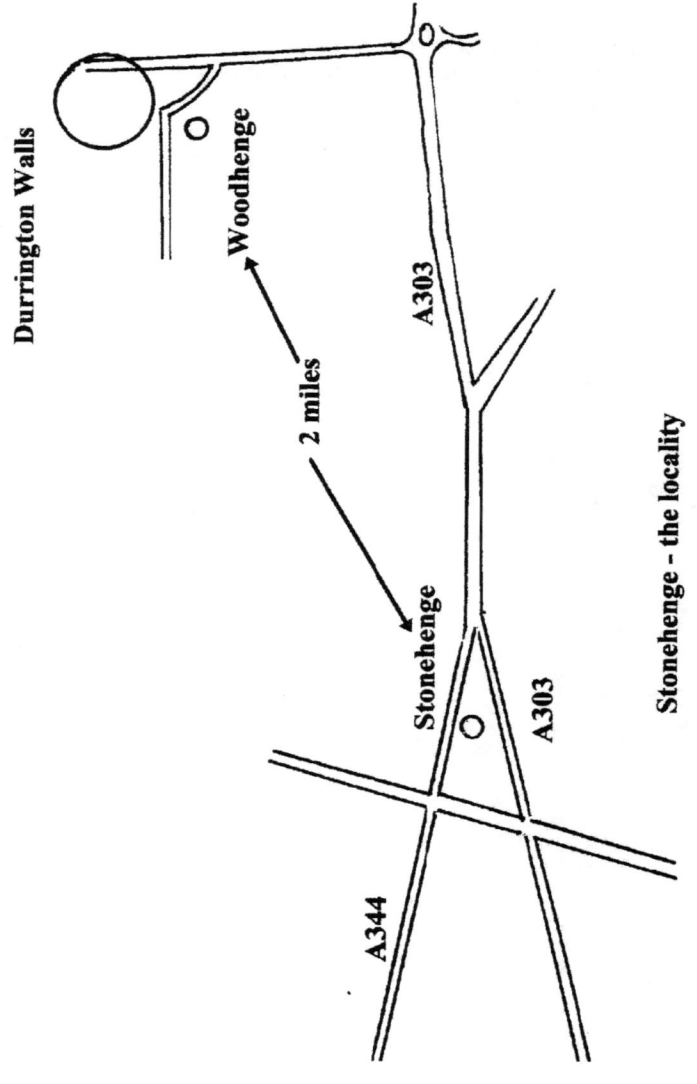

Well away from both sites is another huge treehenge called Mount Pleasant with a diameter of 765 feet. Here also there are 6 concentric rings with Earth as the centre.

It is well known that both treehenge sites were regularly ploughed up until their discovery, for hundreds, if not thousands, of years. Such ploughing destroys every context down to the depth of the plough, and in many stone circles the stones were gleefully smashed and carted off as building material. Banks and ditches were similarly "ploughed out". The immense stone circle with bank and ditches at Avebury, which contains an entire village with pub, church and manor house, and is 1300 feet in diameter, is but a shadow of its original self. Most of the megaliths being broken up a few hundred years ago by the ignorant peasants. But this has not prevented those missing stones from being counted back in again, in the same way that I propose that some of the post holes will also have been missed at the treehenges, and at Stonehenge's outer ring.

The intelligence which built in huge stones, and fully grown mighty oaks, were doing so all over the world around the same time. No civilisation since, including our own, has ever tried to build in mega-units. It is as if we operate on a different scale, and are neither able, nor willing, to attempt the undertaking of moving such massive weights. Yet, long ago, the ancients were apparently doing it on a large scale. The great English cathedrals, built nearly 1000 years ago, were erected using manageable blocks of stone which a fit man could manipulate using levers and a block-and-tackle. Even the modern skyscrapers are built on the principle of bolting lots of small bits together. Huge ships are simply small plates of steel riveted together.

But here is a significant fact - virtually all of the radio carbon dates for stone and tree circle sites in Britain are around 2160 BC. The carbon dating for the enigmatic Silbury Hill, just to the south of Avebury, and the biggest man-made mound in Europe, also comes out at precisely this date. This is the time that the zodiacal circle clicked around to its new position of Aries the Ram, from its previous one of Taurus the Bull, in its eternal Precession of the Equinoxes. That is, the age moved into a new Dawning of the Age of Aries. 2160 years after that a new age came around - the Dawning of the age

HOW WE WERE MADE

of Pisces (the fish), which became our new year zero, and from which we still count. In the year 2160 AD (i.e. in 160 years time), we will change again to the Dawning of the age of Aquarius (the water bearer). The phrase 'Dawning of' refers to the position of that zodiac sign above the Sun as it rises on the dawn of the spring equinox. Hence the Sun is also said 'to dwell in the house of', for example, Pisces, as it forms a 'roof' over the Sun. Please remember that this is not astrology, but an actual fact of astronomy. Clearly, to those builders, the start of this new era (2160 BC) was of enormous importance. And it was so on a global scale, for in Egypt major changes were also taking place at precisely the same time, and I'll touch upon that again later.

I should point out that there are nearly one thousand stone circles in the British Isles, including Ireland, but the whole of eastern England and a large chunk in the centre is totally devoid of them. In Ireland the whole of the centre and the west is similarly bare. Additionally, there are the treehenges, circular monuments such as Maiden Castle, and Long Barrows of megalithic construction, in such profusion that I doubt anyone has ever tried to count them, but we are talking thousands. They are all marked up on the exquisite Ordnance Survey maps of Britain. A pint of beer, a magnifying glass, and one of these maps, is a combination which is guaranteed to bring a deep and profound pleasure to every adult male in the land.

Sitchin, Ref 6, p 374, describes a structure made of stone and wood at the site of Sarmizegtusa in Romania (note the similarity between Sarmi, Suomi (Finland), and Sumer), which he calls "Stonehenge by the Black Sea". A plan view of it looks like some sort of machine made up of punched computer cards and circular rings of concentric post holes. There are five neat rectangles, which are comprised of short stone cylinders which have been named 'lobes', and the two larger ones contained 60 each, arranged in rows four by fifteen, and six by ten. There is also a stone disc made up of ten segments, into which have been embedded six other stones in each segment, giving a total of 60. He notes that researcher Hadrian Daicovciu saw strong links to ancient Mesopotamia, through the recurring use of 60 and the Sumerian number base; and the similarities "could have been neither a coincidence nor an accident". The shock at this site comes from one of the stone circles, which consists of three concentric rings. In particular the central horseshoe shaped central ring of stones, appears to be identical to the same central ring at Stonehenge in their construction. Oh, by the way, this site also dates to around 2160 BC, just like the ones in Britain.

Back in Africa, there is a modern-day instance of a people who have been gifted with extremely arcane data from some time in the distant past. These are the Dogon people of Mali and Upper Volta. They are mentioned in passing in Hamlet's Mill, Ref 1, but Temple devotes a large part of The Sirius Mystery, Ref 8, to them. Both books base their information on the original work by two French anthropologists, M. Griaule and G. Dieterlen, who spent decades in the field seeking and getting the confidence of the tribal elders, who eventually decided to share their secret knowledge with them. Temple includes their article in its entirety as an appendix to his book, and expands upon it greatly. He goes far beyond the study of the Dogon to include research into outlying cultures far off in the Mediterranean and how they might have influenced the Dogon. The four (French) Sudanese peoples are: the Dogon in Bandiagara, the Bambara and the Bozo in Segou and the Minianaka in Koutiala, but the main informants were the Dogon. Their interest in 60 lies in the interval of a ceremony called the Sigui, which they hold once every 60 years, and its purpose is the renovation of the world. The method of calculating these intervals is very complex and one needs to refer to the original research (as mentioned above) if one wishes to fully understand it, and indeed why the need to have a 60 year period. If it were just for this interesting, but very odd, ceremony, they might never have raised further interest in the outside world, but the two researchers discovered that these people were in possession of 'impossible' scientific knowledge. This concerns a detailed understanding of the twin star system, Sirius A, and Sirius B which revolves around it. It happens that Sirius A is the brightest star in the sky and can be easily seen by the naked eye. Sirius B however is "totally invisible" (Temple's words, and he is a Fellow of the Royal Astronomical Society), and is difficult to observe even with a telescope. It was first seen in the late 1800's, and only photographed in 1970.

HOW WE WERE MADE

The Dogon have anciently known about the existence of Sirius B, and the 50 year period of its revolution around Sirius A. They use this 50 year period to help them to calculate the 60 year Sigui ceremony. They also know that the revolution is in the form of an ellipse, and draw this with Sirius A as one of the foci of an ellipse with the path of Sirius B going around it. They also know that Sirius B is tiny compared to Sirius A, and that it is very heavy, and that it revolves on its own axis in one year. It is now known to modern science as a white dwarf, confirming the tales the of the Dogon, who could not possibly have known these facts - unless of course someone told them, in the far distant past. They also say it is made of an extremely dense metal which they call Sagala. We have known since Kepler (d. 1630) that the planets in our solar system move, not in circles, but in ellipses. A circle has a single focal point, i.e. its centre; whereas an ellipse has two foci, which are at the 'stretched' end of what looks like a flattened circle. As already mentioned, many of the treehenges and stone circles in Britain are made up of single or multiple rings of ellipses, and here is an example of an African people repeatedly reproducing ellipses in relation to the stars. These provable facts can not be accidental. But the best exhibit of the Dogon is that they also know about the existence of Sirius C, with a similar amount of detail, the four moons of Jupiter, and the rings of Saturn (all invisible to the naked eye). Temple says that the star Sirius C was only confirmed by astronomers in 1995.

The Dogon do not have a problem coming to terms with the origins of their remarkable learning, for they know it was brought to Earth by beings from the Sirius star system, called the Nommo. The Nommo brought civilisation to earth, gave it to mankind, watched him for some time and then left. They were amphibians with the tails of fishes, and the Dogon drawings of them look uncannily like mermaids, which themselves look like sea cows or dugongs (note the similarity to Dogon) and manatees. And the Dogon live many hundreds of miles from the sea!

The Sumerians also had amphibious beings at their foundation, who had special water tanks built for themselves, in which they could lie during the day, while guiding the Earth beings, but at night they would slip into the sea to emerge again at dawn. The large Babylonian stone carvings in the British

Museum show humans emulating these gods by wearing large cloaks in the shape of a fish with a large fish-tail at the end. The Sumerians described these beings as repulsive for men to look upon. Who knows, perhaps the gods thought that we - soft furry mammals - also look repugnant, I've certainly seen some humans that I don't want to see again.

On these points of dispersement the authors of Ref 1, p 311, have this to say:

> Plato still spoke the ancient tongue, representing, as it were, a living "Rosetta Stone". And accordingly – strange as it may sound to the specialist on Classical Antiquity – long experience has demonstrated this methodological rule of thumb: every scheme which occurs in myths from Iceland via China to pre - Columbian America, to which we have Platonic allusions, is "*tottering with age*", (my italics) and can be accepted for genuine currency. It comes from that "Protopythagorean" mint somewhere in the Fertile Crescent that, once, coined the technical language and delivered it to the Pythagoreans - *(among many other customers)* (my italics). Strange, admittedly, but it works.

Actually, the Pythagoreans received all of their knowledge from the Egyptians, and were quite happy to say so. But the above sentiment is sound if we take it that 'someone' delivered it to certain peoples in ancient times.

HOW WE WERE MADE

V
DIVINE MEASURES

We have already met some of the measures which were given to man at the beginning of his civilisation, and here I will introduce a further one which is still with us today, just as most of the others are. In summary, those so far outlined are:

Time

> The second
> The minute, composed of 60 seconds
> The hour, composed of 60 minutes
> The day, composed of 12 hours of light and 12 of dark
> The week (or Decan), composed of 10 days
> The month, composed of 30 days, or 3 Decans
> The Model Year of 360 days, or 36 decans, or 12 months

Corrections were in place to ensure accuracy of a very high degree; the 5 'Days Upon the Year', the additional day every leap year, and the additional year every 1,460 years.

Circular Geometry

> The second
> The minute, composed of 60 seconds
> The degree, composed of 60 minutes
> The number of degrees in a circle, composed of 360 degrees

HOW WE WERE MADE

Perfect Pi

Is the number 3, which unlocks a whole range of further Divine Numbers, but which, using real pi, would never be apparent. In certain places real pi has also been used, in order to make the decypherment just that little trickier. We can only discern which pi to apply through experimenting. Real pi and Perfect Pi reflect the approach which they took with the year, namely, to have a Model Year of 360 days, against the real year of 365 1/4. In both cases the true values were known, but in those values lay a ragged mess of number strings which did not provide the neat set of factors required in the divine scheme. The Perfect Pi of 3 was used by all of the ancient civilisations, and so using this value now is not a fanciful ploy simply to get to numbers which 'just happen' to reflect, and tie in with, others such as the Model Year. It is said that the Greeks discovered real pi, around 400 BC, a discovery which shook their world of numbers, because up until that time they too had used the Perfect Pi of 3. In fact, part of Greek philosophy was based on numbers, and they believed that numbers were the bases of everything on Earth, so the realisation that pi was not the perfect 3 was a shattering event.

It is now provable that the Egyptians encoded real pi into the dimensions of the Great Pyramid at Giza, whereby its height, multiplied by 2 x pi, is equal to the perimeter of its base. And indeed, it is also encoded into the even larger Pyramid of the Sun at Teotihuacan in Mexico, where its height multiplied by 4 x pi, is equal to the perimeter of its base. It is therefore evident that real pi was known long before the Greeks got hold of it. However, Perfect Pi was also used at the same time; a sort of 'real geometry' and a 'perfect geometry', both in use together, and in parallel; one reflecting the nasty world of reality with messy complicated numbers having long strings of digits after the decimal point, and the other, a neat system where every number is a whole and round one, and where there are no awkward remainders to deal with.

Dimensions

This is the additional measure which I will now run through, although, as will be seen, it should be familiar to all, but it is the origin of these units which may not be quite as well known.

Probably the most interesting measure of all, it concerns linear, square and cubic measure. It is interesting because it is based on man himself. The units are:
> Inch
> Foot, composed of 12 inches
> Yard, composed of 3 feet
> Mile, composed of 1,760 yards

The above units arise from what I shall designate the Paradigm Human Male (PHM). These particular males have measurements on their bodies and limbs which encompass, not only these inches and feet etc, but other numbers which reflect the Earth itself, the moon and indeed the solar system. Clearly, not all males have these dimensions.

The first inkling of this goes back many years to my childhood, and other boys were probably inducted into these facts too - if they appeared to be PHM's, for this only works on such people. When I was 14 and had reached, and stopped, at my present height of 6 feet, our geography master asked those of us of that height to stand up in class. He was also 6 feet and he made a bit of a performance of lining us up, including himself, while another two boys held a long window pole across our heads. Those who did not fit exactly were asked to sit down. He then informed us that this group held some special information, encoded in our bodily dimensions. We were very pleased to learn that we were special in some way, while those who weren't, appeared a little miffed. We went on to learn that we were one fathom in length - 6 feet, and our outstretched arms were the same as our height - one fathom. He continued on to show that the length of our shoes was 12 inches, the width of the pressed thumb was one inch, the stride was three feet, or one yard, as was the distance from the breastbone to the tip of the long

HOW WE WERE MADE

finger, the spread of the fingers was six inches and the width of the palm including base of thumb 4 inches. This last is still used today, called a 'hand', to measure horses -- from ground to base of mane. It is such a person who is a PHM.

    The teacher's name was Mr C, and I looked up to him as a role model. As we both had sandy hair, and were both 6 footers, I used to visualise myself being like him when I grew up, even though he once severely caned me with his 'stick' - a fearsome tree branch, rigid, one inch thick, about 18 inches and polished. He would bring the boy to the front of the class and place the stick gently on the boy's hand. This was to force the hand lower, in order to get a longer swing, so as to inflict maximum pain. I received one strike on each open palm, and I can feel the pain today. As each blow struck home I cried out, at which, some of the girls in the class burst into tears. All because I had been in the school gardens at lunchtime with 'E', and was deliciously fondling her large and exquisite 14 year old breasts, which, with her permission, I had freed from their bra, and brought out to play in the sunlight. Having only recently acquired these twin beauties, she was very keen to have a young man take them in hand, and observe the effect they had on him. Unfortunately our dalliance in this garden of Eden was being spied upon by a snake, another girl, and she reported us. After 'getting the stick', I was sent to see Mr W the Headmaster - a short, plump, and religious gentleman with a most pleasant disposition. He was extremely embarrassed, shuffled his feet a lot, and blushed bright red; no doubt from contemplating the lascivious and drooling retelling of my explorations by my teacher. He asked if I had already been caned, and much to his obvious relief, I said "yes sir". He mumbled something about being naughty, and said I shouldn't do it again. Apparently, my crime was not in worshipping 'E's incomparable bosom, but for being in the forbidden garden. I'll bet! My playmate was not in any way punished. Today, the school has been demolished, the garden has gone, and Mr C and the Headmaster are both dead.
[Postscript to 2nd edition. I have since learned from professor Stecchini's work (see Ref 19, p 305) that the Egyptians were using their thumbs, hands and feet to measure inches and feet 5000 years ago).

    It is therefore apparent that these human measures were once quite well known, and used by adult males (of that size), in their daily lives, for such tasks as stepping out a distance on the ground, or cutting off a piece of rope to a very precise length, the uses are endless. The PHM was (and is) a walking tape measure. However, I was to discover other measures about the PHM, which have not been observed before.

In this respect, an important step forward for me came while I was examining the drawing which is attributed to Leonardo da Vinci. Everyone must have seen this at some point, it's the one of a man with up-stretched arms, and which includes circles and squares. I could never comprehend why I felt there was something not quite right about it. It is not generally known that Leonardo plagiarised this drawing, in every respect, from a first century BC Roman engineer and architect called Vitruvius. It turns out that Leonardo was a serial copier of other's works for which he had, until recently, taken credit, as explained by Jean Gimpel in The Medieval Machine, Ref 12, p 142. This is an informative book which is spoiled by the French author's vitriolic loathing of all things Anglo-Saxon, and his unreconstructed Marxist opinions. The Vitruvius/Leonardo drawing has the man with his arms in the air above his head at a completely contrived angle, and I realised, that it was the subconscious refusal over the years, to accept this, which had been irritating me every time I looked at the picture. It became apparent to me that the arms were at that very specific angle so that a compass point could be placed on the navel and a circle drawn which would touch the feet and the outstretched fingers. In this way Vitruvius/Leonardo could claim that their preconceived notion, that the navel is the centre of the body, was demonstrated by the circle. This is not the case, and that circle only works at that arm angle. It is a bad construction and they were both wrong.

The correct way is to observe the height of the figure, in this case 6 ft, halve this number, and use that as the radius of a circle, which then must clearly encircle the body. The compass is first put at the top of the head and a half circle drawn, and then the same at the bottom of the feet. Where they touch will be the centre of the body. I was amazed to discover after doing this that the geometric centre of the body is at the top of the legs, at the point called the perineum (also known as the crotch). See the two illustrations.

HOW WE WERE MADE

which, yes, I too plagiarised from Vitruvius (but with my corrected geometry), and also shown in an illustration below.

Vitruvius/Leonardo had been looking for a sacred point on which to place their compass, and the navel does appear to be an attractive point, almost designed as a compass point, but it's not.

In fact, in terms of sacred spots, the perineum makes more sense, since this is the entrance, the altar, where new life is initiated, and the very point where the new-born babe first meets the light of day. At the very geometric centre of the mother's body. If more confirmation was needed, it can be seen that the diagonals of the square which encloses the body, also pass through the same point.

Other measures include:

> The 12 inch distance from the top of the head to the centre point of the outstretched arms.
>
> The 36 inch waist.
>
> The crotch is 36 inches from the ground, and 36 inches from the top of the head.
>
> The stride of 36 inches.
>
> The weight of 12 stone.
>
> Water is 0.666 of man's weight, that is, 2/3rds. All mammals on Earth have this ratio.

THE PARADIGM HUMAN MALE

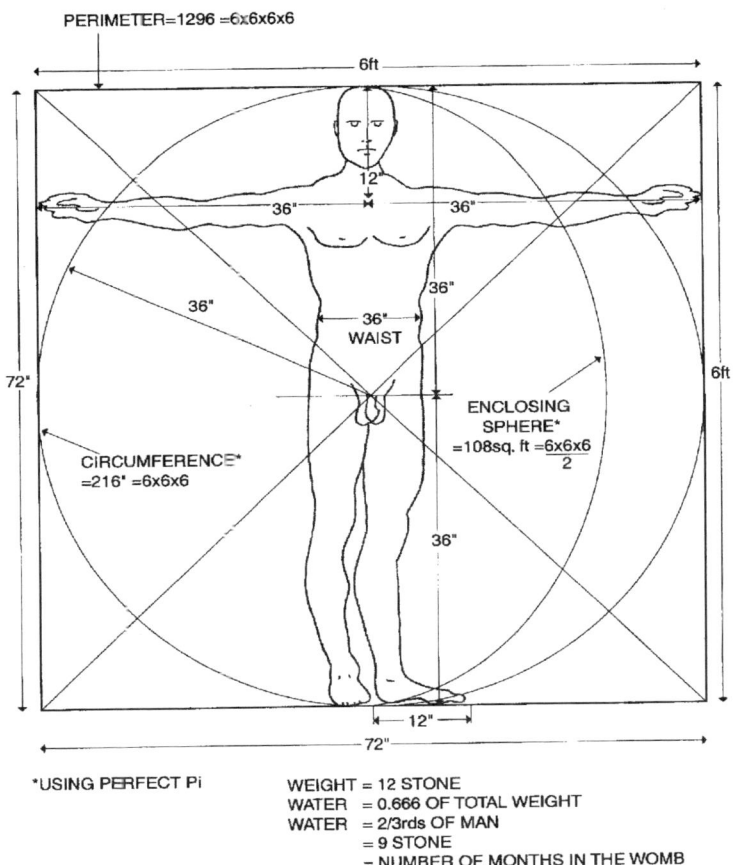

*USING PERFECT Pi

WEIGHT = 12 STONE
WATER = 0.666 OF TOTAL WEIGHT
WATER = 2/3rds OF MAN
= 9 STONE
= NUMBER OF MONTHS IN THE WOMB

HOW WE WERE MADE

MORE PHM NUMBERS PREDICATED ON 6

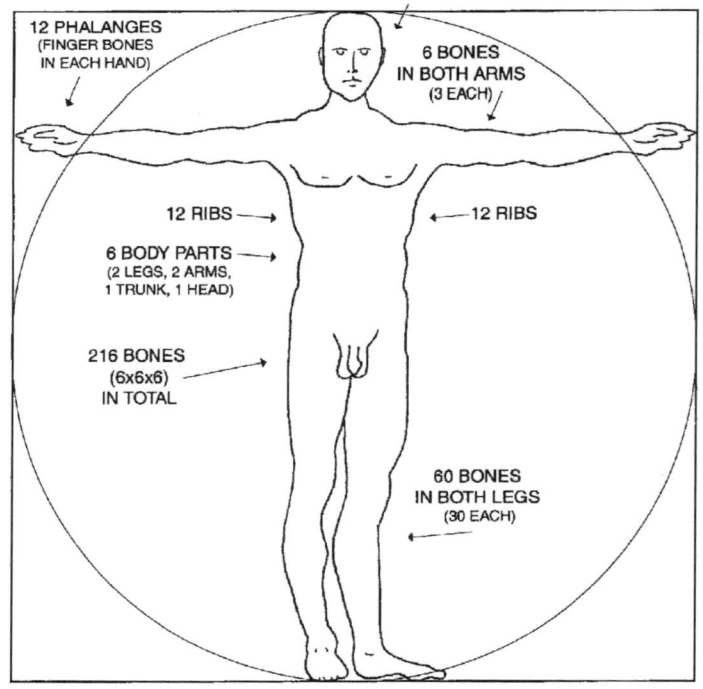

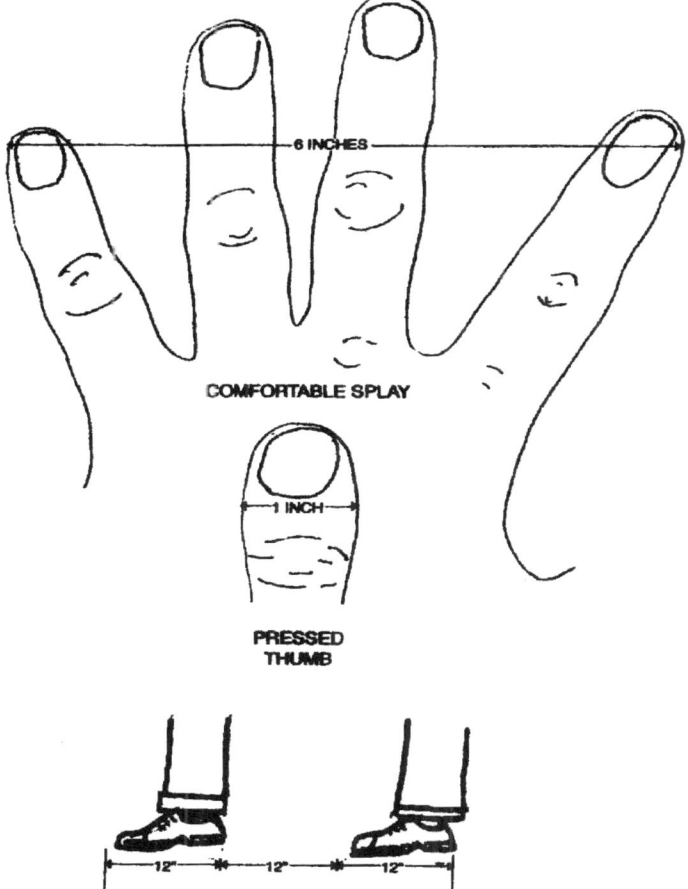

HOW WE WERE MADE

Until the melt-down at the end of the ice age, water was 2/3rds, or 0.666, of the Earth's surface. It is now 70%, and is in an imbalance.

Man's height, and width of the arms, may also be read as 72 inches (6 x 12), another important number which is also the number of years it takes to move one degree of the Precessional cycle in the sky.

The man is made of 6 distinct parts; two legs, two arms, a trunk and the head.

There are 6 openings on the head; two eyes, two ears, one mouth and one nose.

There are 216 bones in in the human (6 x 6 x 6), counting the nine fused vertebrae of the sacrum and coccyx as individuals, and also the enigmatic hyoid bone which sits, unconnected to any other bones, in the upper part of the neck. The number of bones in a person actually varies slightly around this number.

There are 12 ribs on both sides.

There are three bones in each arm – a total of 6.

There are 12 phalanges (finger bones) in the fingers of each hand (not the thumbs).

There are 30 bones in each leg.

It may be that the 12 phalanges in the four fingers were the original reasons for counting in 12's.

I may, moreover, add, that in the healthy PHM the resting heartbeat is 60 pulses per 60 seconds. It does of course vary, but this is the low end of the spectrum of heart rates and it only applies to those with good health, and it is the rate given in medical textbooks. This pulse rate is in complete synchronism with time itself, and in one hour a total 3,600 are pulsed out, giving another total of 43,200 in one 12 hour day. The 'sargal-min' of Sumer is 432,000; and 43,200 is one quarter of ten Precessional Cycles in years; it is also twice the number of nautical miles of the circumference of planet Earth, and the number of years for Earth's tilt to move from the minimum to the maximum.

But even more, I discovered that the circle of man, at 36 inches radius, produces, using Perfect Pi, a result of 216 inches as its circumference. 216 is, it will be remembered, 6 x 6 x 6. Also recall, that Revelation said that 666 is a human number. 2160 years is the time for one change of the zodiac, that is, from one sign to another. 2160 is the diameter of the moon. And of course we have met it elsewhere. This is the mancircle.

The sphere enclosing man with a radius of 3 feet (with Perfect Pi), produces a surface area of 108 square feet, this is half of 6 x 6 x 6. 1080 years is one half of one zodiacal change in the Precessional Cycle. This is the mansphere.

Man's perimeter of four 6's multiplies out to 1296. 12,960 years is one half of a complete revolution of the Precessional Cycle of 25,920 years. This is the mansquare.

The mansphere fills a box, a cube whose sides measure 6 feet. There are 6 sides to the cube. This produces a surface area of 216 square feet, and a volume of 216 cubic feet. Both represent 6 x 6 x 6. This is the mancube. These numbers are shown in the illustration.

HOW WE WERE MADE

Stirling says (Ref 20 p. 27):

"The first measures are said to have been derived from the body of man. God, the world, and man are synonymous terms, and the human body becomes the standard measure of the world"
My italics.

And again on page 247:

"The Doric was the oldest column, and was first made of the proportion 6 to 1, an imitation of the body of a man, as it is said, whose foot was found to be the 6th part of his height."

My surprise can be imagined when, in Ref 1, p 219, I found that this mancube had cropped up in the past, "The first ark was built by Utnapishtim in the Sumerian myth; one learns in different ways that it was a cube - a modest one, measuring 60 x 60 x 60 fathoms ['coincidentally', a fathom is 6 feet], which represents the unit in the sexagesimal system. In another version, there is no ark, just a cubic stone, upon which rests a pillar which reaches from Earth to heaven". I interpret that as meaning that Man is the foundation stone.

The volume of this cube is 216,000 cubic fathoms, which is also the distance in miles, surface to surface, from Earth to the moon at perigee. While its surface area is 21,600 square fathoms, which is the circumference of the Earth in nautical miles. There are 216 cubic feet to one cubic fathom.

The sides may also be written as being 360 feet since one fathom is six feet. This connection between 60 and 360 on Utnapishtim's Cube, is very interesting for it is also the relationship, in a circle, between a radius of 60 ft and the circumference of 360 ft (via Perfect Pi). The illustration refers.

Further, on page 221 of Ref 1, the authors say that even Christ was compared to a "cube shaped mountain, upon which a tower is erected" (in *The Pastor of Hermas*).

Revelations 21.16 says "The city lies foursquare, its length the same as its breadth; and he measured the city with his rod, 12,000 stadia; *its length and breadth and height are equal.*" My italics, and this is the definition of a cube. The holy city is a cube whose volume is thus 1.728×10^{12} cubic stadia (and note the 10 and the 12 here). This number is 66,666,666 Precessional Cycles of 25,920 years! But, even more remarkable, is the fact that 17,280 years is $2/3^{rds}$, or 66.6% of one Precessional Cycle, or the passage of 8 signs of the zodiac at 2160 years each.

The size of the holy city is structured on the Precessional Cycle. Whoever chose the number 12 as the number string for the holy city also knew that it was the cube root of 1728. There are also 1728 cubic inches in one cubic foot.

Stirling (Ref 20 p. 175) says:

> "...... the Holy of Holies being 20 cubits, or 360 inches
> square, with a perimeter of 1,440 inches, while the Holy Place is
> 720 by 360 inches having a perimeter of 2,160, the number of miles
> in the moon's diameter; ...... the measures of the porch are 180 x 360
> inches, which gives a perimeter of 1,080, the number of miles in
> the moon's radius". Surely there can be no doubt that this is simply a
> method of encoding, what had once been, secret data to which the
> 'ignorant and vulgar' were not party.

And on page 333, this rather inscrutable description:

> Roma [from gematria] has the value of 311, the side of a
> rhombus 540 long, and 540 x 4 = 2160. According to the Greek
> valuation of the letters it is equal to 941, and 942 is the diagonal of a
> square whose sides are 666.

At Mecca, in the holy shrine of the Ka'aba, sits the Holy Stone, once a cube of black rock, but now broken, surrounded by a ring of stones and held in place with a thick silver strap, and which the pilgrim must kiss. The

HOW WE WERE MADE

JACK IN THE BOX
THE EXTENSION OF IMAGE 6, MAN STANDING IN THE CENTRE,
WITH THE MANSPHERE TOUCHING ALL SIDES

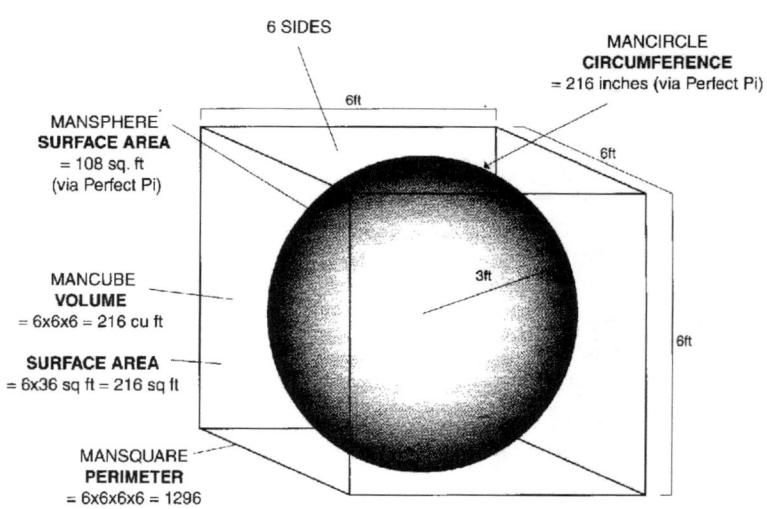

THE ARK OF UTNAPISHTIM, SUMER

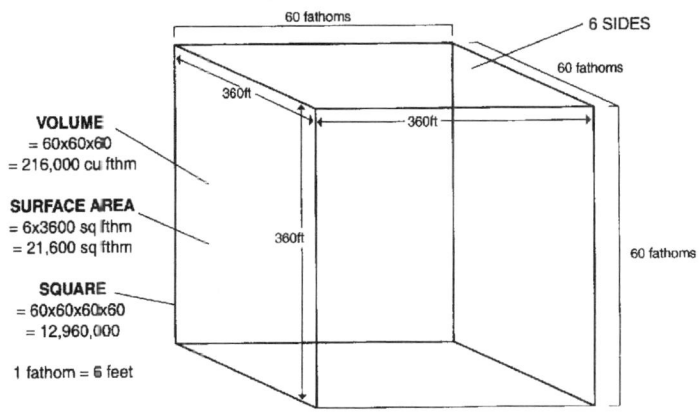

HOW WE WERE MADE

Ka'aba is also a cube shaped building covered with a black cloth. The Holy Stone was either given to Abraham by the Angel Gabriel, or it was given to Adam when he was expelled from the Garden of Eden. Adam is also accredited with building the Ka'aba. Either way, the story goes back to the beginning of time. I do not have the dimensions of the building or the stone.

On page 222 of Ref 1 they note that:

> The cube was Saturn's figure, as Kepler showed in his *Mysterium Cosmographicum*; this was the reason for the insistence on cubic stones and cubic arks...... Sigu's basket stopper was obviously an inadequate version of the cube seen through the eyes of basket weaving natives. .... The other motif is the foundation stone, which sometimes becomes a cubic ark, it needs patience to cope with the cubic stone which dwells in the middle of the sea.

And on page 435:

> Utnapishtim tells Gilgamesh (GE 11.57) about his ark, which was, like the apsu, an exact cube.

Before I leave Sumer, there is another quote I should like to take from Ref 1, p 297: Utnapishtim "describes with great care the building and caulking of the ship [the Ark], six decks, one *iku* (acre) the floor space, as much for each side, so that it was a perfect cube, exactly as Ea [the god] had ordered him to do". So, here are 6 decks, one cube, and the amazing *iku*. I say amazing because this is another example of a word which is still with us, almost unchanged after thousands of years. The acre is an ancient word that is recorded in Sumerian, Sanskrit, Latin, and the Nordic tongues and eventually in English. In England, at least (it may once have had the same definition in other languages), it is still defined, after many hundreds of years, as a rectangle 66 feet by 660 feet. 66 feet are 22 yards, which is also 'one chain', and, an English cricket pitch is the width of one acre. The total size of an acre is 4840 square yards, which is not a significant number. This dimension is shown in the illustration below, which also displays the mirror reflection between the Model Year and the imperial system of measurements.

Shortly after the signing of the Magna Carta, around 1215 AD, a royal decree was issued with the title 'Assize of Weights and Measures', and this defined the standard yard – 'the Iron Yard of our Lord the King'; contrary to predictions, this extremely relevant measure is still in use today. It is relevant because it relates to the Paradigm Human Male, and not some trumped up abstract length dreamed up by a few blood crazed commune dwellers two hundred years ago.

All of the measures we have seen so far concerning the dimensions of the PHM are based on 6, 6^2, and 6^3. We have met them everywhere from Sumer to the Yucatan. These numbers confirm that they are part of the Divine Measures, as are Time etc, and that man himself is the living measuring stick, predicated on the gods' number base of 6, and designed accordingly.

We saw earlier that 21.6 is the date of the Summer Solstice. In the case of man, this figure, in minutes on this occasion, that is 21.6 minutes, is the time taken for the PHM to walk exactly 1,760 yards, or strides, which is one mile, and this is the definition of the mile. To cover one mile in that time the man must walk at 2.778 miles/hour, and anyone holding the PHM dimensions can quite easily check this out for themselves by walking a measured mile at a comfortable rate (which happens to be 2.778). The otherwise odd number of 1,760 makes no sense until it is understood that it has been based on, and calculated around, the sacred number of 666, namely, 21.6. It is also the case that the PHM will jog comfortably at precisely 6.6 miles per 60 minutes.

Oh, by the way, the perimeter of the Great Pyramid at Giza is 1,760 cubits!!

Even the lifespan of man was reduced by the gods, through genetic manipulation, to 120 years, as told in Genesis 6. Prior to that man had been living for many hundreds of years, but they got fed up with his antics and punished him with early mortality. Some have argued that the long lifespans

HOW WE WERE MADE

"THE IRON YARD OF OUR LORD THE KING"

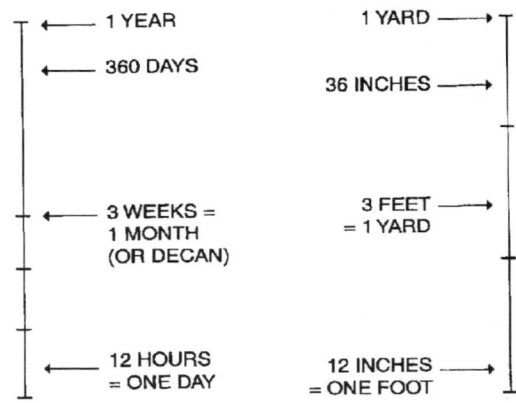

THE ANCIENT YEAR **THE IMPERIAL SYSTEM**

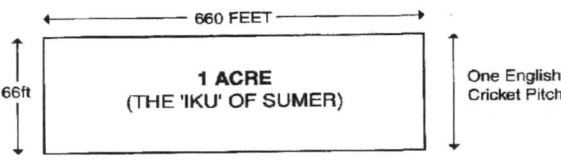

quoted in Genesis 5 were lunar months, not solar years, but that cannot be so, for some of the ages quoted would make the men too young if they were lunar months; for example "when Enosh had lived 90 years he became the father of Kenan". If these were lunar months that would make Enosh 7.5 years old when his son was born. That man was living amongst the gods is also made plain in the same two chapters, for it is explained that when mankind began to breed daughters, the sons of God began to sleep with them, producing offspring that were "the mighty men of old, the men of renown". There is a clear distinction here between man, and gods. Additionally we are told that the Nephilim were on the Earth in those days. But we are not told who these are. A whole menagerie of intelligent beings is here at the same time - man, sons of God, half-caste man-gods, God, and the Nephilim. Not satisfied with reducing man's lifespan to 120 years, He gets really annoyed and threatens to wipe out all of mankind. In reality the average age of life for people on this planet is now more like 60 years.

These days the concept of genetic modification (GM) is commonly known, and we read daily of advances which will allow the elimination of disease. Biologists are already changing plants and animals, and there is absolutely no reason why humans can't also be GM'd, into, let's say, supermen. It is certain that any group of 'gods' who were able to visit this place thousands of years ago, would be well advanced in these arts, and had most probably GM'd themselves into achieving better intelligence and greater longevity. It can only be a matter of time before we do the same to ourselves. Fiddling about with what they found here would surely not have been a problem, and it explains the sudden appearance of modern man about 30k years ago, and the equally sudden disappearance of Neanderthal man at the same time. They did not grant him civilisation however until 3,100 BC. Until 3,100 BC humans can have been little better than clever animals, able to stay alive, but not much more. Even though their brain potential was exactly the same as ours is today, they did not have the kick-starts needed to live some sort of civilized existence. The evidence of how humans perform, or achieve, without the benefit of education, i.e. civilisation, is all around us. It doesn't take much regression for man to become extremely primitive again, in one generation. It is only the constant teaching of the next generation which keeps us civilized. We do not have any innate ability to

HOW WE WERE MADE

pop out of the womb and automatically assume high knowledge and moral standards. Everything has to be given to us, on a plate, by kindly teachers, and with learning comes the ability to use that information in other ways as we get older. So it was with mankind; until someone came along and gave him that teaching, he was nothing.

That the mile itself is a sacred measure will become evident later when I move on to consider larger measurements, which obviously require larger units. I will demonstrate that the distances, measured in miles, conform to the same sacred units that we have already seen in many other fields. The very fact that the measurements which I will highlight are these same numbers, on a different scale, proves beyond doubt that they have been designed, and that their number string is part of a scheme. These numbers are not secret, they are available in many reference books, it's just that no one has noticed before.

Unfortunately, in the metric system there are no larger units, everything is measured in metres, which is only three inches longer than a yard. The result is that large distances end up with hideously long numbers as their measure, eg Earth's diameter is 7,972 miles, but 12,756,000 metres.

We are in danger of losing this last Divine Measure - inches, feet etc, by the onward march of the dreaded metre. The metre is a measure which bears no relationship to anything that we can see or touch with the naked eye or hand. It was a complete invention, made up by a group of deranged revolutionaries in France in the 1790's. These people were crazed with blood and had murdered thousands of innocent fellow countrymen in the name of the revolution. The world has seen many examples of such madness; Russia & Stalin, Cambodia & Pol Pot, China & The Red Guards, Romania & Ceausescu; the list goes on. But there is always a common thread, and that is a mad desire to wipe out everything from the past. To start again with a new rational system, even to a new Year Zero. Ordinary folk (enemies of the people), government systems, buildings, education, *et al*, all is grist for the revolutionary mill. The French behaved precisely according to revolutionary type, and proceeded to dump all measurement systems tainted by association with the hated past; thus the metre was born, stained with blood, on 7 April 1795. It was supposed to be one ten-millionth part of the Earth's quadrant, although quite why that would be more useful to the ordinary man, rather than the length of his foot, is beyond anyone's comprehension. Today that measure is inaccurate, but the original platinum bar has been retained, even though it is unrelated to anything. Napoleon asked why the government was tormenting the French people with these stupid new measures, when they had perfectly good ones already in place - yes, they used inches and feet!

Then they found that the metre was conveniently, almost, a nice round figure for the speed of light - 300,000,000 metres/ sec, so it is now defined as the distance travelled by light in a vacuum in 1/ 299,792,458 seconds. As I have noted, a unit which is useless to anyone. Tellingly, the authors of the Larousse Encyclopedia of Astronomy, Ref 13, have this to say on p. 79, "We, in this country, [France] have been in the habit of *using English measures in our daily lives* (my italics), but the metric system is almost universally used for scientific purposes. In this book, therefore, the plan has been to employ the metric system wherever possible, but where it is felt that English measures would be more easily understood, we have used them". Be assured that the book is mostly in feet and inches.

Tompkins, in Ref 19, p 73 comments:

> Sir John Herschel, one of Britain's most eminent astronomers at the beginning of the nineteenth century, criticized the French meter derived from a curved meridian of the earth as being erratic and variable from country to country because the earth is not a true sphere, and each meridian of longitude would therefore be different. (What's more the French had erred, and produced a meter that was .0002 too short.) ....
> Herschel suggested that the regular British inch – which was officially computed as the length of three grains of barley taken from the middle ear and placed end to end -- be arbitrarily lengthened by a mere one thousandth part in order to obtain a truly scientific, earth-commensurate unit exactly one fifty-millionth part of the polar axis of the earth.

HOW WE WERE MADE

Although Sir John felt that the inch had been corrupted over the millennia and needed lengthening by one thousandth of an inch to make it fit the Earth's proportions, it may also be the case that it is not the inch which has changed, but the Earth. There are observable signs that it is changing almost on a daily basis, and certainly during the 'ice age' the poles were massive compared with today's.

Professor Livio Catullo Stecchini in Ref 19, p 304 says:

> The ancient system of measures continues to be used today in the form of English measures; we find the basic units of the English system, such as the pound .... , used in Mesopotamia [Sumeria] in the third millennium B.C. [3,000 B.C.].

And on page 309:

> The English grain has remained stable as 1/5000 of a Roman *libra*. English weight units have not changed at all since Sumerian times. The oldest weights of which I have found ... at Tepe Gawra in Iraq .... precede by about a millennium the invention of writing. .... These weights are fractions of the English ounce avoirdupois.

Also on page 344:

> ..... a foot equal to the English foot was the basic standard of Russia, ... to the time of the Soviet revolution [see my comments above regarding revolutionaries ditching the old systems]. .... it takes specialised historical training to trace the linear standard of England and Russia to the ancient orient, but I may also observe that there are many Greek temples which have been planned in English feet.

Again on page 345:

> The political conditions of the feudal society of Saxon England were very different from those of Pharaonic Egypt, but the method used by

King Athelstan in order to relate his power to the system of measures and to the cosmic order bears a remarkable similarity to that adopted by the Pharaoh Akhenaten. [He created the 'Amarna revolution', adopted a single god – the Aten Disc (not to be confused with the A10 from London to Cambridge, which is not, apparently, worshipped); had, as wife, Nefertiti, and son Tutankhamun].

These two letters appeared in British newspapers. From the Daily Telegraph, 23.2.2002: "Sir, On holiday in France, I needed a length of copper pipe for a repair to our caravan. I went to a garage and explained as well as I could that I wanted a piece of 12.5mm pipe. Puzzlement, then, "Ah Monsieur, le 'alf inch". H.M., Norfolk". And from The Sunday Times, 24.2.2002: "I have lived and worked in France for the past 26 years, and whenever I have needed a piece of plumbing equipment, be it a pipe or a connection, I have always had to measure and buy it in inches or a fraction of an inch. Throughout France, plumbers recognise no other measurement. C.A.G., Devon". I understand the same applies in Denmark, and, for all I know, may be so across the whole of Europe. As we saw above, it used to apply in Russia too. In Norway an inch is called a 'tum' ie thumb.

It is a fact, that if a young man in this country (GB) who is, say, 6 feet tall, and who has been indoctrinated with metric propaganda throughout his education, is asked his height, he will reply "6 ft". He will certainly not say "1.8288037 metres". Which is what happened when I filled in my passport application form; I put 6 ft, and the passport came back with 1.83 meters on it, which, as can be seen, is incorrect.

A further benefit of the inch is its divisibility by 2 into ever smaller measurements: 1/2, 1/4, 1/8, 1/16, 1/32, 1/64, etc, and multiples of these, e.g. 3/16^{ths}. Within living memory everything in engineering was solely sized in these fractions; bolts, drills, nuts, spanners etc. Now they come also marked in millimeters.

These fractions can also be written another way:- 2^{-1}, 2^{-2}, 2^{-3}, 2^{-4},

HOW WE WERE MADE

2^{-5}, 2^{-6}. Amazingly, this enumeration can be applied to digital systems, in which a variable can take one of two 'states'. For example a coin is a single variable with two states. This concept is also used in digital transmission systems for telecoms, and indeed in digital computers, where the signal can be either '0' or '1', i.e. 2 states. The number of positions of this variable determines the size of the code. For example five coins each having two states (ie heads & tails) will produce 2^5, or 32, combinations (cf. above where 2^{-5} is 1/32).

The Egyptians used this system of division too; in a construction called the Eye of Horus they assigned a fractional value to each part of the eye, as shown in the illustration. When they needed to show a fraction in their hieroglyphs they would show it as that part of the eye. The fractions in the Eye add up to 63/64, or the bizarre number $(1 - 2^{-6})$. Temple, in Ref 3, p 442, feels that the inverse, 64/63, which is 1.01587, is an approximation to the Comma of Pythagoras of 1.0136, but I'm afraid I do not, the difference is too large. The form of $(1 - 2^{-6})$, or, $- (2^{-6} - 1)$ is identical to that of a negative 'Mersenne number' which is written $(2^n - 1)$, where, here, n = -6.

At the small town of East Liverpool in Ohio, just across the border from Pennsylvania, there is a sign which says "The Point of the Beginning". This was the spot where, in 1786, Thomas Jefferson started the measurement of the USA so that it could be divided up, sold, and legally owned in accurate plots. The measure used was a 22 yard chain, and the quest started with axemen going on before, clearing the way, followed by a foreman who held the front, or fore, of the chain while the hindman carried its rear. At each 22 yard point a marker was then hammered into the ground. The way forward was set using a compass. Why the choice of 22 yards? Well, this is the length of an English cricket pitch, and the width of an acre, and a very sensible distance it is too, which Jefferson clearly also thought since he was a keen cricketer. The whole of the USA is now measured in lengths of English cricket pitches! They will be loathe to convert this to metres. This number is very close to 21.6, but, even more importantly, since there are 3 feet to one yard, the length of 22 yards is actually 66 feet, so the USA is charted using the divine numbers of 6 and 6. The USA also uses the English acre to measure land, and this too, as we saw, is 66 feet by 660 feet.

THE EYE OF HORUS

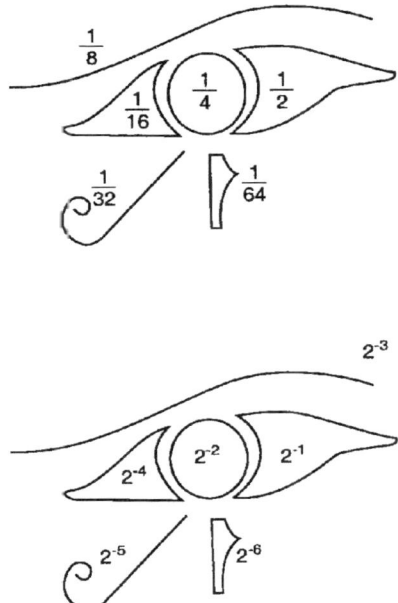

HOW WE WERE MADE

Moving away from the sacred linear measures of feet and inches, to the botched measure of the metre, is a repetition of the tragedy of losing the ancient calender of the Model Year of 360 days, as described earlier. We appear to be quite happily marching towards the same stupid mess of meaningless and unrelated numbers – or at least the bureaucrats do.

This small range of numbers has, then, been used to design and construct mankind, which makes him a marker for the gods. The same numbers have been used in the construction, placing, and movement of, the Earth, moon and the planets. Additionally, certain constants which are fundamental to us have also been so encoded, and I will be discussing these in the next chapters. It is as if, in order to claim their own, they have used these numbers on specific items, so that on return, they can say "oh yes, this is one of ours". A bit like branding cattle really, all the animals look slightly different from each other, but with that one mark placed there by us we can immediately assume ownership. We don't need to mark the whole cow, or give it any sort of complex encoding, that simple mark is instantly evidence of "this is one of ours". This is why not everything needs to be encoded, which would otherwise have been a time consuming and pointless exercise. A sufficient number of essential parameters have been stamped with their marks, i.e. their numbers, and that is adequate. The first act of a bureaucracy is to start assigning numbers to those caught in its clutches, some of those numbers tell a lot about a person, and put together they will give a complete outline of that person's life and style; and yet they are only strings of numbers. Therefore, we do not need to look for the Divine Numbers in every single aspect of material matters, but to find a significant amount of them in important places, like the mark on the back of a cow, or the post code on some personal equipment. In our own lives we may mark up certain things but not others; for example we would mark the video recorder, but not the dining table. Trying to mark all items in the home would be wasteful, and, in the case of a burglary, the police would automatically know to check for only certain missing luxuries.

I mentioned earlier that beings who had the knowledge to arrange matters on the scale which I've been discussing, certainly knew all about the structure of all life on this planet. It is only now that we are becoming able to manipulate the 'artifact of life' - DNA, or Genetic Modification as it is being termed – GM, which I have already mentioned. I read in the national press in 2001 that one laboratory had managed to implant human DNA from sperm, into the DNA of a pig's egg. It had 'taken' and the resultant creature was developing in vitro - a human pig (and please, no jokes about having worked for one, or worse still, been married to one). After a few weeks they decided to terminate the 'experiment', although I am sure that they could have found a willing human female carrier to bring it to fruition, or failing that, an animal. Other work is going on in the field of foodstuffs, one of the latest being to create a GM'd tomato which has three times the amount of lycopene, a substance which has proven cancer protecting properties.

Those carvings from ancient Mesopotamia, and indeed Egypt and Greece, which show creatures which are combinations of two or more others, begin to take on a new life. We can observe that they are on leashes, and are walking beside their owners precisely in the same manner as we take the dog for a walk. From the example which I quoted above, the reality that such cross-species development can in fact take place begins to look more and more possible. It is a well known fact in the agricultural world that the staples of rice, maize and wheat are examples of food sources which strangely 'evolved' around 3000 BC to produce very much larger grain crops than had ever been possible with their wild ancestors, just in time for 'civilised' man to emerge onto the world scene. This was done for us in order that humans could move away from a hunter-gatherer existence and settle into societies, which would develop and support civilisation.

That the gods knew about the structure of DNA is actually shown in the stylised representation of it in Sumer, in the form of entwined serpents. For example Sitchin in Ref 14, p 176, describes how one god was given the title of NIN.GISH.ZI.DA and awarded the symbol of Enki (one of the founder gods of Sumer). This symbol was the pair of serpents which the god is shown wearing, and his name means 'Lord of the Artifact of Life', i.e. DNA. I have adapted Sitchin's sketch and this is shown in the following illustration. Similarly, King Gudea of Lagash (Sumer, circa 2160 BC) also used the symbol, as shown in the illustrations, of the entwined serpents, and this time the serpent/DNA is guarded by two creatures who are themselves

HOW WE WERE MADE

obviously the result of genetic modification. This sketch is adapted from a vase in the Louvre Museum.

The association of the these two entwined serpents with human health and 'medicine' is still with us today. It came down to us via the Greeks and then the Romans, it was called either, the Caduceus of Mercury or the Caduceus of Hermes, and was used as a symbol by medical practitioners in those far off days. Today many medical institutions use it as their sign, for instance the Public Health Service in the USA. A strand of DNA for comparison is shown in the illustrations, from which the similarities are evident for all to see.

On the 16th November 2002 the BBC broadcast a programme called 'Britain's Best Buildings', it was one of a (excellent) series, and this 55 minute episode gave us a view of Durham Cathedral. The series is also available in a book: 'Britain's Best Buildings, by Dan Cruikshank, published by BBC Worldwide Ltd, 2002, London'. The writer and presenter of the show is also the author of the book. In the nave of the cathedral he showed us a series of 6 unique columns, of a rather strange shape, for they were all as tall as they were round, and were arranged in 3 pairs, each pair having the same design cut deeply into the surface. Of particular interest was the pair with a net design made up from individual lozenges, which I have sketched in. The presenter made the following observations " Each lozenge is 12" x 12" = 144" square. The columns are 12 lozenges high and 12 lozenges in girth, so each column has 144 lozenges. The book of Revelations chapter 21 says that the holy city had 12 gates and its walls measured 144 cubits. The holy city is a mighty cube. The nave columns are 22' 3" high and round. Two have the net pattern and two have a chevron design [sawtooth]. There are 12 chevrons per column, and 8 peaks per band. [nb this gives a total of 72]. But see it another way; the net pattern is also a double spiral, [a] double helix, and of course this is a discovery [of] DNA. The double helix has become the geometry of life itself. So the medieval science of sacred geometry gave the masons of Durham Cathedral a vision of perhaps the most important scientific breakthrough of the modern age - the double helix of DNA". Cue sacred choirs and whirling strands of DNA. Apart from the divine numbers of 6, 12 and 72 displayed above, notice that the height and girth of all of the

6 columns is 22' 3", this is almost the number string for the present tilt of the Earth itself, 23.3^0. These are shown in the sketch below, which, I should point out, does not do justice to the actual spiral shapes on the columns, in this sketch they look like flat straight lines, but seen on camera they really are beautiful spirals.

HOW WE WERE MADE

NIN.GISH.ZI.DA "LORD OF THE ARTIFACT OF LIFE"

STANDARD OF KING GUDEA OF LAGASH, SUMER

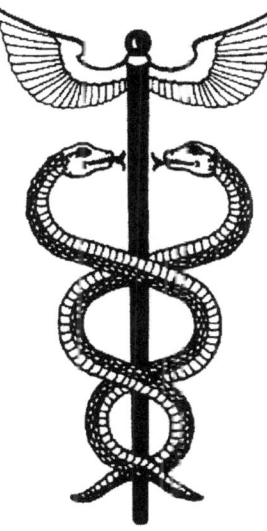

**MERCURY'S CADUCEUS
ALSO HERMES' CADUCEUS**

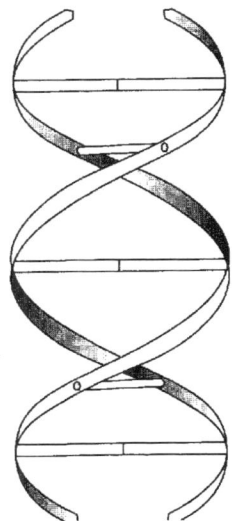

**DNA - DEOXYRIBONUCLEIC ACID
"THE ARTIFACT OF LIFE"**

HOW WE WERE MADE

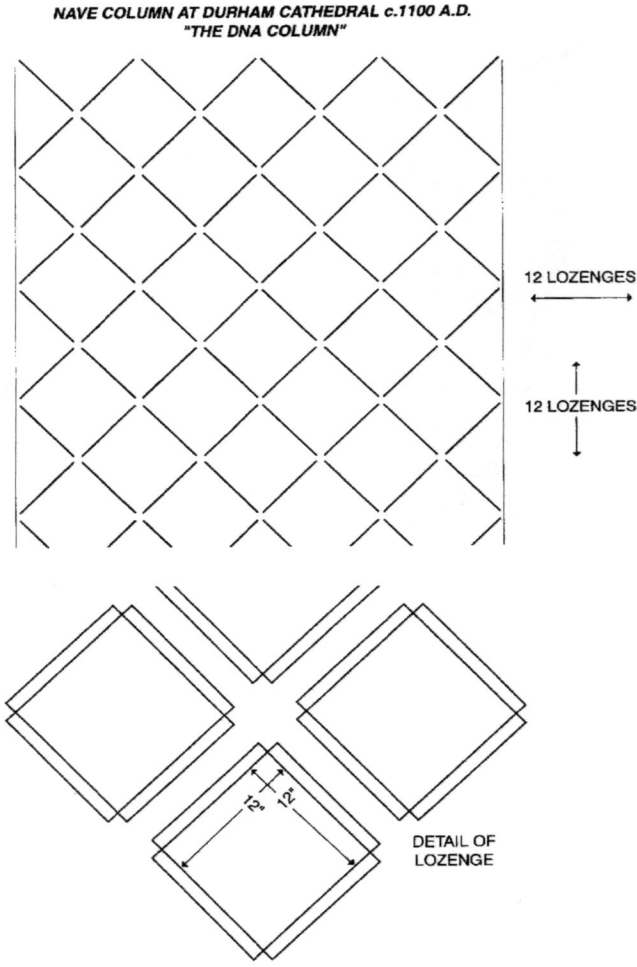

VI
SPECIFICATION EARTH

Has the Earth itself been designed? Are there any sacred geometrical measures which might point to such a project, which may be discovered by inquiring about numbers which reflect those we have already seen elsewhere?

Well, let's have a look.

Around 10,500 years ago, when the ice had finally finished its meltdown, the Earth assumed the approximate geography that it has today, and its tilt of 23.3^0, called the Obliquity of the Ecliptic. This tilt gives us the Arctic Circle and the Antarctic Circle, which both measure 23.3^0 down from the actual points of the poles. It also gives the measure to the Tropics of Cancer and Capricorn, which are 23.3^0 up, and down, from the Equator respectively. First, I'll just outline a few points about the Tropics as they will become quite important concepts in my discussion of the Earth's location. These two are given those names because at the summer solstice, on 21 June in the northern hemisphere, the Sun appears directly over the Tropic of Gemini; but, long ago, it appeared over the constellation Cancer, and was given the title Tropic of Cancer, which has been retained to this day. Similarly, on the summer solstice in the southern hemisphere, the 21 December, (ie the winter solstice in the north), the Sun appears over the constellation Sagittarius, but, long ago, it appeared over Capricorn, which name has also been retained. The lines are decided because it is on these two dates that the Sun reaches its greatest journey to the north, and to the south, after which it turns, and proceeds back again. Put another way, the angle of 23.3 is the northernmost latitude reached by the overhead Sun (and ditto for the south). The Tropics mark the turning points of the Sun. The word 'tropic' is from the Latin

HOW WE WERE MADE

'tropicus', and means 'turning of the Sun'. It is only between these Tropics that the Sun can be seen directly overhead. Hence we have have phrases like "in the tropics" which means that area that lies between the two Tropics, and is the warm parts of the planet – the tropical locations.

That the Sun has moved from Cancer to Gemini is due to the circular motion which the Earth's axis is slowly making around its own tilt of $23.3°$. This circular motion gives rise to another effect called the Precession of the Equinoxes, and a complete revolution takes 25,920 years. As there are 12 constellations in the zodiac it therefore takes each sign 2,160 years for a transition from one sign to another. (I promise that the two phenomena – Obliquity and Precession - are as hard as it gets!). The Sun moved into Gemini around the start of our year zero, some 2000 years ago, and before that it was in Cancer. It will move into the next constellation of Taurus in about 160 years, ie the Sun will then cover Taurus on the summer solstice in the north (but the tropic will still be called Cancer in honour of the past). I hope you have noticed that magic number of 2,160 years, as we have met it several times already in different guises.

We have now established some facts about four of the imaginary lines around the planet, and its tilt, so I will put that to one side for a while to consider another factor which is related to their positions, namely the tilt of the Earth. The obliquity of the Earth is not a fixed angle, which is presently $23.3°$, it varies over a very great period of time believed to be about 41,000 years (of which, more shortly). These measures are summarised in the illustration.

Messrs Bauval and Hancock in Ref 15, p 305, have this to say about the angle of obliquity:

> An intensely mathematical treatment of the matter [obliquity] is given by Laskar, Joutel and Boudin in the Journal of Astronomy and Astrophysics, na270, pp 522 –533 (1993). From their findings, the apparent limits of the obliquity are $22°$ to $24.5°$, though values are far from certain.

THE EARTH TODAY

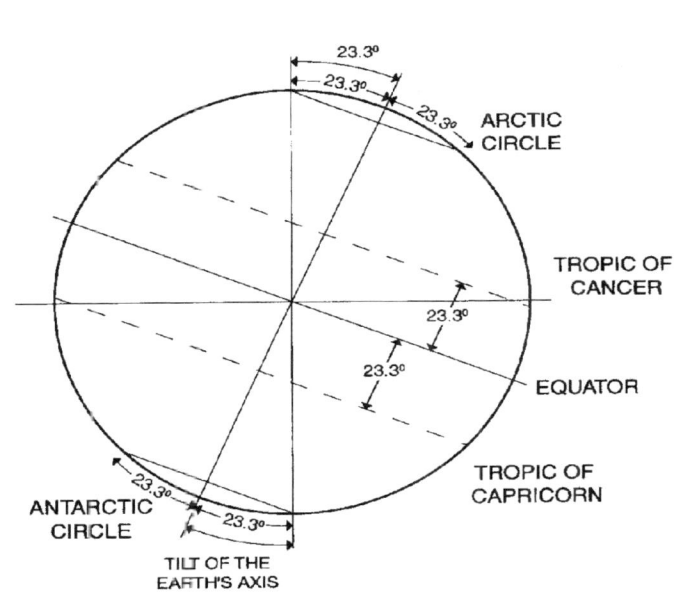

HOW WE WERE MADE

Knowing what we now know about sacred numbers (and there is a lot more to come), I felt absolutely certain that the minimum angle of 22^0 proposed by the above mathematicians, and remember it is an acknowledged approximation, is very slightly out. Several other books as well point to it reducing to only 22^0, including Ref 13 the Encyclopedia of Astronomy. This was disappointing for me because my hypothesis is that it needed to be reduced further by 0.4^0. That would then bring it into line at 21.6^0 (which is 6.6.6).

Then came vindication. I decided to also check in Ref 16, the Encyclopedia Britannica (in the Ask Britannica box, type in 'obliquity', then click on 'atmospheric sciences: Climate change and its causes'; I have put this instruction in because I had enormous difficulty relocating the data). To my amazement I saw that it quoted a figure of 21^0 39', which is 21.65^0, for the minimum angle of obliquity; virtually the same as mine – 21.6^0. I had started out in the belief that I would just make the claim about my feeling of the minimum of the obliquity, without being able to produce any proof, and now here was the same figure in the encyclopedia for all to see. That was a very comforting confirmation. Later, when I produce the Earth/Moon dimensions, it will be very hard to resist such a beautiful symmetry, as it will become obvious that the whole mechanism is part of a unified system of measurements, to a high specification. The same source gives the maximum angle as 24.6^0, thus the angle varies 3^0 (6/2) between max and min, and 3^0 is also 10,800 seconds.

As I said earlier it is this tilt that gives us the seasons of the year in the temperate zones – they have made it as pleasant as possible for us! Without the tilt there would be no seasons; no spring in which to see new buds and flowers growing again, no autumn in which to observe the changing colours of the leaves, and no lovely white snow in the winter crisp and crackling underfoot and all silent and clean. Such beauty. A changing of scenes four times every year, and of course 4 is 0.666 of 6. Oh, and without the tilt the days and nights would be the same length all of the time, and there would be no seasons.

There are several theories as to what caused the meltdown at the end of the last "ice-age". I have put ice-age in quote marks because there is strong evidence that there never was an "ice-age" at all, but that the polar regions were shifted into different zones by a phenomenon which caused a catastrophic re-alignment of the planet. Professor Charles Hapgood has published such a theory in his books Path of the Poles, and Earth's Shifting Crust (the latter with a foreword by Einstein in 1953 supporting his ideas). In short, his hypothesis is that the Earth's crust was caused to slide around the core through an imbalance brought about by the huge mass of ice at the poles in pre 15,000 BC. The sea level was 426 feet lower than it is now and so that volume of water stored as ice would have meant that the polar icecaps were indeed very much thicker than they are today. These monstrous weights at both ends of the planet led to a need to re-balance, and this was brought about through the "skin" sliding around to a new position so that the gyroscope which is Earth was now spinning correctly, in effect a self-correcting mechanism. Unfortunately, in so doing the old poles were pushed into warmer climes which then started them melting. New polar positions were located at the places they are today, but the old ones continued to melt for about 3000 years thus giving rise to the flood legends which occur in all cultures

The figure given by the Encyclopedia Britannica for the sea level pre 15,000 BC, is that it was 426 feet lower than it is today, that is, it has risen by that amount to the level we have today. With the sea rise went a large amount of estuarial and low lying land. This type of land is usually prime fertile soil fed by deposits of silt from up country, which would therefore be growing dense greenery and thereby attracting large numbers of animals. The shallow warm waters around these low lying coasts would also be teeming with marine life. So, rather than living in a hostile "ice-age" mankind was inhabiting a rather more beneficial and productive land than is available nowadays. All of that was lost, and, in addition to the floods, there would have been earthquakes, storms, tidal waves etc; their settlements in those areas would have been wiped out as the people, who could, fled to higher ground. Because those settlements are now under the sea we do not know what the population of the world was then, nor will we probably ever know since they are now all covered with thousands of years of silt, and

HOW WE WERE MADE

below-seabed archaeology is not something that has ever been tried as yet. Some large structures have been spotted, such as: the "pyramid" off Japan, the city off the western coast of India, the Malta "cart ruts" which run all over Malta and also continue out to sea cut into solid rock, and the Bimini "road".

I have diverted away from numbers for a moment simply to show that the meltdown was certainly not caused by climatic changes. Graphs of sea level rise produced by oceanographers all show that the rise was not gradual, it came in two, or possibly three, catastrophic meltdowns that occurred very suddenly, which itself is implicative of a change in the orientation of the Earth's position. There are archaeological proofs of this suddenness which are described in Professor Hapgood's books that I mentioned above. One of his examples may suffice to convince. During excavations in Siberia a frozen mammoth was found with foliage in its stomach which had come from trees that only grow in warm climates. But even more startling was that the acid in its guts had not had time to dissolve the greenery before the animal was quick frozen. One moment it is eating warm leaves from a tree in a pleasant habitat, the next it is frozen to death. A bit like a polar explorer taking his clothes off and stepping outside his tent! That is how quickly the earth moved.

However, I must part company with the professor on the mechanism of the move. That the Earth juddered is beyond doubt in my view, and is well supported by the evidence which he puts forward, in the books which I mentioned above. I am not convinced though, that his thesis that the skin of the Earth, the crust, can slip around the whole core, as such a move would surely tear the planet asunder. The crust is 3 miles thick on the ocean floor, but 19 miles thick on the continents. This skin is connected to the mantle which is some 1800 miles thick. No holes have ever been drilled through the crust, even though we drill for oil. The only information we have of the mantle is that which is obtained from seismic surveys. How the crust is connected to the mantle is not fully understood, but of course, connected it must be. To separate the two seems impossible. My hypothesis for the movement is much simpler, and I do maintain that elegant simple solutions are far more credible than complex ones. I do not suppose we will ever know the true solution, but I believe that the Earth moved because its axis moved, to a new tilt of 23.3°, from its old tilt of 21.6°.

Hancock draws attention to a similar view in Ref 17, p 512:

> While he was at the University of Cambridge the geologist S K Runcorn published an article in *Scientific American* which made a pertinent point:
>
>> There seems to be no doubt that the Earth's magnetic field is tied up in some way to the rotation of the planet. And this leads to a remarkable finding about the earth's rotation.... [the unavoidable conclusion is that] the earth's axis of rotation has changed also. In other words, the planet has rolled about, *changing the location of the geographical poles.* (my italics).

Furthermore, if the old tilt had been more vertical, at 21.6°, then the poles would have always been further away from the Sun during each polar summer, thus making the poles colder than they now are. During each colder summer the ice would remain in the formation stage, rather than melting slightly, or at least not forming. Over a long period of time the poles would have enlarged, depositing more ice, and taking water away from the oceans which would have lowered their levels. Eventually, the point was reached whereby so much ice was piled up at each end of the Earth that the planet was made to wobble, and to move to a new angle of tilt, leading to the meltdown.

The previous tilt of 21.6° would of course have other effects on the Earth. The two polar circles would also now be at 21.6° down from the polar points. The Tropics of Cancer and Capricorn would also be 21.6° up and down from the equator.

Just imagine then, before the meltdown started, that on midsummer's day – 21.6 (21st of June), all of these circles, and the Earth's tilt too, were all on the same number – 21.6°! This is of course 6.6.6. Just a perfect day. The illustration refers.

HOW WE WERE MADE

AND AS IT ONCE WAS ON A MIDSUMMER'S DAY - 21.6, THE SUN ROSE AT 21.6°, A PERFECT DAY!

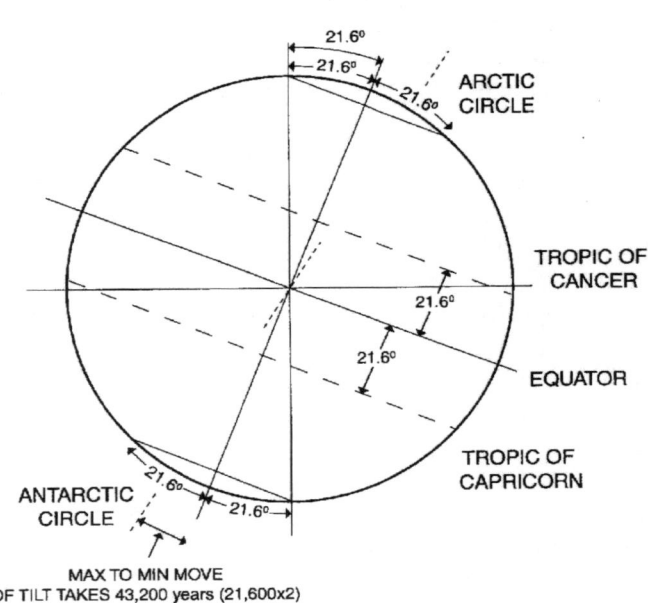

MAX TO MIN MOVE
OF TILT TAKES 43,200 years (21,600x2)

There is another hidden coding in 21.6^0, for I can also write it another way. 21.6^0 is a decimal, but if the 0.6 part of it is stated as minutes instead of part of a degree, i.e. 0.6 x 60 minutes, we have 36' which is read as 21^0 36' - note the 36. Taken further, the 36' is also 36 x 60 seconds, which is 2160"; we therefore have 21.6^0 which can also be presented as 21^0 2160". Furthermore, in its 21^0 36' form, the ratio 21:36 is an expression of the ratio 6:10 (21 divided by 36, is 0.6 divided by 1, multiply both by 10) which is the bringing together of the gods' number base of 6 beside the human digits of 10 – the decimal system of man.

Equally remarkable, is that, before the meltdown, the lower oceans occupied exactly 66.6% (there's that 666 again) of the earth's surface (two-thirds). Since then, with the rise in sea levels, this ratio has changed to something around 70%. This water figure (66.6%) is interesting for it is also the volume by weight of the amount of water in a human body. All other mammals have the same figure – 66.6%, and so the surface area of water on the planet is (was) the same percentage as the weight of water in the mammals walking around it.

There is another factor involved with the tilt of the planet, and that is the time it takes to move from its minimum to maximum angle of tilt, ie from 21.6 to 24.6 degrees. The time is "believed" to be about 41,000 years. This movement is not to be confused with the other, circular one, which gives rise to the Precession. However, my hypothesis in relation to the tilt, is that it will eventually be found to be 43,200 years, not 41,000. Why this strange number? Well, quite simply because it is twice 21,600, or twice 6.6.6 (x 100). Do remember that the "guesstimate" figure of 41,000 is just that, no one yet knows the correct figure; I feel convinced that mine will be found to be the correct one. We saw earlier that this number string featured in Sumer as 432,000, the 'sargal-mir'; and also as 4,320,000, the 'sargal-u-min'. Across the world the number is also 6 katun of the Mayan system (and note well the 6 here), that is, 6 x 7,200 days = 43,200 days. And of course, the ancient Hindus too had the string as the kaliyuga, 432,000 human years; and also the mahayuga, 4,320,000 human years.

HOW WE WERE MADE

Remarkably, there is another confirmation of 43,200, which is related to the Precessional Cycle, half of which is 12,960 years. If I now call this 12,960 feet instead of years, then, as there are 3 feet to every yard, this number is also 4320 yards. Here we have a chain of measures connecting feet, yards, the Precessional Cycle, the tilt of the Earth, and 666; for 432 is twice 6 x 6 x 6.

So, perhaps the ancients knew and revered these number strings, and gave them special names, for the simple reason that they referred to actual measurements related to the planet.

I would like to quote here, verbatim, a rather astounding relationship about this number, presented in Ref 15, pp 39 – 40, (they take the discovery from Professor L C Stecchini in the Appendix to the book *Secrets of the Great Pyramid* by P. Tompkins, Ref 19), but since they give all the calculations I will reproduce their comments here (it refers to the Great Pyramid):

> Equally 'impossible' – at any rate for a people like the ancient Egyptians who are supposed to know nothing about the true shape and size of our planet – is the relationship, in a scale of 1:43,200, that exists between the dimensions of the pyramid and the dimensions of the earth. Setting aside for a moment the question of whether we are dealing with coincidence here, it is a simple fact, verifiable on any pocket calculator, that if you take the monument's original height (481.3949 feet) and multiply it by 43,200 you get a quotient of 3938.685 miles. This is an underestimate by just 11 miles of the true figure for the polar radius of the earth (3949 miles) .... Likewise, if you take the monument's perimeter at the base (3023.16 feet) and multiply this figure by 43,200 then you get 24,734.94 miles – a result that is within 170 miles of the true equatorial circumference of the earth (24,902 miles). Moreover, although this sounds a lot, it amounts.... to a minus error of only ¾ of one percent.

They also point out, on p. 41, that the pyramid is located barely a mile south of the latitude of 30° (another number we're familiar with), being actually $29°$ $58'$ $51''$. This is almost precisely two-thirds (0.666) of the way down from the north pole.

If I add $21.6°$, or $21°$ $36'$, to this highly accurate figure just quoted above, another latitude of $51°$ $34'$ $51''$ is produced. The latitude of Stonehenge is $51°$ $10'$ $50''$, which is an error of 0.8%. Or, putting it another way, Stonehenge is $21.6°$ north of The Great Pyramid to an accuracy of 0.8%, highly accurate when we consider that the face of the planet is being stepped out. Since both monuments were erected many thousands of years ago their relative positions will no longer be as they were at the time of construction, due to Continental Drift, which is about 0.8 inches per year, and which is the same rate that our fingernails and hairs grow.

And so it may well be that, once, at the beginning, they were indeed exactly $21.6°$ apart.

The latitude of Stonehenge, at $51°$ $34'$ $51''$ (that is, with error of 0.8% corrected) is, in its decimal form, $51.58°$. Now, the Precessional Cycle time of 25,920 years multiplied by 2 comes to 51,840, which is the number string 51.84 - the latitude of Stonehenge with a very small error. 518,400 is the number of minutes in the Model Year, and the number of seconds in 6 days – the time to create the world. It also took 8,640 minutes to create the world which is the string 6.6.6 x 4

There are other connections between Stonehenge and the Great Pyramid; for the slope angle of the north face of the pyramid, as measured by Sir William Flinders-Petrie, is $51.84°$, on page 12 of his 'The Pyramids and Temples of Gizah', originally published in 1885, with a reprinted edition published in 1990. Not only is this angle unique in tying the height to the perimeter via pi, but it also connects it to the Precessional Cycle, as does the 43,200 ratio mentioned above. How does the Precessional Cycle tie in with this angle? Because twice this Cycle of 25,920 years is 51,840 years. These two facts are truly dazzling; that is, the angle of the Great Pyramid reads out the relationship between height and perimeter, and this can only be so at this

HOW WE WERE MADE

very specific angle, which then also ties into the Precessional cycle. The Precessional connection is my own finding.

In fact, if the two numbers (ie twice the Precessional Cycle and the angle) are laid out together it can be seen that the comma and decimal point are interchangeable; while the zero becomes a small degree sign:

$$51,840 \text{ years}$$
$$51.84^0$$

As if that were not enough, the gods then find another remarkable universal number constant which fits with this angle, and that number, called The Golden Section, or the Golden Number – Φ (the Greek letter phi) comes from the Fibonacci series. This series, discovered in 1202 AD by the eponymous Italian, is simply a chain of numbers whereby each one is the sum of the two in front of it, ie:

$$1\ \ 1\ \ 2\ \ 3\ \ 5\ \ 8\ \ 13\ \ 21\ \ \text{ad infinitum}$$

Φ is found from the ratio of a pair of the numbers, and the larger the two numbers the more accurate is Φ. Here we may take 21/13 = 1.615, which is inaccurate because 21 and 13 are too small. If sufficiently large pairs are chosen (not shown here) then the correct value of this number is known to be 1.618. Curiously this number looks like the inverse of itself :- 1.618 = 1/.618. Fibonacci numbers also 'crop' up in botany (pun intended) in the arrangement of whorls on a pine cone, the petals on a sunflower, and lots of others. Φ also has strong connections with √5 ,
for Φ = (√5 + 1)/2, and 1/Φ + Φ = √5. The King's Chamber and the 'sarcophagus' inside the Great Pyramid are awash with the dimensions √5.

What a surprise then to discover that the Cosine of 51.84^0 is 0.618 = 1/Φ. Which of course applies to both the Great Pyramid and Stonehenge, as the first has this angle and the second has this latitude. There are still further associations, for the sine of 51.84^0 is 0.786, which, like numerous other encoded strings, does not appear to display anything of interest; however,

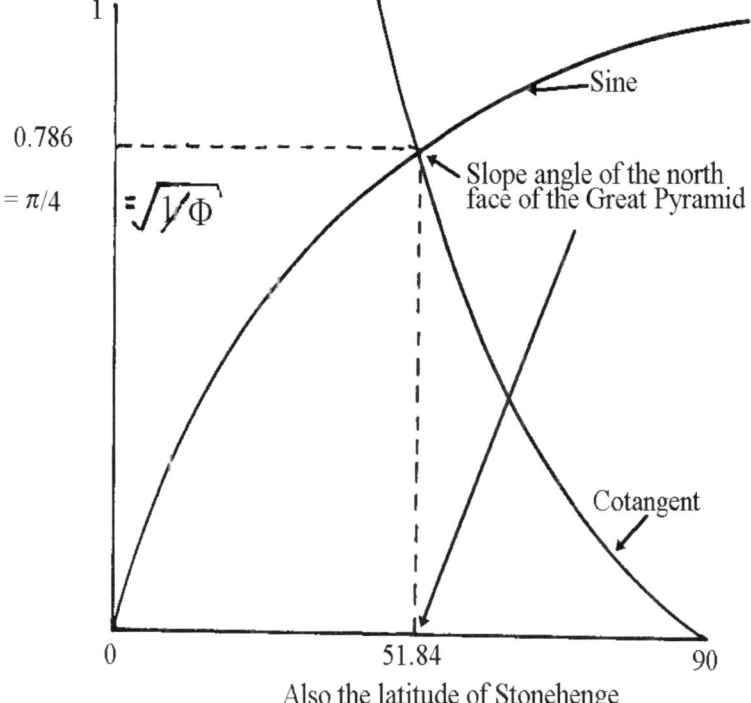

$\Phi = 1.618$ (The Golden Section)

Not to scale

HOW WE WERE MADE

this is also $\pi/4$ and $\sqrt{(1/\Phi)}$. In addition, the cotangent of $51.84°$ is also 0.786 and therefore has these same two numbers attached to it. To round these magical matches off, the tangent of $51.84°$ is 1.272, which is the square root of Φ, which, itself, is $(e - 1)$. It might be thought that there are several values of sines and cotangents which match each other, but no, it is only at this unique angle. Of course, these numbers apply to Stonehenge too since it has this angle, so that this structure is encoded with Φ as well. The sketch shows plots of the graphs of cotangents and sines, emphasising the uniqueness of this angle. These values are my own discoveries.

They are, in summary:

$$51{,}840 \text{ years}$$
$$51.84°$$

$$\text{Cosine } 51.84° \;=\; 0.618 \;=\; 1/\Phi$$

$$\text{Sine } 51.84° \;=\; 0.786 \;=\; \pi/4 \;=\; (1/\Phi)^{1/2}$$

$$\text{Cotangent } 51.84° \;=\; 0.786 \;=\; \pi/4 \;=\; (1/\Phi)^{1/2}$$

(this is the only angle at which the sine & cot are equal)

$$\text{Tangent } 51.84° \;=\; 1.272 \;=\; \Phi^{1/2}, \text{ and also } (e - 1)$$

So, the north face ties in the Prec. Cycle, Φ, π, and e, all in one angle !!!

By the way, $\pi/4$ (see above) in radians, is equal to $45°$, which of course is the angle of the diagonals across the base of the pyramid.

Another baffling Φ ratio is in the size of the pyramid – and this was known to Herodotus. A cross-section of it is shown here (from Ref 19, p 196).

However, I have never seen it put in the following form, by using Pythagoras (the square on the hypotenuse is equal to the sum of the squares on the other two sides):

$$\Phi^2 = (\Phi^{1/2})^2 + 1^2$$
$$\Phi^2 = \Phi + 1$$
$$\text{or, } \Phi^2 - \Phi - 1 = 0$$

This is the standard form of a quadratic, and is usually written:

$$X^2 - X - 1 = 0$$

And, lo and behold, the roots of this equation are 1.618 and 0.618 !!!!! **Half of the cross section of the Great Pyramid is a quadratic equation whose roots are Φ & 1/Φ.** This is my discovery.

Stirling (Ref 20 p. 216) also notes:

> "It is well known that Herschel the astronomer ascertained that the entrance passage of the great pyramid pointed to that part of the heavens occupied by the pole star in the year 2160 BC. But Professo Piazzi Smyth calculated that it passes the same point every few thousand years".

And on p. 227:

> (on the Great Pyramid) "The perimeter of the first step, inclusive of the ledge, is 687.56 feet, this is the diameter of a circle whose circumference is 2,160 feet - the moon's diameter". Let's remember that 2160 is 666 x 10.

HOW WE WERE MADE

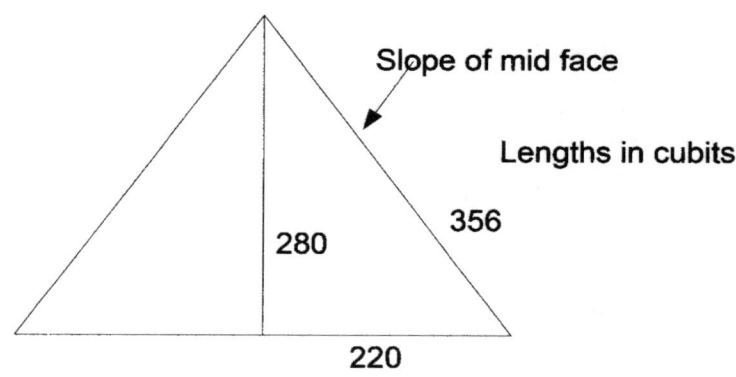

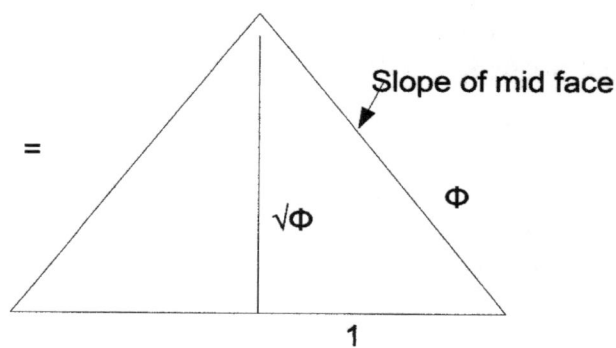

Cross section of Great Pyramid

Yes folks, the 'experts' would have us believe that this mathematical masterpiece was knocked together by stone age folk rubbing granite together to get a smooth surface. Let's face it, this is blatantly and obviously the work of the 'gods' - with humans doing the basic graft.

Herodotus, around 400 BC, knew that Φ was somehow keyed into the Great Pyramid, but did not know how, and Professor Stecchini in Ref 19 expands on the number but does not mention the points which I have outlined above and summarised in the sketches. This also means that the Fibonacci number was known a long time before he rediscovered it.

This is probably an appropriate place to bring in other relevant numbers to do with Egypt. In the 1850s an Englishman called Taylor put forward his theory that the height and perimeter of the Great Pyramid were linked in the same way that the radius and circumference of a circle are linked, that is Circ = 2 π x radius, or perimeter = 2 π x height. It did indeed turn out to be correct. Then, in the 1860's, Charles Piazzi Smyth, the Astronomer Royal Scotland, noticed that when the length of the perimeter was converted to inches it was 36,522, which he then immediately said represented the number of days in the year, as 365.22 (x 10^2). He spent several months at Giza with his wife, measuring and clearing the pyramid. Then another Englishman, William Flinders-Petrie, hove to in 1880 and proceeded to measure the pyramid with great accuracy, as he was an accomplished surveyor. He 'proved' that the previous measurements were inaccurate, and sarcastically opined (referring to Taylor and Smyth's theories about the year and the perimeter being the same) "what a pity that an ugly little fact can spoil a big beautiful theory". This, from a 26 year old about the elderly Astronomer Royal. W F-P had his camp in an old rock cut tomb, and camp may be rather appropriate since he used to carry out his work wearing only a pink singlet and pink underpants – to scare off the tourists apparently – and it worked. What a queer to-do. Can one buy men's underclothes in those colours today? Poor old Smyth died thinking himself a fool. Another Englishman, David Davidson, arrived twenty odd years later, and this man was a professional Structural Engineer and a corporate member of the Institute of Structural Engineers. He was determined to lay to rest, once and

HOW WE WERE MADE

for all, the silly theories about the year and the perimeter, and also to confirm W F-P's measurements. In fact he did the opposite, and showed how W F-P had forgotten to take into consideration the hollowing out of the sides of the pyramid when he allowed for the replacement of missing casing stones at the base of the pyramid. When this was taken into account then the perimeter was indeed 365.24 (x10^2) inches. Furthermore, going around the base of the pyramid means that 4 right angles of 90^0 must be passed, which therefore requires passing through 360^0. So, here is a measure which connects both the Model Year of 360 days with the real year of 365.24 days, **the two magnitudes of the two years stated in one length**. The circumference of the Earth is laid out in exactly the same lengths as we shall see later in this chapter.

The circumference of Stonehenge is the same number string as the Great Pyramid – 365.22 (x10) inches, and so it too encodes the real year with the ancient Model Year of 360 days, since of course it is round and there are 360^0 degrees in a circle.

There is yet another encoding about the perimeter of this pyramid, for its sides are 440 royal cubits, which gives a total length of 1760 royal cubits. What a number – for, as has already been pointed out – this is also the number of yards in a mile! (Sir Isaac Newton defined the royal cubit as being equal to 20.63 British inches, but I can find nothing in that number). So, the perimeter encodes the length of the year and the Imperial mile.

It is hardly difficult to understand that those who can devise the planets can also design what is upon them. We will see further confirmation, in due course, that the Earth has been built to specified numbers, so is it any more demanding to observe that the land of Egypt itself is also designed? The French invaded Egypt in the 1790's, and were thrown out by the English shortly after, but in the meantime performed some very good measurements of the Great Pyramid and northern Egypt, in addition to slaughtering many thousands of Egyptians, for no particular reason, but that is what dictators do. They noted, in particular, that the diagonals of the Great Pyramid pointed to the east and west points of the coast and also neatly enclosed the many estuaries of the Nile, and, if a compass was put onto the pyramid a circle could be drawn between the two points on the coast which again tidily encompassed the coastline. The Greeks knew this and observed that the resulting shape looked like their letter Delta, which is why some river mouths today are called deltas. A line drawn from the pyramid up through the centre of the arc around the coast formed a precise longitude pointing to the north. These facts have been known to the modern world now for over two hundred years, but clearly someone knew about it thousands of years ago, since 'they' surveyed and planned it.

However, I wondered what would appear if I extended this line down the page into Sudan, that is, into, and beyond, upper Egypt. I applied my measurements to a map of Egypt to follow this, what is in reality a line of longitude, and noted that it passed through a feature of the Nile called the Second Cataract (the second coming up river from the delta). At first I thought this was just a 'coincidence', but then realised the full implications of this locale – it is right on the line of longitude which is very accurately aligned north/south; it passes through the centre of the Great Pyramid and then through the centre line of the horizontal delta line. These line-ups can be seen on the following outline sketch of Egypt, whose shape and numbers I shall describe. I also noted that the present-day southern border of Egypt is about 30 or so minutes of latitude north of the Second Cataract, which was somewhat disappointing as it would have been rather elegant to have yet another tie-in with those I have just described. Applying the same approach that I used when investigating the original tilt of the planet, I decided to explore this southern border through time, to see if it had always been there or was a modern creation. In fact, Professor Stecchini says (in Ref 19, p. 299), "In a new imperialistic spirit, Egypt in a wide sense was understood to end at the Second Cataract". Thus, the Second Cataract also defined the limit of Upper Egypt, in addition to its other functions – by the way, it is big, and was also known as the Great Cataract. And then the biggest surprise of all; for on measuring the latitude of this waterfall, I discovered it to be no other than 21.6^0! As this was indeed the original tilt of the Earth, it was therefore the ancient Tropic of Cancer too! And so the old boundary of Egypt was actually the latitude of the Tropic – which makes a lot of sense, until it is remembered that it has not been at that latitude since at least before 15,000 BC. This fact shows that the origins of Egypt go back a lot further

HOW WE WERE MADE

than we think. Extending this ancient boundary to the east across the Red Sea shows that it just passes just to the north of Mecca, which is 10^0 east of the Second Cataract and hence the centre line of Egypt, and 10^0 south of the very top of the curve of this line – on the coast where stood the lost city of Behdet. In fact this also states that the length of Egypt from Behdet to the Second Cataract was 10^0 of latitude.

Because this boundary is a parallel, or a latitude, and the north/south line through the cataract and the pyramid is a longitude, it follows that they cross each other at precisely 90^0, and it is, in itself, another quite improbable combination. At this point it becomes evident that Egypt must have been designed from a 'blueprint', which would reward further investigation. On this issue Stecchini comments Ref 19, p 292, "He [another Egyptologist] resisted the notion that Egyptians conceived of their country as having an exact geometric shape. They believed that when the gods created the cosmos they began by building Egypt and, having created it perfect, modelled the rest around it".

It can be seen from the sketch that a line drawn parallel to the Red Sea coastline cuts both the southern boundary and the centre point of the horizontal delta line, just skimming the promontories of Ras Banas and Ras Hadarba, and forming an angle of 60^0 with the base line. A similar line at the western boundary terminates between the peaks of Jebel Uweinat and Jebel Kissu, while crossing the base line and the western vertical longitudinal boundary at an angle of 60^0, noting here too that the base line and the western boundary cross each other at 90^0. The angle at the top of Egypt in the centre of the delta is therefore also 60^0, resulting in an equilateral triangle of 60 x 60 x 60 degrees. This is the Greek's Perfect Number of 6 expressed in two dimensional form, as we saw in Chapter I.

The distance from the centre line of Egypt to each of the west and east limits is 360 miles, thus providing a base line boundary of 720 miles. Each half of this magical boundary encodes the number of days in the Egyptians' Model Year of 360 days, while 720 is 1/3 of 2160. 1/3 is half of 6 and 2160 is the number of years for one click of the Precessional Cycle to move from one zodiacal sign to another. Likewise, the lengths of the other two sides are

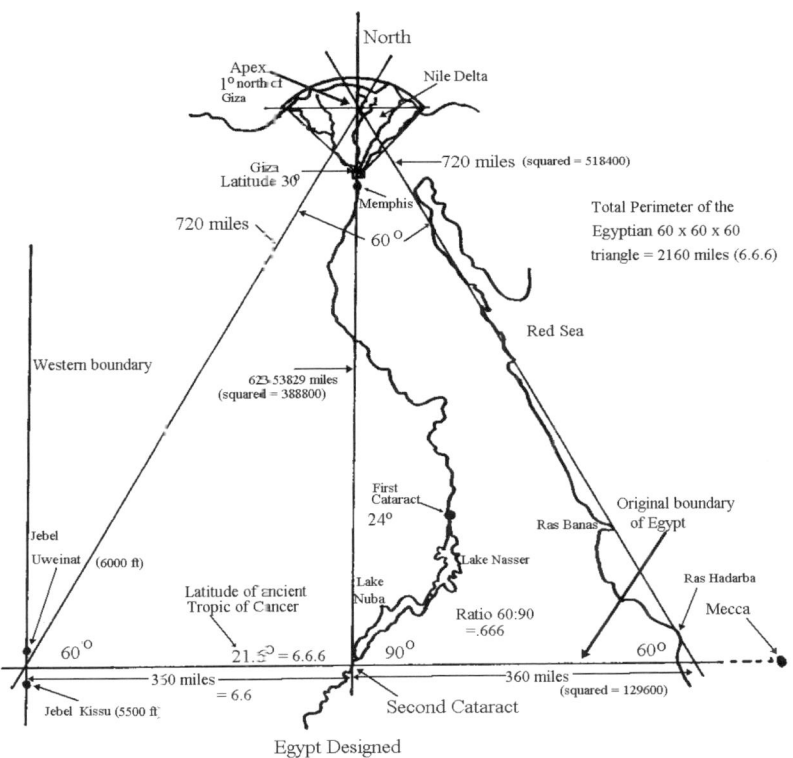

HOW WE WERE MADE

720 miles as well. As there are 3 sides to this triangle (and we have just seen that 720 is 1/3 of 2160) it follows that the total length of the perimeter of the triangle must be 2160 miles!

The length of the vertical longitude from the centre of the delta to the Second Cataract is 623.53829 miles, which does not look very promising for any hidden encoding; but, let one of the two 90^0 triangles, which make up the two halves of the bigger one, have its side lengths written down in the familiar way of Pythagoras (the square on the hypotenuse is equal to the sum of the squares on the other two sides). So we see:
$$720^2 \ = \ 360^2 \ + \ 623.53829^2$$
which multiplies out to

$$518,400 \ = \ 129,600 \ + \ 388,800$$

From which it can be immediately observed that 518,400 is $1/5^{th}$ of 100 Precessional Cycles of 25,920 years, and 129,600 is ½ of 10 of these same cycles. The real stunner here is in the number 388,800, for this number is the sum of 10 Precessional Cycles plus ½ of 10 Precessional Cycles (259,200 + 129,600). Additionally, it may be recalled from earlier in this section that 518,400 encodes 51.84 which is the angle of the Great Pyramid and two Precessional Cycles. The whole of Egypt laid out according to the stars; is it any wonder that they knew they lived in perfection!

We have already seen that the Second Cataract delineates the ancient boundary of Egypt and the original Tropic of Cancer, but the First Cataract just north of present day Lake Nasser, also called the Little Cataract, had an important function too. Not only was the Great Pyramid situated at the symbolic latitude of 30^0, it was also an incredible 6^0 of latitude north of the First Cataract! From the Great Pyramid to the horizontal line which joins the two diagonal lines of the delta together, is an exact 1^0 of latitude. This is the latitude of 31^0, which, as will be confirmed later, is also the cube of π. It is an accepted proposition for many researchers that the original prime meridian (ie 0^0 longitude) was in fact through the centre of the Great Pyramid. It is rather startling then to observe that its present day longitude

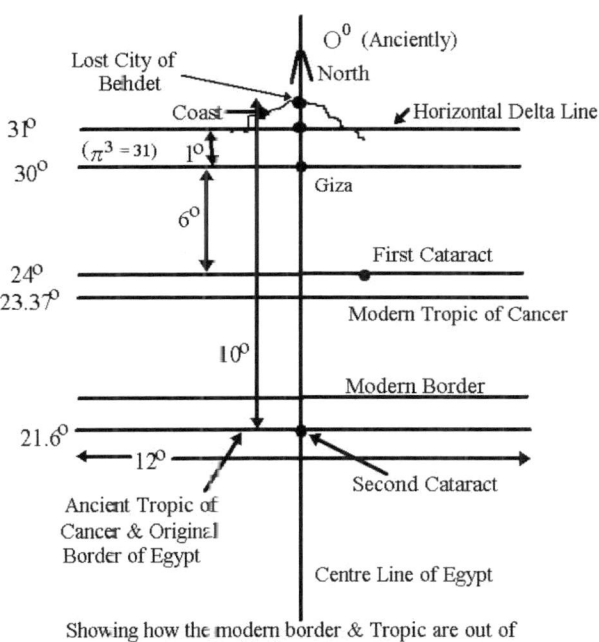

Egypt's Modern and Ancient Borders

HOW WE WERE MADE

east of Greenwich (which is now the prime meridian of 0^0 longitude) is also 31^0, which neatly matches its (the horizontal line just mentioned) latitude of 31^0. Putting it another way, the prime meridian has been moved 31^0 to the west.

At some time in the remote past the First Cataract would have been marked out by the movement of the Tropic of Cancer in its cycle of up and down marches over 43,200 years. As the Tropic moves at the rate of 3^0 per 43,200 years (or 10,800 seconds of latitude per 43,200 yrs), it is a simple matter to calculate the exact time, in years, when the Tropic would have stood at the First Cataract. Carrying out this little sum provides a rate of movement of 0.25" (that is 0.25 seconds of latitude, not inches) per year. In other words, since (our) last year the tropic has moved 0.25" (seconds) closer to the equator. The present latitude of the Tropic is 23^0 27', while the latitude of the First Cataract is – to quote Professor Stecchini (Ref 19, p 293) - "The upper edge of this cataract is on the perfect latitude of 24^0 00'." The difference between these two figures is 33'. Hence 33', or 1980 seconds, divided by 0.25" per year yields a time of 7,920 years before the present day, or about 6,000 BC. This figure is quite close to the Dawning of the Age of Gemini in the year 6,480 BC (that is, 2,160 x 3 – for 3 'ticks' of 2,160 years on the Precessional Cycle clock, BC).

It has already been shown that the base line of Egypt is split precisely into two equal halves, each of which is 360 statute miles. If these are stated instead as nautical miles (these are described shortly) then, as there are 60 nautical miles per degree (at a certain latitude, see above), it follows that 360 nautical miles are equal to 6^0 of latitude either side of the central dividing line.

The length of the original boundary line (through the Second Cataract) is just short of 12^0 of longitude, at this latitude of 21.6^0.

The sketch above provides a summary of these planned latitudes and longitudes.

On the other side of the world, and referring to the Pyramid of the Sun at Teotihuacan, Ref 17, p 190, points out:

> A more curious but equally deliberate effect could be observed on the equinoxes.... then the passage of the sun's rays from south to north resulted at noon in the progressive obliteration of a perfectly straight shadow that ran along one of the lower faces of the western façade. The whole process, from complete shadow to complete illumination, took exactly 66.6 seconds. It had done so without fail, year-in year-out, ever since the pyramid had been built and would continue to do so until the giant edifice crumbled into dust.

In discussing planet Earth, I earlier described how the numbers of warriors who emerged from Valhalla was 432,000, on which the authors of Ref 1, p 162, comment:

> That makes 432,000 in all, a number of significance from old. This number must have had a very ancient meaning, for it is also the number of syllables in the *Rigveda*. But it goes back to the basic figure 10,800, the number of stanzas in the *Rigveda* (40 syllables to a stanza) which, together with 108, occurs insistently in Indian tradition. 10,800 is also the number which has been given by Heraclitus for the duration of the Aion, according to Censorinus (*De die natalie* 18), whereas Berossos made the Babylonian Great Year to last 432,000 years. Again 10,800 is the number of bricks of the Indian fire-altar (Agnicayana)..... Shall one add Angkor Wat to the list? It has five gates, and to each of them leads a road, bridging over that water ditch which surrounds the whole place. Each of these roads is bordered by a row of huge stone figures, 108 per avenue, 54 on each side, altogether 540 statues.... and each row carries a huge Naga serpent with 9 heads. The whole of Angkor thus turns out to be a colossal model set up for..... a continuous one-way Precession from west to east.

HOW WE WERE MADE

I have to note however that they appear not to have seen the connection here with 666, for 432 is twice 216 (which is 6 x 6 x 6), while 108 is half of 216. And it follows that 54 is one quarter of 216 and one half of 108. Additionally they seem to view 10,800 and 108 as different numbers, whereas in my scheme they are one and the same number string. However, their observations about Angkor have an echo of my comments about Stonehenge etc being models of the solar system. These numbers are also reflected in the dodecahedron of Plato, which I shall come to.

Someone, at some ancient unknown date, was on this planet hauling mighty stones about, and not just any old stones but the hardest they could find, even if that meant transporting them over huge distances. Not content with that they then carve them to specific shapes with remarkable accuracy and to a high degree of engineering tolerances, put them together without mortar and then arrange them into models of the planets and stars. The stones were meant to last a very very long time.

But back to the planet's dimensions. The polar diameter of the Earth (it's slightly different from the equatorial diameter because the planet is a bit flat at the poles) is 7,900.1 miles, and, converting this to inches by multiplying it by (1,760 yds x 3 ft x 12 inches) gives a figure of 500.55 million inches. If I call it 500 million inches, instead of the accurate one, then a remainder of 550,000.0 inches is left over, which converts back to 8.7 miles different from the stated figure of 7,900.1 miles. This is an error of only $1/10^{th}$ of one percent – which is $1/1000^{th}$ - a quite remarkable model of accuracy, and this allows me to say with confidence that the diameter of the Earth is 500 million inches. This also confirms the inch as a sacred measure, as did the Paradigm Human Male. There may be another reason why this tiny 'error' exists, and that could be that the planet has actually changed shape by $1/1000^{th}$ of its original diameter, in the same way that the continents are apparently moving apart. Also I do not know if the diameter counts in, or out, the extremely thick ice cover on Antarctica, which is also the highest continent. There is no land mass at the north pole and the ice there is quite thin in comparison.

There is something else which is significant about the number 500 too.

For, when multiplied by the length of the Precessional Cycle of 25,920 years we see the number 12,960,000. Putting this in words rather than numbers, it spells out a passage of time equal to the passing of five hundred Precessional Cycles. This, as we saw earlier, is the Sumerian number 'sargal-su-nu-tag', or 'unit greater than big sar', a number so special, and huge, that it has its own name. In the Mayan system it is 3,600 tuns of 360 days, which gives the same total; as does 10 tretayugas of the Hindu method, which, by the way, itself equals 36,000 divine years! If we look at 500 in its other form of 0.5 and multiply this by 25,920 years, then naturally we obtain half of a Precessional Cycle, of 12,960 years, a number which can also be conjured up quite easily from the maths of the ancients.

(Before the next paragraph, I should just put in a reminder here that real pi is 3.141592, while Perfect Pi is 3.)

Furthermore, if we look at the way the equatorial circumference has been divided up using the divine number of the circle – 360, then other standards also become apparent. The equatorial circumference is 24,901.55 miles, which, when multiplied by (1760 yds x 3 ft) produces 1.3148 ($\times 10^8$) ft (which is not of any significance). But, if this is taken further and a degree is examined, look at what comes out. As there are 360 degrees in a circle, that number must be divided by 360 to produce the length of a degree of longitude at the equator. The result is 365.22 ft ($\times 10^3$) per degree. This result is incredibly close to the year of 365.25 days; in fact the difference between the two numbers is a minuscule 0.008%, and it is immediately apparent that one degree of longitude, at the equator, encodes the length of the year. 365.223 ($\times 10^3$) ft = 365.25 days.

It is evident that one degree of equatorial longitude joins together both the Model Year of 360 days and the real year of 365.25, for the degree is $1/360^{th}$ of the Earth whereas it actually measures 365.22 ($\times 10^3$) feet; **the two magnitudes of the two years stated in one length**. This is precisely the same result as found in the perimeter of the base of the Great Pyramid, where both years are stated in one measure, as described earlier, and at Stonehenge. The gods were showing off here, but brilliant nevertheless.

HOW WE WERE MADE

In the next chapter I will demonstrate that the number string of 365.25, is, as well, the ratio of the circumferences of the Earth and the moon.

Let us look at the width of a minute, on the equator, which is $1/60^{th}$ of one degree. 365.223 ft (x 10^3) divided by 60 produces 6.087 (x 10^3) ft per minute. If I call this 6 instead of 6.087, then I introduce an error of 1.43%, which, on a planetary scale, is negligible. So, one minute of arc at the equator encodes the number 6;   6 (x 10^3) ft per minute. As a matter of fact, reference   books, such as dictionaries, often contain tabular data about measures and will quote 1 nautical mile, which is the width of one minute of longitude, as being equal to 1000 fathoms, which is 6000 feet since there are 6 feet to one fathom. 3 nautical miles equals one sea league. And so, in showing the small error in my calculation here, I am being rather harsh on myself.

Let me explain the importance of this fact that a nautical mile is 6000 feet here on Earth. All planetary bodies, including the moon and the sun are measured using the system of 360^0, 60 minutes and 60 seconds. That means all bodies have a 21,600 nautical mile circumference. This results therefore in the length of a nautical mile in feet being different on each body. But, uniquely, here on Earth it is connected to the number 6 in the measure of 6000 feet. Can there be any doubt that this has been caused to be?

But, what about one second of arc at the equator? Well, this is again $1/60^{th}$ of one minute, which means dividing 6.087 (from above) by 60. The answer is 101 ft per second, which is within $1/100^{th}$ of the number one, that is, one percent. Again, I am justified in saying that one second of arc at the equator is 1 (x 10^2) ft per second, or 100 ft per second. This particular rate has a resonance, for this is almost the speed of the planet's rotation in miles per hour, ie 1037.6 miles/hr.

While discussing the Earth's circumference I should further highlight the measure which is used, mainly by mariners, the 'nautical mile', which I mentioned above. When Europeans started mapping the globe, and the English invented longitude, (with the help of Harrison's Chronometer) the Earth was to be measured on longitude and latitude in the ancient system of

360 degrees with the usual sub division of 60 minutes and seconds. From this an international unit was devised – the Nautical Mile, defined as "the length of one minute of the meridian through Greenwich [London], ie 1/60th of the degree of latitude". In other words the circumference of the Earth is 360 degrees x 60 minutes, which is 21,600 nautical miles. Each degree width of latitude at 45 degrees is therefore 60 nautical miles. So, it can be seen that the Earth is also measured in the ancient system of base 60. As there are 21,600 nautical miles, and the number of statute miles is 24,901.55, there are then 1.153 statute miles to one nautical mile, which, we may note in passing, is the 16th root of 10.

But, more remarkably, when this number of 1.153 is multiplied by the universal number e (2.72, see p. 124) the result is π (3.14). Or, put another way, the ratio between statute miles and nautical miles is π/e (1.154). BUT, only here on planet Earth, as other bodies have different dimensions then their ratios to each other will obviously be dissimilar from ours. That is how unique this ratio is, it applies here, and only here, on this unique planet. I am not aware that this ratio is known to science.

Now, investigating the width of latitude, and applying the the same method as was used when looking at longitude, we can note first that the length of the circumference which passes through the poles is 24,818.896 miles, this is smaller than the equatorial circumference due to the poles being slightly flat. Turning this into yards, feet and inches, and doing the usual division, we find that there are 120,000 yards per degree, 100 feet per second, 6000 feet per minute, and 360,000 feet per degree, of latitude. But more; there are 4,320,000 inches per degree, 72,000 inches per minute, and 1,200 inches per second. In order to arrive at these perfect numbers, with which we are already very familiar, an adjustment of 1.1% is needed to the polar distance quoted above, otherwise the figures just calculated come out slightly skewed by 1.1%, a tiny percentage on a global scale. With this adjustment of 1.1% on 24,818.896 to give 24,545.455 miles, a conversion shows that this figure is also 43,200,000 yards and therefore, 129,600,000 feet – two very common sacred number strings.

HOW WE WERE MADE

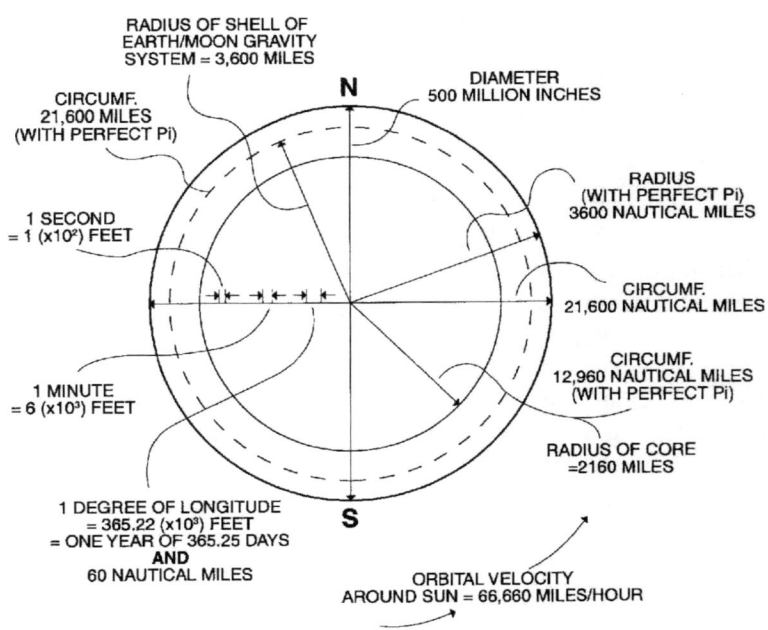

Earth Numbers (1)

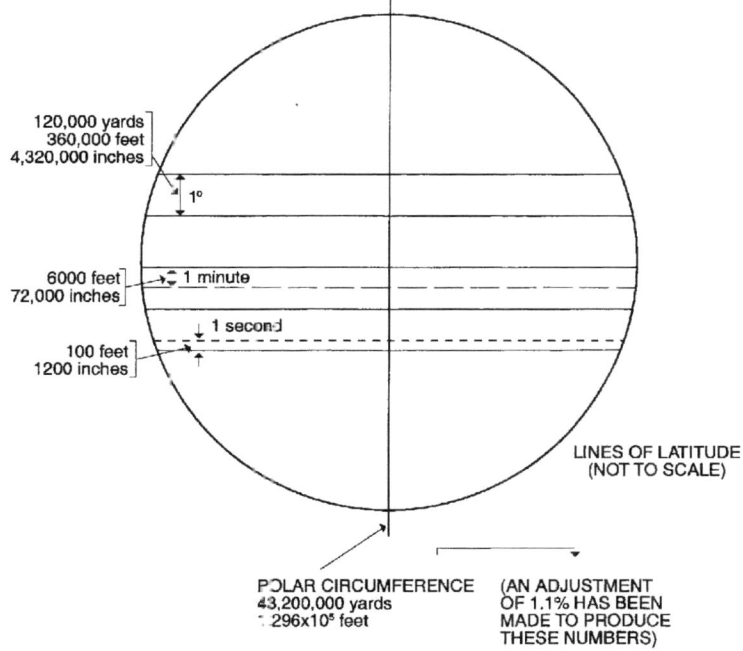

Earth Numbers (2)

HOW WE WERE MADE

The magnitude of the Earth has other familiar numbers:

Its core is 2160 miles in radius – how repetitive this number is! If I now use Perfect Pi on the core, its circumference turns out to be 12,960 miles, which is one half of the Precessional Cycle in years.

To echo what I said when discussing the use of pi as used by the ancients, once the original figure for pi, namely 3, is brought in, then all of these same numbers come tumbling out time and time again.

The radius of the shell of the Earth-moon gravity system is 3600 miles from the centre of the Earth. Again bringing in Perfect Pi, I discover that this shell has a circumference of 21,600 miles.

As the circumference of the Earth is 21,600 nautical miles it follows that the radius of Earth in nautical miles is 3,600, using Perfect Pi.

Why not have a guess at the orbital velocity of the Earth around the Sun, by covering up the rest of the page, before I give the answer below? The Times Atlas of the World (1996) on page 51, gives the 'mean orbital velocity of Earth' as 29.8 km/ sec. Converting km to miles by multiplying them by 0.62137, gives 18.516826 miles/sec (almost the number string for the speed of light - 186. (Actually around 186,281 miles/sec depending on the reference book consulted; the five I have give 5 different speeds – pedants arise). Multiplying 18.516826 by 60 x 60 to convert seconds to hours, results in 66,660 miles/hour going around the Sun. I think double exclamation marks are called for here!! This figure naturally also means that it is moving at a rate of 1111 miles/min. Accordingly, the moon is being pulled around the Sun by the Earth at the same speed. These figures are summarised in the two illustrations below. But please note how meaningless and useless the measure of 29.8 km/sec really is, because it conveys no sense of their sacred number scheme.

So, here we all are, sitting comfortably on a sphere, that is spinning around at over 1000 miles per hour, which, at the same time, is hurtling through space at 66,660 miles per hour, and there's not a wobble, not a ripple on the mill-pond, and we are not flung off into space but kept on the surface by a force which we call gravity and which is defined as one of the weakest of the forces in the Universe (compared to the atomic bond, and the electromagnetic force for example). There are machines which are designed to simulate the effects on man of increasing the force of gravity. They take the form of a chair placed at the end of a long rigid arm which is then spun at certain high speeds to see what happens when the man undergoes, say, twice the force of gravity. If he was not strapped in he would be flung off the chair rather violently. A similar machine used to feature in fairgrounds as a deep cylinder about 40 feet across, volunteers would then pay to step inside and the whole device was then started spinning. As it got faster the thrill-seekers became pressed hard against its wall, to the point where they could crawl up it and defy gravity; of course, there was a lip at the top to stop them reaching it, otherwise they too would have been flung out. But we are not thrown off this spinning machine. Very strange indeed.

By way of another achievement of harmony the escape velocity for a body to leave the earth is 24,979 miles per hour, compared to the equatorial circumference of 24,902 miles, this is a difference of barely 0.29%.

The *piece de resistance* of the Earth's construction numbers could very well be the ratio between the radii of the core and the Earth/moon gravity shell, namely 2160:3600, for this is the ratio 60:10. It is the ratio between the gods' number base of 60 and mans' number base of 10, the number of his digits. These two numbers side by side state explicitly the association between the ancient number system of Sumer and the decimal system. In this respect I am reminded of the part in the legend of King Arthur, where all is desolation, the land is barren, all is lost, for the Holy Grail cannot be found; and then one of his knights receives The Word in a vision. He tells the King that he has found the Holy Grail. The King asks him to explain, and the knight pronounces The Truth. The Holy Grail is a piece of knowledge, it is: The Land And The King Are One. The King then rides through his kingdom touching the land, the waters and the people, and all blossom again, for he had forgotten his old duties while searching for a false Grail. And here we have a number system which shows that Man and the Earth are one, both

HOW WE WERE MADE

designed to the same sacred dimensions, by them.

As if that was not enough it can moreover be noticed that the Earth's circumference in nautical miles - 21,600, when rated to the Precessional Cycle of 25,920 years, produces the proportion 10:12.

This is the ratio of man's digits and the decimal system to the other counting base which we use – the number 12; for example, a not exhaustive list of this number's universality would include the following:
12 phalanges in the fingers of one hand. NB. A thumb is not a finger.
12 people on a jury
12 lunar cycles per year
12 months per year
12 menstrual cycles per year
12 signs of the zodiac
12 hours per day
12 hours per night
12 inches per foot
12 pennies per shilling (gone now alas, a victim of metrication)
12 units per dozen
12 dozen per gross
12 fruits on the tree of life (Rev. 12.2)
12 disciples
12 knights of the Round Table (initially)
12 eggs per carton.
And, in Revelations 21, the holy city shall have 12 gates, each with 12 angels, inscribed with the 12 tribes, 12 foundations with the 12 names of the apostles, and its walls will measure 12,000 stadia.

Allow me to highlight a strange fact about the Earth's surface. The authors of the Larousse Encyclopedia, Ref 13, pp 84-85, produce a sketch which shows the Earth as a tetrahedron (their Fig 180), of which they have this to say:
> Most of the land masses of the Earth lie in the northern hemisphere, and they may be divided into three massifs: Afro-Euro, the Asian with its prolongation into Australia, and the

American continent. They form three triangular 'bosses' pointing to the south pole. The latter is occupied by a vast continent... This constitutes a further 'boss' corresponding to the depression occupied by the oceans around the north pole -- more than 10,000 feet deep. I have partially copied this as below.

THE EARTH AS A TETRAHEDRON

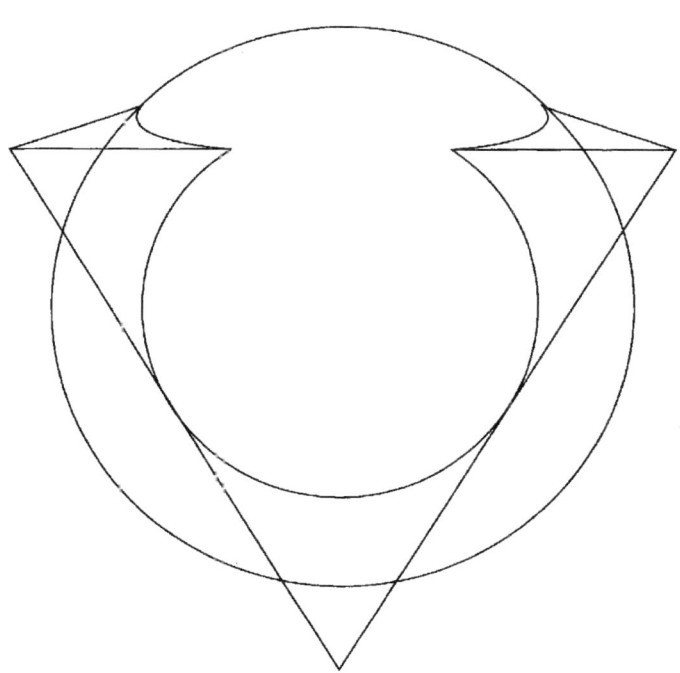

HOW WE WERE MADE

VII
BUILDING AND PLACING THE MOON

Our really large neighbour, which is actually a small planet, to the extent that together they have been called a twin planet system, is a very strange dancing partner indeed. The dance which they twirl to together, with their various bobbings and tiltings and spinnings, is a ballet which has been choreographed to the music of numbers; numbers we have already met with. It is extremely odd that something as big as the moon should approach us and yet not crash into us, but instead take up a position only some 250 thousand miles, at maximum. This distance as we saw earlier is the polar radius of Earth measured in inches. Newspapers, and TV documentaries, are always trying to scare us with horror stories of meteors and comets which are close to Earth, but these are inevitably many millions of miles away. But the moon is really very close (by comparison the Sun is 93 million miles distant). If anything like it ever came towards us from space then we would be doomed without a doubt. But of course it never will, because 'they' – the gods - do not want their special game spoilt.

Not only does it take up its position almost nudging us, but does so in order that the size of its disc in the sky is then made to be identical to the size of the Sun's disc; well, sometimes it is very slightly larger or very slightly smaller, but mostly it is exactly the same size. This is why there are eclipses, because the moon can exactly cover the Sun. One astronomer I heard on the radio said that this was not only unique in the solar system, but it may well be the only case in the entire universe, so peculiar is it. The apparent size of it which we see at night is a complete optical illusion as it appears to be very large, whereas it, like the Sun, is actually quite small. So small in fact that if a hand is held out at arm's length and compared to the moon it can be seen that it is only the size of half of the finger nail on the

HOW WE WERE MADE

little finger. Another illusion is that it is larger when on the horizon than when high in the sky; but no, it is the same size all of the time, and anywhere in the world. All of those cowboy films which showed a colossal moon hanging over the campfire are just 'special effects'. I have spent my whole life thinking the moon was larger in the warmer climes, but it is not.

The moon's cratered surface is another curious feature, because there are very many more craters on the side facing us than there are on the invisible side. Clearly any rock missiles heading towards the twins would hit the other side of the moon not the side facing Earth, or they would miss the moon and hit the planet. In fact it would be nearly impossible for a meteor to hit the moon on the side facing us, for the simple reason that the earth's gravity is 6 times that of the moon (please note the 6 here), and any incoming space rock would be turned towards us, not the moon. There is an interesting observation which has been made about the craters, which at first sight appear to be randomly dispersed across its surface, which is what should be expected from irregular arrivals of meteors, but this is not the case. The Encyclopedia, Ref 13, p 134, has this to say:

> .... turning the surface into an indescribable confusion as if the moon had been the subject of violent convulsions. But this chaos is only apparent. Close study........ shows that relationships are to be found among the formations there. Indeed,... London University and others have discovered and begun to map what they call a 'grid system' of features. This is essentially a natural network linking up craters..... into a pattern.

Or is it a 'natural' network? Accordingly, here is a body which is not quite what it seems to be. Are the craters designed? Or, has the moon turned on its axis in the past to show us a face that once looked out into space and took the splats of debris which came its way, and protected Earth at the same time? Or was the whole affair planned? Whichever way we look at the strange position, and state of, the moon, we must conclude that it is indeed most wonderful.

In addition to the beautiful seasons brought about by the Earth's tilt, we also get the tides and the moonlight from the Sun's opposite number – the moon – identical in size and shape in the sky; one hot and red the other blue and cold. What amazing symmetry. And all obeying the divine number system measured in minutes and feet. We tamper with these at our peril!

In fact the first number to be observed about the moon is its diameter, which, as is to be expected, is 2,160 miles. This has to be one of the most stunning exhibits so far, and confirms the mile as a sacred measure.

Because nautical miles apply to any spherical body it will be evident that the latitude and longitude on the moon may be mapped using the same plan as on Earth; that is, to divide it up using the 360^0 system with 60 minutes and 60 seconds. There are therefore, just as on Earth, 21,600 nautical miles around the moon's equator, but of course, these nautical miles will be much smaller than the Earth's equivalent. So, here is a small planet whose diameter is 2,160 statute miles and whose circumference is 21,600 nautical miles. This is a ratio of 10 and represents the number of digits on our hands, and consequently the decimal methodology used in arithmetic here on Earth.

The circumference of the moon is obtained simply by 2160 x pi (ie pi x diameter), which gives 6785.8401 statute miles, and, as we have just seen, this is 21,600 nautical miles over the same distance. If I wish to know what is the number of statute miles per nautical mile on the moon, I simply divide 6785.8401 by 21,600. The answer is an incredible 3.141592 (x 10^{-1}) statute miles per nautical mile on the moon. This is real pi to a very precise accuracy – a number string seven digits long. Such beauty! Statute miles, nautical miles and pi all connected in one simple statement.

We saw in the previous chapter the that the ratio of statute miles to nautical miles was π/e, on Earth; whereas here on the moon the ratio of statute miles to nautical miles is π. To find the ratio of Earth nautical miles to moon nautical miles we simply divide one by the other, to give e. Unbelievable though it may sound, the relationship between Earth and moon nautical miles is the universal constant e. Putting that simply, one nautical

HOW WE WERE MADE

moon mile which is 3.141592 (10^{-1}) statute miles, divided by 2.72 (*e*) gives 1.154 (10^{-1}) statute miles. And here on Earth one nautical mile is indeed 1.153 statute miles. Showing yet again that the two are linked together as securely as Siamese twins. The little diagram below may help to make this easier to visualise.

That is, $0.3141/2.72 = 0.1154$ statute miles.

Put another way – ratio of: Moon Nautical Miles/ Earth Nautical Miles
 (both stated in statue miles) = $0.3141/0.1153 = 2.72 = e$

The circumference is coded another way too, for if Perfect Pi is used instead to calculate it (3 x D), a figure of 6480 statutes miles is obtained, and this is, literally, exactly one quarter of the Precessional Cycle of 25,920 years.

Let us check out the width of longitude, at the equator. As we saw above the circumference is 6785.8401 statute miles, so dividing this by 360 we obtain 18.84956 miles, which does not mean much. Let that be divided by 60 to measure the width of a minute, and it will be discovered that one minute of longitude is 0.3141592 statute miles, real pi x 10^{-1}. Once again, this is perfection. Putting it another way, a walk of 10 minutes of longitude at the equator is exactly pi statute miles. This is a clear connection between pi and the decimal mode of 10. But that is only for longitude at the equator, whereas, it astonishingly, applies to all of the minutes of latitude across the entire surface of the moon. Looking at the moon from top to bottom, every one of the 21,600 minutes (nautical miles) of latitude measures 0.3141592 statute miles, real pi x 10^{-1}. One minute of longitude at the equator, all the minutes of latitude, and one nautical mile, all are equal to π x 10^{-1}. The moon is quite literally 'Pi In The Sky'.

Let that be spelled out absolutely clearly: one minute of equatorial longitude is one nautical mile and 3.141592 (x 10^{-1}) statute miles, as is every one of the 21,600 minutes of latitude. Utterly incredible. This is compelling evidence of design.

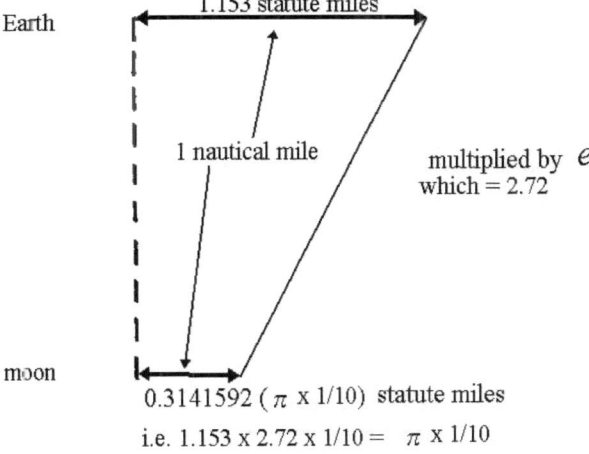

Statute & Nautical Miles on Earth & Moon

125

HOW WE WERE MADE

The situation at the moon's equator, where the minutes of longitude are the same width as those of latitude, is fascinating. These crossover minutes form squares whose sides are each pi statute miles (x 10^{-1}) in length, so that the area of each square is pi^2 square statute miles (x 10^{-2}). There are 21,600 of these pi^2 squares around the moon's equator. Circles inscribed in these latitude/longitude squares obviously have diameters of pi, and their circumferences are therefore pi^2 miles x 10^{-1}, (not square miles of course). These squares also have an area of 3,600 square seconds. This is not so much a string of pearls but a string of pi's around the middle of the moon which is beaming out its message to us, for all to see.

It is worthwhile re-visiting the figure for the width of a degree, 18.84956 miles, as shown above, to investigate any other hidden numbers. Multiplying this by 1760 yds x 3 ft yields a figure 99525.655 feet, which is 100,000 ft for every degree of longitude at the equator; one hundred thousand feet to a very acceptable error of only 0.474%. These same figures also apply to all of the degrees of latitude, so, without repeating the explanations used above in outlining the string of pi's, each square degree of longitude/latitude at the equator is 10,000 million, or 10^{10}, square feet. Neat.

These measures are brought together in the illustration below.

There is another very odd problem to do with the moon's mass, which is $1/81^{st}$ of that of the Earth, for the decimal version of this fraction is the amazing 0.012345679012345679012345679 recurring. Notice that 8 is missing from this string, and also that 8 is the only non-unity integer in the fraction form. This weird fraction of 1/81, when divided out to become a decimal, actually spells out all of the numbers in man's decimal system. At first sight there does not appear to be any connection with the number 6, but a moment's contemplation reveals that 81 is also $(6/2)^4$, or in words, half of 6 raised to the fourth power. Or, it can be written as $(8 + 1)^2$. It is also our old friend 1,296 divided by 16.

Looking at this from another angle, it can be seen that 6/2, which is 3.0, is the number string for the number of days in the month of the Model Year -

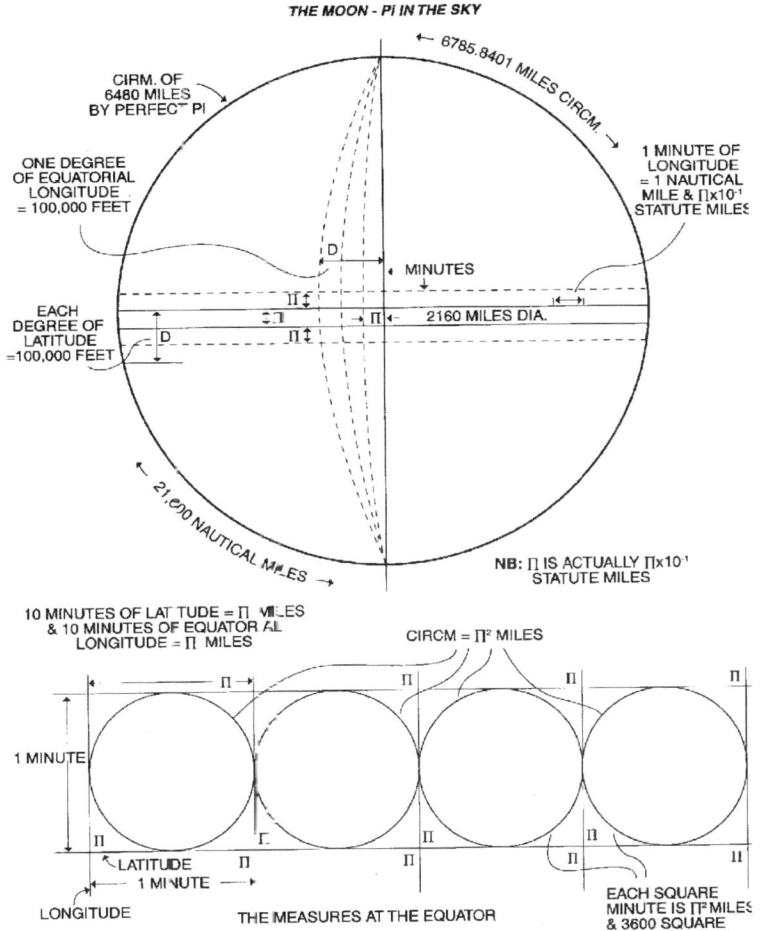

HOW WE WERE MADE

30, while 4 is 2/3rds, or 0.666 of 6. And 4, or 40, was the number of Gilgamesh - Shanabi (40).

So, the Earth's weight is 81 times larger than that of the moon. Now just let us stop there for a moment to consider weight and volume, and their relationship before I comment upon the next step. If we take one pint of water in a glass (i.e. volume of water) and place it beside another larger glass containing two pints of water, it is apparent that the second one is twice the volume of the first, it is equally apparent that the weight of the second is twice that of the first. This is so obvious that it hardly needs saying, but let me say it anyway, an increase in volume will lead to an equal increase in weight of two similar bodies. However, if a thin and hollow glass globe is placed in the container of the one pint of water and glued to the base, and then water is poured back in again up to the one pint mark, it will appear that there is a normal full one pint of water present, as the globe will not be visible. The volume of the second will still appear to be twice that of the first, but lo, on weighing them it is found that the larger one now weighs much more than twice, say one and a half times, that of the one pint container – because there is now less water in the one pint container. This may once have been the basis of a conjuring trick.

Now, back to the Earth moon relationship, for this is the very situation which exists between these two heavenly bodies as well. The Earth is 81 times heavier than the moon, but its volume is only 50 times that of the moon. These two figures may be confirmed from a perusal of any decent atlas. There can be only one of two explanations for this, either the moon is made up of rock which is significantly lighter than that of the Earth (almost certainly not the case), or, like the one pint container cited above, the moon is partially hollow.

On this point Ref 13, p 145 has this to say:

> The exact composition of the rocks forming the Moon's surface is still unknown; all that can be said is that the rocks reflect the light very poorly, in a manner *similar to basalt* " (my italics).

Basalt is described in books on minerals and rocks as very hard and solid, with its weight being the same as granite. So, the argument that the moon is lighter than it should be due to a lighter density of its body, does not apply.

This then, leaves no other alternative; how hollow is the moon? We know from gravitational physics that the Earth is 81 times heavier, but, as we can not see into the moon we have to *assume* that it is solid. We start from taking 81 as accurate but 50 as incorrect. So, if we divide the Earth's volume by 81 we will get the *real* volume of the moon – that is, its shell. If we then take that volume away from the *assumed* volume, we will be left with the volume of space in its centre. The result will present a moon shell which is then the same ratio – 81 – in weight, as it is in volume, to the Earth.

To sum up, the simple equations are:

$$\text{Earth Vol}/81 = \text{real vol of moon}$$

$$\text{Hole in moon} = \text{assumed vol of moon} - \text{real vol of moon}$$

The volume of Earth ($4 \pi r^3$) is 7.958^{11} cubic miles, from which, by the above equation, we get the real volume of the moon as 9.8251^9 cubic miles. The moon's radius of 1080 miles gives an (assumed) volume of 1.583^{10}. From which the size of the hole (the void in the centre) is then 6.004^9 cubic miles, and putting this into the ($4 \pi r^3$) form results in a hollow sphere in its centre with a radius of 780 miles. Take this figure away from its observed radius of 1080 miles, and a shell results which is 300 miles thick – which is 6 divided by 2. Or, put another way, to pass through the moon an object would go through two thicknesses of rock – yes, 600 statute miles of rock! With this new knowledge both the volume and the weight of Earth are now 81 times those of the moon. It's all rather like a tabletop model globe of the Earth – which is hollow inside. The illustration refers. Some years ago NASA did also claim that the moon was hollow as it rang like a bell when impacted by equipment, but they later withdrew that statement.

HOW WE WERE MADE

THE HOLLOW MOON

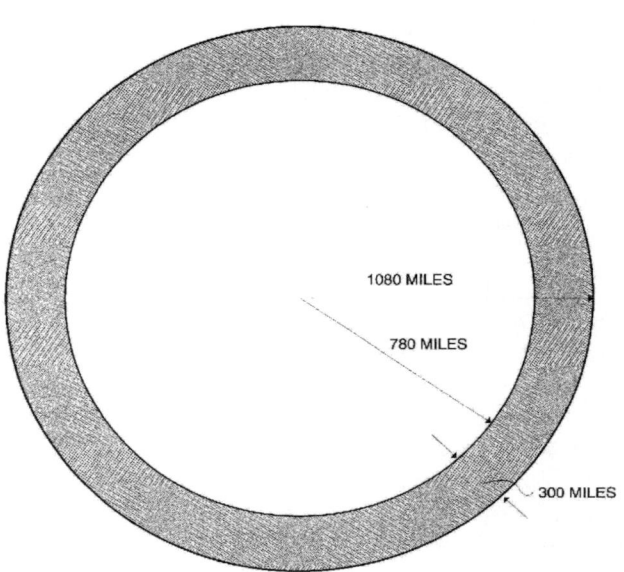

Now behold these magical little equalities:

$$\text{Cosine } 216° = \text{Cosine } 36° = 0.81$$
(The moon's diameter is 2160 miles and
1/81 is the ratio of Earth-moon mass)

Don't $216°$
and 2160 miles or years
look the same?

The gods have used this device before; remember from the previous chapter that the slope angle of the Great Pyramid is tied to twice the Precessional Cycle in the same way:
$$51.84°$$
$$51,840 \text{ years.}$$

$$\text{Sine } 21° \: 6' = 0.36$$

also
$$\text{Sine } 6° \: 12'' = 0.108$$
(in this one the numbers 6, 12 and half of 216 are joined)

plus
$$\text{Tangent } 12° \: 12'' = 0.216$$

The connections, via geometry, of the key numbers of 6, 12, 216, 108, 36 and 81 are quite extraordinary.

HOW WE WERE MADE

Further, from Professor Stecchini (Ref 19, p. 377), we have:

$$\sine 18^0 = \cos 72^0 = 1/2\Phi$$
$$\sine 54^0 = \cos 36^0 = \Phi/2$$
$$\secant 36^0 = \cosec 54^0 = 2/\Phi$$
$$\secant 72^0 = \cosec 18^0 = 2\Phi$$

I shall now consider some aspects of the moon's location, and why, placing it where it is, also involves the divine number strings.

The moon performs a very peculiar orbit around the Earth and its distance from Earth is a variable, and so the 3 distances usually quoted are the maximum (apogee), the minimum (perigee), and the mean.

Firstly, the mean distance of the centre-to-centre Earth moon system is 238,000 statute miles, which is exactly 60 times the radius of the Earth; this is the number base of Sumer.

Secondly, the nearest the moon ever comes to the Earth is 216,420 statute miles surface-to-surface. This is our old favourite 216,000 correct to three figures, which is a difference of a tiny 0.2%; not bad on placing two planets side by side. Well done them. 216,000 is the Sumerian number 'Sargal'.

Thirdly, with the Earth and moon still in this perigee position, we may note that the distance between their centres is 221,463 miles. Now then, before I continue, I need to clarify a universal constant here, it is called 'e', and it is the base of Natural, or Naperian logarithms (after Napier, the genius who discovered them). These are different from 'common' logs whose base is 10. Common logs were always used in arithmetical calculations before the advent of the ubiquitous pocket calculator, whereas Natural logs were, and are, used in the differential and integral calculus. The value of e is 2.72, and, like pi, it is an irrational number, that is, it has no end to it and cannot be expressed as a fraction. If I now multiply e by real pi, that is, 2.72 x 3.141, to give 8.54352, and then multiply this by the Precessional Cycle of 25,920 years, I get 221,448 which is the centre to centre distance Earth to moon at perigee to an accuracy of 0.007%. Another piece of clever encoding to a stunning degree of precision.

There is also a significance for the apogee distance of 252,710 miles to centres, which is also 247,667 miles surface to surface. This is the number string of the polar radius of Earth in inches to an accuracy of 0.96% (the radius is 250,275 (x 10^3) inches).

The circumference of the moon is 6785.8401 statute miles, while the polar circumference of Earth is 24818.896 miles, and the ratio of these two partners is 365.7 (x 10^{-2}), the number string of days in the real year on Earth, to a tiny error of one tenth of one percent.

I have to bring in some complicated concepts here in order to justify what I highlight later, otherwise it would be simply 'a claim'; they are not my concepts however, as I am not an astronomer, but they are well known in that fraternity. The general understanding is that we on Earth only ever see 50% of the moon's surface, as it does not rotate; but both of these perceptions are wrong, as we shall see below. The moon's regular rotation, coupled with irregular revolution produces what is called "libration in longitude", and this allows an observer on Earth to see first further round the east side and then further round the west side of the moon. The moon also varies north and south of the ecliptic so that one can see over one pole and then over the other pole, this is called "libration in latitude". The two, taken together over a period of time, allows us to see rather more than half, and in line with all of the other 60's we've come across so far, it is hardly a surprise to learn that we can actually see 60% of the moon's surface from Earth.

The second generally misunderstood observation, about the moon not rotating, which I mentioned above, can best be seen in the illustration.

The moon does in fact rotate once for every revolution which it makes

HOW WE WERE MADE

**THE MOON'S ONE ROTATION
FOR EVERY ONE REVOLUTION OF THE EARTH**

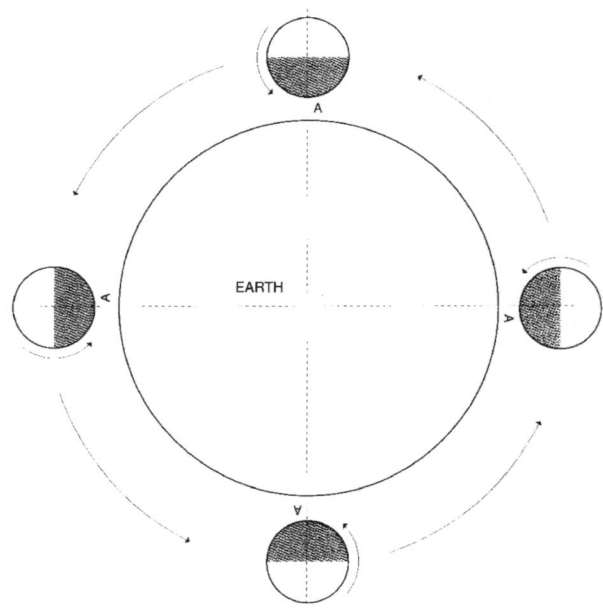

around the Earth as shown in the sketch, which is self evident and does not require any further explanation. The same effect can be demonstrated in the home. Walk around a circular table always facing the centre of the table. When you arrive back at the starting point you will have completed one complete turn on your own axis, and anyone sitting at the centre of the table will not have seen the back parts of you. This same motion was noticed by Archimedes who observed that a man standing on the top of the world, would, were he to walk to the bottom of the world (notice they knew the world was round), have his feet pointing in the opposite direction. He called this concept of the opposite sides on the globe the 'anti-podes', anti meaning opposite, and podes being the Greek word for feet; we now pronounce this as antip-oh-deez, but it should really be anti-podes.

The moon could have made a different number of rotations, such as one half, or three, or five or in fact any number, but no, it makes one; beautiful, simple, one; and in so doing shows only one side of itself (well, 60%). What symmetry, what precision, what a message.

But hold on here, what is its speed of rotation? The circumference, as we have already seen, is 6785.401 miles, and it turns on its own axis in precisely 27.3218 days. Therefore its speed is 6785.401 miles/27.3218 days. Converting this to inches and hours shows a hidden code of 660,000 inches/hour. The actual figure is 655,646.4; so, to two significant figures of 660,000 we have a tiny error of, bizarrely, 0.66%.

At what speed is the moon moving around the Earth? I will not go through all of the calculations regarding its period of revolution and the circumference of its circular-ish journey about us, but will simply say that it is of course 0.66 miles/sec. In fairness I should point out that this is its maximum rate; the minimum is 0.62, but the speed is normally quoted as an average at 0.64. Please compare this number with the Earth's speed of 66,660 miles/hour. The two planets are rotating, one about the Sun and the other about the Earth, at speeds which have the same number string. Observe also the earth's speed of 66,660 miles/hour with moon's rotational speed of 660,000 inches/hour. These numbers are shown in the illustrations.
Let the moon's three states of motion be said quite plainly:

HOW WE WERE MADE

Rotation   660,000 inches per hour
Orbiting the Earth   0.66 miles per hour
Orbiting the sun (with Earth)   66,660 miles per hour

All of these number strings discussed so far are also summarised in the illustrations above.

The radius of the moon is 1080 statute miles, a highly significant number which I discussed further back, and would just point out again that this number has an ancient lineage, it is half of 6 x 6 x 6, and is the 'sar es', that is 10,800, of Sumer.

The moon, as I said at the start of this chapter, performs a somewhat odd orbit around Earth, such that each month's appearance is never the same for some years, until, that is, it returns to its starting position again, it is its 'back to square one' position. This cycle takes 18.6 years and is known as the Saros Cycle; a quick calculation using the coded multiplier method, produces: 18 x 6, which is, 108.0, an old favourite and of course the radius of the moon.

I can also identify 18.6 as the number string for the speed of light which is approximately 186,000 miles/sec (actually around 186,281 depending on the reference book).

If I divide this number by 6 then I obtain the answer of 31, and, on taking the $6/2^{th}$ (cube) root of 31, was utterly surprised to find 3.1414 – real pi itself (it's actually 3.1415). However the actual value of the speed of light is usually given as 186,281, and, on doing the same sum, achieve an answer of 3.143 and this real figure is pi to an accuracy of 0.03%, a quite astonishing piece of perfection when dealing with such a large number. So here are three key numbers all shown to be connected to each other – the speed of light, pi, and the gods' number 6, by the equation described here - the $6/2^{th}$ (cube) root of (186/6) = 3.141 = real pi.

The actual speed of light (186,281) has another astonishing connection, this time with 666, for its square root is, to three significant places, 432. A number found all over the place, and which is twice 6 x 6 x 6! The string

4320 years is one sixth of the Precessional Cycle.

Burl in Ref 11, p 132, describes how certain investigators have estimated that the entrance to Stonehenge was used for measuring the 18.6 year cycle:

> the posts had been temporary sighting devices for recording the moon's northerly risings from its minor at the ENE, 61^0, to its major at the NNE, 41^0, and back over its 18.6 year cycle, with the Heel Stone standing at 51^0, the midpoint between those extreme risings.

Coming back for a moment to the question of coincidences, I will take a quote here from the authors of Ref 1, p 162:

> "To quibble away such a coincidence," remarks Schroder, "or to ascribe it to chance, is in in my opinion to drive skepticism beyond its limits" [F. R. Schroder, *Altgermanische Kulturprobleme* (1929), pp. 80F].

I could not have put it better myself.

So, the moon bobs around the Earth quietly beaming down on every square inch no matter where that square inch may be, its movements are such that it monitors the whole surface of this planet, and only one side of it ever faces towards us, as if, indeed, it was an observatory. If the face of the moon was instead to be the lens (possibly multiple lenses) of a telescope then its positioning and stare could not make more sense. When these facts are coupled with the probability, as explained above, that it may well be hollow, can there be any doubt that this satellite, the moon, has been manufactured, placed where it is, and given its system of movements? A further question must then be, what is inside the moon? Unfortunately I do not have any additional data which I could use to analyse this further.

HOW WE WERE MADE

THE PARTNERS DANCE THE PAVAN

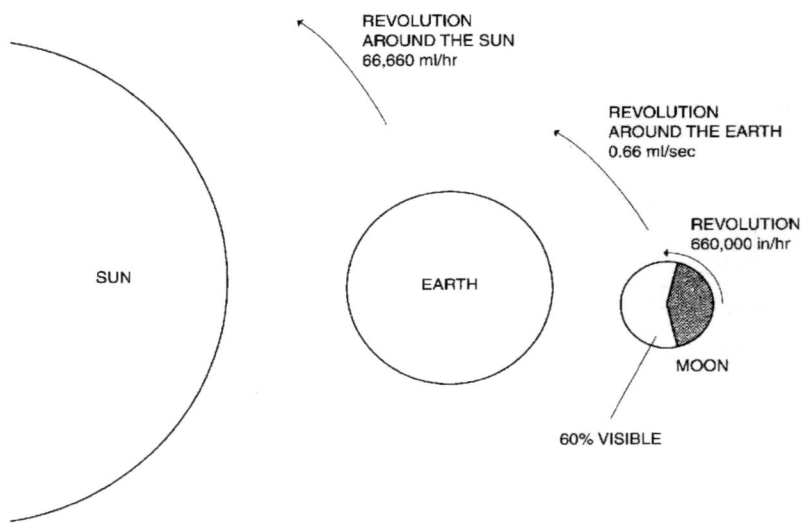

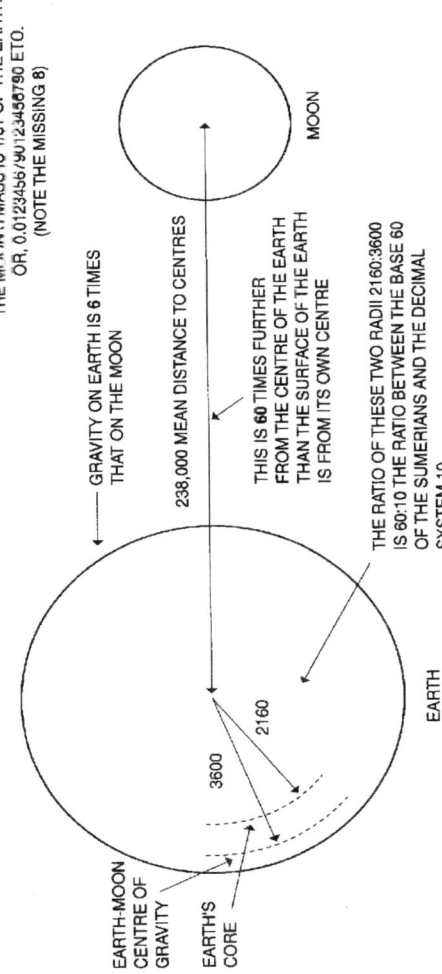

HOW WE WERE MADE

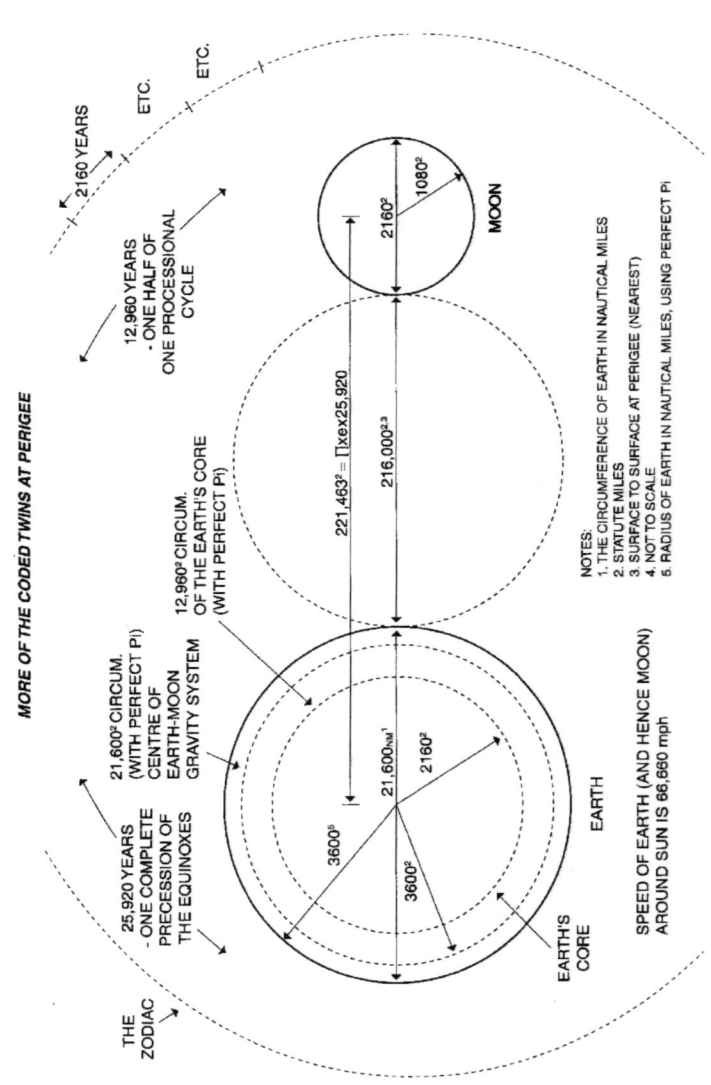

VIII
AD ASTRA
to the stars

At the beginning of this book I made mention of the Precessional Cycle. This is a circle of constellations of stars in the sky, which, because of the sunlight, we can only observe at dawn, dusk, and nighttime. It is commonly known as the zodiac, but let me add that today this Cycle has nothing to do with astrology, although two thousand years ago, and more, it, and astronomy, were the same thing. Nowadays astrologers (these are folk who use a zodiac chart to tell the future, or your fortune) are still using a zodiac alignment from the far distant past. Of course the cycle of stars has continued to turn inexorably through remote space over great periods of time, and so the zodiac alignment today is not the one used by astrologers (today). The zodiac has been with mankind forever, as far back as we can go we find evidence that man had knowledge of it, so much so that we now treat it as if it were as natural as the moon or the Sun; something fixed and immutable, unchangeable, eternal and constant. In fact we think of it as something which is as solid and unalterable and as easy to observe as the moon and stars; something that any creature can do no matter their intelligence or education; even your pussycat knows the difference between the Sun and the moon.

But this is not so The zodiac is not evident, clear-cut, or conspicuous; it is not in plain sight, or apparent or clearly defined, it is not an obvious body in the heavens, it is not distinct or discernible. Nor is it prominent or pronounced, in fact it is hardly observable or perceptible. In reality then, the only way to know about the zodiac is to be taught about it, like learning the alphabet. In other words the zodiac, like the alphabet, is a construct, an

HOW WE WERE MADE

invention, a creation. It is an artifact, an arrangement which has been sought out after scanning the stars to find an array which would obey the system of numbers which the gods had chosen. The clusters which they alighted upon are strange, to say the least, in that most of them bear no relationship to the shapes which the groups are supposed to represent. When I was younger and was learning about star arrangements, I used to wonder why I appeared to be the only one who felt that the shapes that were pointed out to me appeared to be shapeless. I was told that imagination had to be used, with the aid of a pencil and paper whereby the remaining part of the animal could be sketched in. I'm afraid I remained extremely sceptical, and spent my life pondering on how anyone could possibly conceptualize the supposed constellations, although I could just about buy The Plough. It gradually became apparent to me that these had been given to mankind long ago, like the Model Year, as part of the sacred knowledge that man would need in order to measure time; these asinine, asymmetrical assemblages were invented specifically for use on planet Earth, and were given to several first civilisations. These tortuous plans were difficult to learn, and even today there are few people about who can easily point out all of the constellations, mostly they are astronomers. Hence our ancestors had to have these written down, painted and even carved into rock, so important was it to the gods that this knowledge be hammered into us. This is why there are so many ancient records still around. What possible use could a species have for spending large amounts of intellectual energy on a subject which could have no possible benefit to its existence, and indeed how could man possibly know of the colossal lengths of time which the zodiac takes to complete one revolution in the sky? By the way it's 25,920 years – a number we've already met elsewhere. The answer is apparent; that these vast timescales between zodiacal constellations were never meant for mankind at all, they were left as an astronomical clock for the gods, a clock which they ensured would always be available for them on Earth, with man simply as its custodian to care for and maintain its imprint. But why? Why would they need a clock with such lengthy 'ticks' between each sign? I'll come back to that question later.

Consequently, a set of constellations was chosen which could be viewed from the Earth and which would have the coded numbers contained within their 'mechanism' as they revolved painfully slowly around the sky like a huge clock face, whose pointers creak through space driven by the gear wheels of time itself, or rather they appear to move. In fact it we who are moving. But this cycle would have the coded numbers conveyed as time because the zodiac is just that, the reflection of a clock face in the sky, which, like a clock, contains a 360^0 movement. The twelve numerals on your analogue watch face are a perfect mirror of the zodiac, no matter whether they be in Arabic or Roman numerals, or even simply marks on the face, they still mark out the Precessional Cycle, which, through the gods' careful planning and placing, are still with us today, and as close as our wrists.

Before I look at the positioning of the imaginary star shapes, first consider why they appear to move around the sky. Everything in the sky appears to move around us, the Sun, the moon and all of the stars. This is because the Earth is both rotating on its own axis and is also travelling around the Sun; in the case of the moon it is of course moving around us. As an interesting aside here, the philosopher and mathematician Bertrand Russell (joint author with Whitehead of *Principia Mathematica*) once said that we will never know for certain whether we are going around the Sun or the Sun is going around us. But the Earth has another movement too, one whereby its axis is very slowly rotating in a circle. If one imagines the axis elongated out into space then two imaginary circles can be drawn out in space forming two cones whose points touch each other at the centre of the Earth. These imaginary lines are sketched out by Earth as it performs this eccentric circle. It performs this particular motion while actually tilted, which tilt I've already mentioned, so here we have an axis which is tilted over at 23.3^0 and is simultaneously slowly rotating, and this is in addition to its daily rotation. A sketch of this motion is shown in the illustration.

Also shown are two sketches made by people living in North-West Africa and reproduced in Refs 1 & 3, but ultimately taken from the work by Griaule and Dieterlen. These drawings have been with those Africans for a great deal of time and are passed down the generations as explanations of how the Earth and its position were put into place by the creator being. Their explanations and the drawings that go with them are an inescapable fact that these folk have knowledge of the Precession, even to the arrows indicating

HOW WE WERE MADE

revolution of the axis. It beggars belief that a hunter-gatherer tribal group should ever have had the technology to measure such vast time scales, and there certainly is no evidence of a past astronomical science base. It seems to me that the most logical explanation is that at some time in the very distant past they were *given* this information and warned that it contained a great secret, and to ensure its transmission down through time. It is interesting too that an ancient method of measuring time is the 'hourglass' a device with the same inverted cones touching in the middles, through which pass the *sands of time;* sand is made purely of that material which I talked about at the start – quartz, but we'll come back to that. Both the Precessional path, etched in space, and the hourglass, have the same shape, and both measure out time. The time that the axis of the Earth takes to complete one revolution of the circle shown in the illustration, is 25,920 years. Note here that this number is twice 12,960, which, as we have already seen, is the Hindu tretayuga of 3,600 divine years or 1,296,000 human years. It is also, in Sumer the sargal-as and the sargal-su-nu-tag, and, in the Yucatan, 36 tuns (36 x 360 days).

Now to the signs of the zodiac themselves. I've already pointed out that their shapes bear little resemblance to the figurines they are supposed to represent, but, in addition, their sizes are also totally unrelated to each other. Some overlap, and some are higher in the sky, and there are larger and smaller gaps between them, as shown in the illustration.

It was difficult to create such a strange set of signs, bearing in mind that the signs drawn in the illustration must also be seen against a backdrop of a sky glittering with thousands of other stars, (we can normally see with the naked eye about 3,200 stars) and with other constellations which are far more obvious than those in the zodiac. They have clearly been 'forced' to be apparent, so that they can measure time in synchronism with the earth's 25,920 year wobble; this would allow the gods to leave and return thousands of years later and be able to tell at a glance how many years had passed on Earth. Each 'age', which lasts for 2160 years, could also be an indisputable marker, a 'stop and start again' period which could broach no argument; when that sign's time is over it is the moment to step aside and hand over to the next god – and the evidence is in the sky – there can be no dispute.

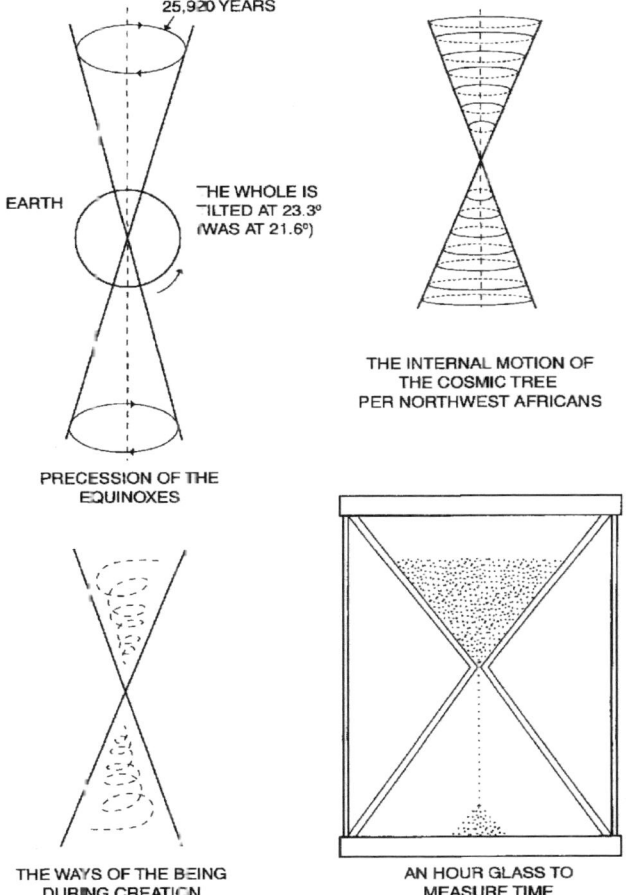

THE CONES OF TIME

HOW WE WERE MADE

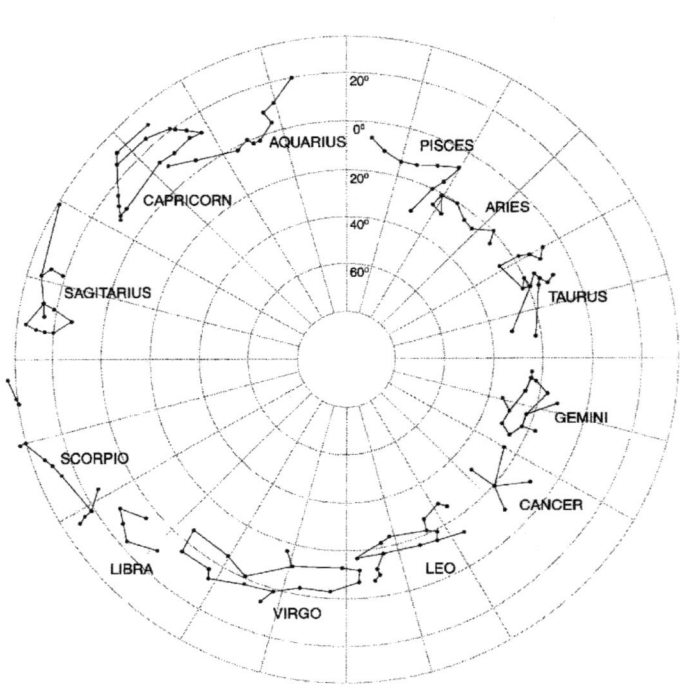

Because the axis of Earth is describing a circle in the sky (over the period of 25,920 years) it follows that that circle must contain 360^0, which then provides for 30^0 for each of the 12 constellations. However, because the signs are of different widths as viewed from Earth, this means that it is difficult to decide when one sign has passed and another has started. It is not a simple exercise, and the observer has to be taught how to measure the actual width of 30^0, as opposed to any apparent width. But, so essential was it to get 12 signs in the circle, that this problem was something that they, and us, had to learn to live with. The numerals on your clock also have 30^0 between each one, because there are 12 hours in the day just as there are the 12 signs in the sky. Furthermore, between each of the clock numerals there are 300 seconds, which match the 30^0 that mark them out, and notice here too that writing 30^0 is the identical string to 300 i.e. three zero zero; with the little 'degree sign' as a small zero. As there are 12 signs which take 25,920 years to rotate in a full circle, a little bit of arithmetic shows that each sign must have 2160 years assigned to it. Back to the watch or clock again, is there any significance in the concept of 6 minutes, as 6 is one of the divine numbers? Well, yes, for 6 minutes is precisely 360 seconds. Asking a similar question of 6 hours, which is a predictive number as it is a half of one day, exposes a total of 2160 seconds!

Let us not forget that Genesis tells us that the world, and man, were created in 6 days, which is also 144 hours; this is also 518,400 seconds or 720^2 seconds (Steven Screen emailed to point out that 72 is the square root of 5184). Now 72 years is the length of time it takes for the zodiac to click round one degree, this is because there are 360 degrees in its circle which takes 25,920 years to rotate. 72 is also twice 36, as is 720 twice 360. It seems impossible, but 518,400 seconds is also the same number string exactly as 20 revolutions of 25,920 years. We also saw earlier that 518,400 is the number of minutes in the Model Year. Does this encoding actually tell us that the number of seconds in 6 days, in reality states the number of years it took to form the Earth – 20 revolutions of the Precessional Cycle of 25,920 years? I do not believe in coincidences of this magnitude. And 20 is one third of 60.

HOW WE WERE MADE

As already explained 51.84^0 is the latitude of Stonehenge, and 51.84^0 is the slope of the north face of the Great Pyramid as measured by Flinders-Petrie.

As the Earth revolves around the Sun through the twelve months, the Sun is said to be in a different 'house' for each month. The house refers to the 'roof' which sits over the Sun just before dawn, and it is this 'roof' which is a particular zodiacal constellation that is over the Sun for that month. If you get up early on a clear dawning and observe the east at the point where the Sun is due to rise, then, providing you have trained yourself to recognise the sign that you are looking for, there you will find it acting as a roof over the coming Sun.

The ancients chose the spring equinox or vernal equinox (which means equal night (and day)) to determine what "age" or house the Sun was presently in, because they knew that these signs were very slowly revolving backwards and that the positions of all the signs would, in 2160 years move one place back. The Precession of the Equinoxes was given this title by the Greek Hipparchus in 127 BC, although it is well established that it was known eons before this. Precession means to go backwards, and as the Sun moves from east to west, the signs move from west to east, so, compared to the Sun's journey, they appear to be going the wrong way. In ancient times the spring equinox marked the beginning of spring and the start of a new year with crops to be sown, and so choosing that date makes sense, although, clearly, they could have chosen any of the four corners of the year.

Unfortunately, the signs are not distributed in an even way around the sky, so that it is not possible to know where the 30^0 segments, which should be allotted to each sign, are supposed to be. There is a way however of assigning this angle by the process of allowing the segments to overlap. This leads to an impossible circle, because in a circle equal segments must not overlap but must of course be conterminous with each other; however, this overlapping methodology does work between individual signs so long as the viewer knows, that is taught, in advance, which stars in adjacent signs are the marker-stars which define the edges of the 30^0 segment. This necessitates learning to recognise 23 of the stars in the 12 signs, and then seeing these as the boundaries for each pair of signs – not a difficult exercise. In reality the marker-stars need not even be part of the constellations, so long as it is agreed that they are the ones. I have actually produced star charts to demonstrate this point but it was not feasible to include those in a book of this size.

Pisces

We know for certain that the time slots of 2160 years for each sign used to have a purpose, in the distant past. These periods were known and recognised by those priests and intelligentsia who watched their movements and waited with bated breath as the time of one sign's ending and the dawning of the New Age approached, for each change of sign was indeed the dawning of a New Age. The coming of each New Age was anticipated with great apprehension, because they were able to foretell, from historical events, that enormous changes would be ushered in with the new star sign, for this is what had always happened at such a time in the past, and which had been recorded and was, therefore, to be expected.

The last historically documented occurrence happened at our year zero, with the passing out of the sign of Aries – The Ram, and the dawning of Pisces – The Fishes. But our year zero, is just that, ours. It is not the real year zero for mankind, that occurred many thousands of year before. Pisces was awaited, and we know that Virgil, in the run-up to zero commented " a new great order of centuries is now being born....", for which he acquired the title of the prophet of Christianity, which was awarded long after he was dead. Naturally he was prophesying no such thing, except that some great change would come about – because it always had on such occasions. In fact, nearer year zero, what was being hailed was that a 'messiah' would arrive and by this time it was was common knowledge. John the baptizer had stirred up the Judeans and had many of them baptized in the river Jordan to repent of their sins. Now John was a man "clothed in camel's hair, and had a leather girdle around his waist, and ate locusts and wild honey", but no sandals apparently, and, he lived in the wilderness. Now, call me cautious if

HOW WE WERE MADE

you will, but this sounds to me like a description of someone who needs care and attention, and yet here are large numbers of folk rushing forward to beg someone who looks 'differently challenged' (to use today's' politically correct non-judgmental form) to dump them in the river. Psychologically, this also says a lot about the state of mind of those coming forward, not only of the douser. Clearly they knew that something was going to happen that would change society dramatically, and they were scared. Yet here was possible salvation, a man was claiming to be able to save them from the imminent unknown, so why not take his offer, after all it could do no harm, except getting wet. The lesson here is important, they knew, everyone knew, that a New Age was impending, Pisces was due.

John tells them "After me comes he who is mightier than I, the thong of whose sandals I am not worthy to stoop down and untie. I have baptized you with water; but he will baptize you with the Holy Spirit". Three wise men from the east had also turned up, following a 'star' which eventually hovered over the birthplace of Jesus; they leave three presents and then decamp secretly to avoid Herod who is so afraid of this birth that he is going to murder all male babies, to ensure that he gets the right one. The only 'star' which could guide someone to a specific spot as small as a stable would have to be several things; low flying, slow, and bright, and of course, controlled. The appellation 'star' is simply a convenient nomenclature for a small bright thing above their heads, moving at a pace which they could follow. Someone was directing these three to a known location, with, yea, and mock ye not, an unidentified flying object. Such devices are common today in the military, they are remote controlled very small aeroplanes about the size of a toy version. They are called drones and are used to overfly enemy territory for obvious reasons. I have seen them used to similar effect for archaeological purposes in order to get a good overview of the terrain, including in town centres.

God had also appeared to several people, and here we must observe that He physically appeared, it was not in a dream, he walked beside them; additionally, there were 'angels' everywhere, speaking in normal voices and standing beside those they were addressing. These were flesh and blood entities who were the midwives of the New Age – and Jesus was to be the chosen emissary, who would be the go-between; that is, between the new god and mankind.

The age of Pisces was to be the time of a new rule by the god whose turn it was to run the Earth, with the power to also influence or manipulate the affairs of man. The old age of Aries had passed and that god's reign was over, and so, by agreement between themselves, it was now someone else's turn. This new god made a decision to run Earth by proxy, via a son which he would produce from an Earth virgin, and it was a girl called Mary who was impregnated, without her consent, (is this not usually called rape?) by this new god, who must have committed this act while she was sedated, by artificial insemination, in which case she would have remained a virgin. She would have been impregnated with an already fertilised egg donated by a 'goddess' who did not wish to bear a child by the new 'god'. Thus Mary would have no genetic connection with the baby, as she was not its mother. This is a procedure which is very common today. He even sends an 'angel' to instruct her that she has been lucky enough to be the mother of his son, and also what name to give him; which, in the original Aramaic language, was Yeshua (not Jesus), and the description of him as a 'christ' was the Greek translation of 'messiah'; so he would then have been Yeshua Messiah (notice that it was known in advance that it would be a boy) This surprises her as she did not even know she was pregnant. The same 'angel' has a word in her future husband's ear to warn him that this is the pregnancy of a god and that he'd better not ditch her just because she is expecting a little matter of a baby. The followers of Jesus would adopt the sign of the fish – Pisces – as their symbol, for that was also the sign of this god; and the fish (the baby) had emerged from the sea – mare – or Mary (as in maritime, marine, mar(i)sh).

The insemination (ie IVF) of the Earthling Mary by a god is something we have met with before now, as it will be recalled from my earlier observations from Genesis 6, "the sons of God saw that the daughters of men were fair; and they took to wife such of them as they chose ...... when the sons of god came in to the daughters of men, and they bore children to them. These were the mighty men that were of old, the men of renown". Here, with Jesus, is an exact repetition of those previous births, and he was certainly set to be a man

HOW WE WERE MADE

of renown!

It is a sobering thought that, in a piece heavy with symbolism, the next sign on the zodiac is Aquarius (the water bearer) which will supersede Pisces. That is, Pisces (the fish, the baby, Jesus) having emerged from water (mare, Mary) is destined to re-enter it again, in Aquarius (The Water Bearer). 2160 AD may well signal the end of Christianity, because the term of the Piscean god and his son, has run its course.

The date of Mary's impregnation is also not an accidental piece of timing; its timing is performed by one whose motives are driven by what is happening in the sky, in the stars. It should be no surprise to learn that the act of conception took place on the night of the Spring Equinox, the 21 March. This is not only a very significant date, but it also allows the birth of Jesus to take place at another such date. He was born 40 weeks later on the Winter Solstice, 21 December, and, due to the importance of this event, I propose that his delivery would have occurred at the equally conspicuous time of 9.36 pm, which is also 21.6 hours. So, his birth time is 21.6 hours on the 21.12 in year zero, the start of Pisces. We know it was during the night from Luke, who says that an 'angel' told shepherds ("keeping watch over their flocks by night") to leave their flocks and go and see him. Pregnancy is usually quoted as 9 months; in fact it is 40 weeks, give or take a few days. I had suspected that there was something symbolic about his birthday, but couldn't put my finger on it due to my layman's believe that the incubation time was 9 months, or 36 weeks, which was incorrect, and prevented me from making a connection between 21 March and 21 December. It was only when I quizzed a midwife member of my family and she said, "40 weeks", that I said "you have just solved a puzzle". This 40 weeks is, moreover, 280 days, which is also the number string for the menstrual period of 28 days. The lunar cycle is near enough 27 days 8 hours, and the true menstrual cycle may actually be this figure, rather than the rounded 28 days. In fact, the moon is customarily quoted as being on a 28 day cycle anyway. Just as the Paradigm Human Male is locked into the divine measures of the planet and the moon, so is woman tied to the complex motion of the moon through her gift of bringing forth new life by the processes of menstruation and pregnancy.

When he 'died' 32 years later, and was taken up, now alive again, into space on a 'white cloud' accompanied by 'angels', the date chosen for this event was again abundant with symbolism. For this was, once again, the Spring Equinox, the 21 March. He went back again on the same date that he had arrived; how elegant, how planned, how obvious.

This also means that men thought Jesus half human and half alien. Although, as all ancient texts inform us that we were made (that is, Genetically Modified from the Neanderthal pre-human stage) in the likeness of 'them', and, in fairness, if they created this planet system, I can hardly refer to them as aliens. In fact it is us who are the interlopers, introduced onto the Earth by them. They have always been here; we, a mere thirty thousand years, most of it spent in cold, misery, and eternal toil – just to stay alive. As one philosopher commented earlier in the twentieth century, "we, are property".

The Council of Chalcedon in 451 AD decreed that Jesus was indeed composed of both divine and human 'nature' (i.e. DNA), but this doctrine caused a split with the Coptic church in Egypt as they viewed him as wholly divine (how right they were). Whatever the phraseology he was certainly a 'god', with the genes of his father up in space (heaven) that would have (has) guaranteed him immortality just like his father. His appearance, which has come down to us through the ages via Greek icons, is certainly not that of a middle eastern man; with his tall stature, pale skin, golden hair and blue eyes he looks more like someone from northern Europe, and he probably had (has) the dimensions of the PHM. If my deductions are correct, then he walks among us.

There are many references to Jesus Christ (JC) communicating with people from space (or heaven): Matthew (Mw) 3.13 "..... the heavens [space] was opened and he saw the Spirit of God descending like a dove [he saw his father arriving in a space vehicle] and alighting on him; and lo, a voice from heaven [the space craft] saying.....". And, a few verses on, the devil "set him on the pinnacle of the temple", which means that he flew him there in a craft, after which "the devil took him to a very high mountain and showed

HOW WE WERE MADE

him all the kingdoms of the world", a crystal clear reference to a trip high up in the sky and around the world in an aircraft. This devil, or Satan, is also referred to as an angel, with his own band of subordinate angels, but JC's father, the god up in space, does not appear able to give orders or command this angel who tempts JC to desert his father and come over to his side; or maybe Satan had been instructed by JC's father to do his best to corrupt him – to test his loyalty. So here is a band of other angels [spacemen] who do not see eye to eye with the god. But the devil (the spaceman leading this breakaway group of cosmonauts), do not harm JC in any way and leave him alone after tempting him, following which the spacemen on the side of the god ('good' angels) come to talk with him (Mw 4.12). In fact (in Matthew at least) there are no bad words about Satan, nor that he is evil in any way – he appears to be someone with a specific task.

The sea, and fish, figure significantly in JC's progress; in Mw 4.18 he walks by the sea and spots two fishermen to whom he says "follow me and I will make you fishers of men". Further along the shore he takes on another two fishermen, and then performs a few miracles. It is at this point that he starts to enunciate, to the crowds, the policies of this new god for the New Age, the familiar list of Blessed are the poor....... etc. This approach is another piece of evidence of the markedly different way that this god would be running mankind compared with his predecessor, who was a vengeful, angry, killing god, a god who gave Moses permission to kill every man, woman, child and animal in the promised land. This philosophy is how the god intends to run Earth during his reign. These are strengthened by his continuing to demonstrate his advanced technological know-how to perform many more miracles, and which really helped to swing the populace in behind him.

At Mw 8.23 he is again on the sea with his disciples, where the boat is in danger of sinking due to a storm, but he is not worried and is sound asleep. They wake him and he asks why they are afraid, and then rebukes the wind and the sea, "and there was a great calm". They ask "What sort of man is this, that even winds and sea obey him". Well, he is the sort who has a father who is in charge of the planet and controls the weather. In the next chapter he is once again on the sea, and in 9.14 he brings a dead girl back to life, something we ourselves are now achieving to a small extent and providing they have not been dead for too long. Rather startlingly in 10.1 he devolves his powers down to his 12 disciples and gives them "authority to heal every disease and infirmity"... "heal the sick, raise the dead.... You received without pay, give without pay, take no gold nor silver ..... etc" These people are to be the mediums through whom the god will address the crowds, because in 10.19 JC says to them "Do not be anxious how you are to speak or what you are to say; for what you are to say will be given to you in that hour; *for it is not you who speak, but the Spirit of your Father speaking through you* (my italics).

He gets very tough in Mw 10.34 and warns that he has not come to bring peace, but a sword, and he will set son against father unless they agree that he is more important than their closest relatives. This is a muscular god who will brook no disobedience. There is constant reference to my Father who is in heaven, which means, my father who is up in space.

In 13.2 he is back on the sea in a boat, and in 13.47 where once again he talks about fishing. In 14.13 back he goes to the sea where he also performs a miracle involving loaves and fishes. In 14.24 he sends the disciples to cross the sea, which is rough, he joins them later by walking across the water to the boat and this terrifies them. He invites Peter to get out of the boat and also walk on water – which he does, he then calms the storm and off they go. This water walking ability is an echo from ancient Egypt, for one of the 42 confessionals in the "I have not" sequence (which I outlined at the start), was, "I have not walked upon the water", which was, therefore, obviously something that was not favoured by the gods. He repeats the loaves and fishes miracle again in 15.35, and in 16.16 refers specifically to his father being a living god, that is, flesh and blood and walking talking.

In 17 there is direct contact with the people from space, when, as we have already seen, he once again ascends a high mountain this time with two of his men, where he is transfigured by a strong beam of light " so that his face shone like the Sun, and his garments became white as light". Two cosmonauts then appeared and held discussions with JC. He was still speaking when a bright cloud [spaceship] appears overhead and they are all

HOW WE WERE MADE

addressed by the god's voice from the spaceship, then it flies up and away, and is gone. He warns his two companions "tell no one of the 'vision' ". If one lives at a time when there is no such thing as airships, and therefore no name for such a machine, then one is driven to use familiar analogous phraseology like 'bird' or 'cloud', to describe that which is in the air. A similar description, using existing words for something for which there is no known word, occurred in the USA when the English shipped over the first locomotive for the Americans; the Indians called it an 'iron horse'.

In 17.27 they are sent fishing again, this time to hook the first fish, which will have money in its mouth.

Finally, in chapter 24 the 'end of the age' is discussed, which is a clear reference to the end of Pisces; and at the end the god is going to take his revenge on mankind for not worshipping him enough, and he will create mass destruction before handing over to the next god in line. And in heaven [space] "the Sun will not give light, and the moon will not give its light, and the stars will fall from heaven [space], and the powers of heaven [space] will be shaken. Then they will see JC coming on clouds [spaceships] of heaven [space] with power and great glory and he will send out his angels [fighter pilots].....".

JC feels his end is nigh on this Earth because he has upset a lot of people, but in 26.53 he tells his disciples not to fear for him because "Do you think that I cannot appeal to my father, and he will at once send me more than 12 legions of angels [fighter pilots]". This is a quite astonishing statement, for here he says explicitly that he is in constant contact with space HQ and can request troops to launch an attack on Earth. A legion was a common concept in those times as the Romans were ruling the country, and each legion consisted of 6000 men, and each was an army. This gives a total of 72,000 angels [fighter pilots] he says he can call up. So here we have three important divine numbers, 12, 6 and 72 (72 years is the time for the Precessional clock to tick one degree). But something goes wrong and his father is not aware that they are going to execute him, we know this because as he is dying he says "My God, my God, why hast thou forsaken me?". This is a clear indication of his belief in a different outcome. But remember that raising the dead is one of the miracles that 'they' can perform. Sure enough, after he is put into a tomb, the descent of an angel [astronaut] from heaven [space] causes the earth to tremble "His appearance was like lightening, and his raiment [flying suit] white as snow". JC has been healed and is well again and talks to the women and the disciples. Yet again he directs them to a mountain, which is his pick-up point for his departure into space, but before he goes says " All authority in heaven [space] and on Earth has been given to me, and lo, *I am with you always to the close of the age [the age of Pisces]"* (my italics). So his father had tested him twice, the first time with one of his 'angels' called Satan, and then to suffer a temporary death. He had passed these with flying colours and was given full authority to rule. Acts 1.6 gives some more information about his final departure "And when he had said this, as they were looking on, he was lifted up, and a cloud [spaceship] took him out of their sight. And while they were gazing into [space] heaven as he went, behold, two [space]men stood by them in white robes, and said, "Men of Galilee, why do you stand looking into heaven [space]? This Jesus, who was taken up from you into heaven [space] , will come in the same way as you saw him go into heaven [space]". That is, he will be brought back down again, in a space vehicle, to walk among us. And, most probably, still is, reporting back to space HQ on our progress.

In John 18.33 He spells out his origins quite plainly "My kinship is not of this world, ... but my kinship is not from the world". And John 7.33 -34 "I shall be with you a little longer, and then I will go to him who sent me; you will seek me and you will not find me; where I am you cannot come". In John 8.22 "Where I am going, you cannot come. *You are from below, I am from above; you are of this world, I am not of this world"* My italics.

Jesus 'died' when he was 32.2 years of age, which is also the acceleration of a body falling to the ground due to the gravitational pull of planet Earth – 32.2 feet/sec^2, and is called g, another universal constant for this planet.

In the Old Testament the prophet Ezekiel gives an extremely detailed description of a spacecraft, around the time of 600 BC (The Book of Ezekiel 1.4 to 2), and from which he is spoken to by the 'god' (this is the one who would be ruling in the age of Aries). His description of it runs to over six

HOW WE WERE MADE

hundred words; here are some extracts, ".... a stormy wind came out of the north, and a great cloud [spaceship], with brightness round about it, and fire flashing forth continually, and in the midst of the fire, as it were gleaming bronze. And from the midst of it came the likeness of four living creatures. And this was their appearance: they had the form of men...... In the midst of the living creatures there was something that looked like burning coals of fire, like torches moving to and fro among the living creatures; and the fire was bright and out of the fire went forth lightening. And the living things darted to and fro, like a flash of lightening...... I saw a wheel upon the earth beside the living creatures, one for each of the four of them. As for the appearance of the wheels..... like the gleaming of chrysolite... their construction being... a wheel within a wheel. When they went, they went in any of their four directions without turning. The four wheels had rims and spokes; and their rims were full of eyes round about. When the living creatures rose from the earth the wheels rose. Over the heads of the living creatures there was a likeness of a firmament, shining like a crystal, spread out above their heads. Above the firmament and over their heads, there was the likeness of a throne, in appearance like sapphire, and seated above it was a likeness of a human form". This personage then speaks to him and holds out his hand with written instructions, which he then orders Ezekiel to eat and swallow! The prophet is then taken for a ride in the spaceship and he describes the thunderous noise which was like an earthquake, as it "arose from its place". A NASA Chief Engineer – J Blumrich even wrote a book about it based on this description in 1973, *The Spaceships of Ezekiel*.

With the immortality of these 'gods', the chances are that Jesus, and his Father, and the 'angels', are still on the planet, but prefer not to make themselves known to us, and may well be guiding some of the affairs of humanity. Several of the biologists working on the Genome project are already saying that they should be able to identify the 'death gene' which has been designed into us to kill us off at the early age at which we now die. The problem for the 'gods' is that, if we did live hundreds or thousands of years, we might soon catch up in science and inventions and be as knowledgeable as they are, which they would not want. If geniuses like Sir Isaac Newton were still alive today I'm sure that we would have progressed even farther than we have in the last three hundred years.

Aries

So, when the father of Jesus took over at the start of his reign, the reign of the Aries god had come to an end, and, as I have mentioned before, they were two very different people. The Aries god's reign began in 2160 BC, and it is to that date we must look to see if there were any other major changes introduced by him (or her) when (s)he too started out after assuming control at the cessation of the rule of the god of Taurus. I will use the masculine from here just because it is easier, but we must remember that the ancient gods were (are) equally male and female, just as we are.

Precisely at this date (2160 BC) in Egypt, the Old Kingdom is struck down. The last ruler of the Old Kingdom in the king lists is Pepi ll, also known as Neferkare, who reigned for 94 years up to 2181 BC, but from then until 2160, i.e. 21 years, the kings were shadowy figures about which nothing is known, and even after this date through to 2050 very little is known about those kings on the king list. But at 2160 a new king emerged – Meryibre Achthoes (Khety l), and the king list is re-established, but the whole period from 2181 to 2050, around 130 years, was a time of great internal chaos with a complete collapse of central authority, and political anarchy. There is very little evidence about Egypt during this extremely turbulent time, which is known as the First Intermediate Period. At the end of Pepi ll's reign the central administration finally collapsed. The events which brought about the dissolution of central control are not known to historians. It is odd though that the state should fold in on itself without any sign of an internal revolution. True, its borders were being nibbled at, by the Bedouin in the north and the Nubians in the south, but Pepi ll had always shown a vigorous face to these snipers, and they were not anything like a real threat. During this period Egypt broke up into self ruling nomes, until 2160 when the twentieth nome, with its capital at Heracleopolis in Upper Egypt, subdued all of the other nomes in that area. The nomarch (ruler of the nome) of this city claimed the northern part of the kingdom of Egypt and established a new dynasty. His name was Archthoes with the throne name of Meryibre, as noted above. After gaining control, Memphis once again became the administrative capital of northern Egypt. Within about 30 years

HOW WE WERE MADE

of 2160 a southern king – Inyotef Sehertowy 1 arose and became regarded as the man who initiated the reunification of the whole of Egypt, and founded the eleventh dynasty. Following a further 10 years a successor called Nebhepetre Mentuhotpe ll completed the reuniting. This king took the Horus-name of Smatowy 'He-who-unites-the-Two-Lands'.

This break up, and then reunification, is very strange; but of course, in my scenario, the assumption of power by the new god of Aries, who wished to stamp his own authority on the land, may well have been the real reason. I have noted before that revolutions always involve a "lets start again at scratch" mentality, as the rebels who win, or the 'new boy' who takes over command, feel superior to the system they have deposed, which itself has usually evolved slowly over time - evolution versus revolution. Clearly the 'gods' are no different from man in this respect. The influential Carl Jung, who died in 1961, had also observed the same association of catastrophic changes taking place in Egypt, with the change from Taurus to Aries.

Confirmation of this occurrence is presented by the change to the worshipping of the Ram, as the official new god of Egypt at exactly this time. Prior to that the Bull had received the required reverence. The god Knum was the most prominent of the ram deities, and was revered as the creator of mankind. He is shown as a human figure with the head of a ram, and eventually Amun himself was also displayed as a ram headed man god. There was also a ram god at Mendes called Banebdjedet who was seen as the spirit (the Ba) of the god Osiris, one of the earliest and most important of their gods; and at the city of Herakleopolis the god Heryshef had the head of a ram. There is a photograph in Ref 5 page 31 of King Taharqo between the front legs of a seated ram which is protecting him, it is in granite and over three feet high, and dates from circa 670 BC. Various temple entrances had whole avenues of seated rams on the approach road. Curiously, a beautiful effigy of a ram was dug up from the grave of a queen, in what had been Sumer, early in the twentieth century by a British archaeologist. It is of a ram standing on his hind legs with his head in a bush eating the leaves, a very fine piece of work in gold filigree with other precious materials. It is only 18 inches high and can be seen in Room 56 at the British Museum. It has however been 'dated' to around 2700 BC, but I do not know on what grounds, as carbon dating was not available at the time. I actually saw an instance of this activity when I was out walking by the Thames one day. Going along the tow-path with the river on my right I came to a section of fencing about six feet high with a tall may-tree or bush, perhaps 15 feet high, on the other side. Something caught my eye and I looked up, to see a ram in the tree above the fence. I asked him if he usually climbed trees, and was even more startled when a voice answered 'yes'. But this was from his owner on the other side of the fence, who went on to tell me that the ram had just been to the very top of the tree. This bettered my previous first, of watching a sheep climb a dry-stone wall in the Cotswold Hills, walk along the top, and jump down to the other side, where the grass was obviously greener.

Taurus

During the age of Taurus the bull (4320 to 2160 BC), the bull had, as was to be expected, been worshipped in Egypt. This highly revered cult object was known as the Apis Bull, which was a single, living, bull and was regarded as the Ba of the god Ptah. All authorities agree that this dates back to the beginning of Egypt, and the bull's head features four times, at the top, and above the king, on the famous Narmer Palette which is dated back to the Protodynastic period. Apart from receiving adoration during his lifetime, when he died there was national mourning, and the embalmed corpse was taken from Memphis to Saqqara along the sacred way to be buried in a sarcophagus made from granite (a material I will return to). The burial catacombs are known as the Serapeum. Quite naturally there was, and is, a large number of these mummified Apis Bulls. His mother was also venerated as the goddess Isis and she was treated similarly, but was buried in a different location – the Iseum. The offspring of the Apis were also buried with dignity but their tombs are unidentified. This deity was so popular, and ingrained so far into the Egyptian psyche and religious practice, that the incoming god of Aries the Ram had great difficulty in dislodging him, and worship of the bull continued well into Aries before he was finally ousted. No doubt the same will happen with the fish in 2160 AD, when the Aquarian god ousts the Piscean.

HOW WE WERE MADE

There is a wonderful example of this changeover in the expulsion of the Hyksos (pre-Jews) from Egypt, under the command of the Egyptian army general Moses, circa 1700 BC. The name of Moses comes from the Egyptian Rameses; meses means 'born of', therefore 'born of Ra', which means that Moses on its own is somewhat puzzling. He and the other Hyksos eventually reached Mount Sinai, where their new god lived in a 'cloud' (spacecraft). There is much ascending and descending of this god in his spacecraft, accompanied by fire, thunder and ground tremblings. Moses is not allowed to see the god, who is always 'in a cloud' and after one visit Moses comes back down with his face shining so brightly it frightens the people. In Exodus 33.11 the god gets very close, "When Moses entered the tent, the pillar of cloud would descend [from space] and stand at the door of the tent...... thus the Lord used to speak to Moses face to face, as a man speaks to his friend". The rest of the people could observe this and would rise up and worship. In 32.4 they had become fed up with waiting for Moses to come down from the mountain and so had made ' a molten calf' (that is, a model of an Apis Bull) to worship and dance around. This caused the god of Aries to murder three thousand of their men (32.28), and also to send a plague upon them (32.35). In their wanderings they are to be guided by an 'angel' who is in touch with the god and who walks in front of them to show the way. Ref 1, p 60, comments " The preceding age, that of Aries had been heralded by Moses coming down from Mount Sinai as "two horned", that is, crowned with the Ram's horns, whilst his flock disobediently insisted upon dancing around the "Golden Calf" that was, rather, a "Golden Bull", Taurus".

It is also at the start of Aries that the new god destroys the cities of Sodom and Gomorrah, as described in Genesis 18 to 19, " because the outcry is great...... I will go down [descend from space] to see...". Later that evening two 'angels' [military commanders] arrive at Sodom, on foot, and Lot invites them into his house for a feast. The townsmen demand to be allowed to deal with them, but Lot offers his two virgin daughters if they will desist, "do to them as you please". The men are then blinded by the 'angels', who invite Lot to leave, "for we are about to destroy this place... the Lord has sent us to destroy it". "Then the Lord rained out of heaven [space] fire and brimstone, ... and the smoke went up like the smoke of a furnace". Today we are all unfortunately familiar with our own ability to destroy entire cities in exactly the same way. The town of Tell Ghassul was also totally annihilated, and archaeological evidence of extensive burning supports this.

Abraham is also brought, with his people, from his birthplace of Ur in Sumer, at this time, to Jerusalem.

So, the newcomer god of Aries takes Egypt and ruins it, carries out a major bombing attack on several cities in Israel, moves the nation of the Hyksos over a huge distance and over many years, and does a similar thing with Abraham and his people; and yet these are only a few of his activities, the bible is full of others. This god waded in blood, and contrasts dramatically with the next one to come along – the god of Pisces, Jesus and peace; except, that as we approach the end of his reign, so the violence increases. In the twentieth century in Europe, Russia, China, Africa and India, many hundreds of millions have died by the sword.

The bible is littered with references to 'gods' descending from heaven [space] in 'clouds' [aircraft of some sort] with their subservient 'angels' [military personnel], and demonstrating their awesome abilities, that is, technologies, on a population that was still quite backward, and susceptible to 'magic' tricks, or miracles. It was the Royal Air Force in 1922 which created the symbol of a pilot's ability to fly an aircraft – a pair of wings with a disc in the middle. He had 'earned his wings' and could fly! This symbol is identical to those from ancient Sumer. This is what the 'angels' were – pilots.

Before I leave the gods alone, there is another reference which I should mention, and that is to the hero Gilgamesh from Sumer. Quoting from Ref 1 p 288:

> Gilgamesh is claimed to have been one of the earliest kings of Uruk (or Erech). The circumstances of his fabled birth make him two-thirds [0.666] god and one-third man, which makes him – in the sexagesimal system of Mesopotamia – two-thirds of 60 (= Anu) = 40, the number which characterised Enki-Ea, whence the latter's

HOW WE WERE MADE

denomination of "Shanabi (= 2/3, ie of 60), and Nimmin (Sumerian = 40)".

Again, on page 296:

> Gilgamesh faces Urshanabi, expecting to be ferried across the waters of death. The boatman demurs: the "stone images" have been broken by Gilgamesh. But at length he instructs the pilgrim to cut down 120 poles, each sixty cubits (thirty yards) in length [to punt the boat].

And page 324:

> ...... one finds oneself dealing with utterly unknown ancestors, whose biblical rages and passions have to be read in an entirely new context.

Much later, the Greek goddess Athena, whose mighty golden statue once stood in the Parthenon, in Athens, which was itself named after her, had her number too – it was 60. Opposite the Parthenon is the Erechtheum, a name which is mentioned in the above quotation, from Sumer.

I said earlier that the dating evidence for many prehistoric megalithic monuments, including Stonehenge, also indicates their foundation to this very time. This confirms that whoever they were (are), they were (are) operating on a global scale.

IX
JOURNEYS INTO SPACE

We saw in chapters VI and VII that the Earth and the moon have some identical measurements to them, and if I now extend that to looking at the Sun, further similarities are in evidence. For the Sun moves around its galactic centre at 186 miles per second, which chimes with the moon's complete cycle of the Earth of 18.6 years (the Saros Cycle), and also the speed of light at 186,000 miles per second (actually around 186,281 depending on the reference book). Incredibly, this Cosmic Year, as it is called, takes 2160 (x 10^5) Earth years for the Sun to revolve about its galactic centre; that is also 2,592 million months (the Precessional Cycle is 25,920 years). Just how amazing is that? And please remember that these numbers are only available in the the divine measuring system, they are rendered invisible if quoted in the metric mess.

Moreover, the Sun is also moving at a speed of 12 miles per second towards a point on the star sphere in the constellation Lyra, not far from the first magnitude star Vega. With a little bit of arithmetic it can be seen that 12 miles per second is also 720 miles per minute; and 43,200 miles per hour, which is 21,600 x 2 (or (6 x 6 x 6) x 200). We have met these numbers everywhere.

Stirling quotes (Ref 20 p.18):

> The diameter of the Earth's orbit around the sun is 220 diameters of the sun ..... This statement is to be found in Galileo's System of the World. [as is] The diameter of the sun containeth the diameter of a fixed star of the 6th magnitude 2,160 times (both

HOW WE WERE MADE

of these relationships are shown in the attached diagrams).

Now 220 yards is one English furlong, which is 660 feet which is 7,920 inches – the mean diameter of the Earth; that is, the sun's diameter multiplied by the English furlong is the diameter of Earth's orbit around the sun.

and, on page 28:

A mile contains 1760 yards, and an equilateral triangle [60, 60, 60,], inscibed within in the orbit of Saturn measured by the diameter of the sun, measures 1,760 diameters on each of its sides. *Therefore the British standard records three important measures of the cosmic system. Assuming that these coincidences are the result, not of accident but design, we are led to the conclusion that at some time, possibly very remote, that the dimensions of the cosmos were ascertained, and introduced into the standard measures inherited by the English people.* (My italics).
The reader must be asked to assume that a standard measure, corresponding to that in use in England, was known to the Egyptians, Hebrews and Greeks.

Furthermore, the three sides of the triangle add up to 5,280 feet, which of course, is 1 statute mile! The diagram shows these figures.

How accurate are these statements? Well, we can test them with the data we have today.

The sun's diameter is 865,000 miles, and this, times 220, is 190,300,000 miles. The maximum diameter of the Earth's orbit around the sun we know to be 189,029,880, and so the claim is correct to an error, or tolerance, of 0.67% - very low.

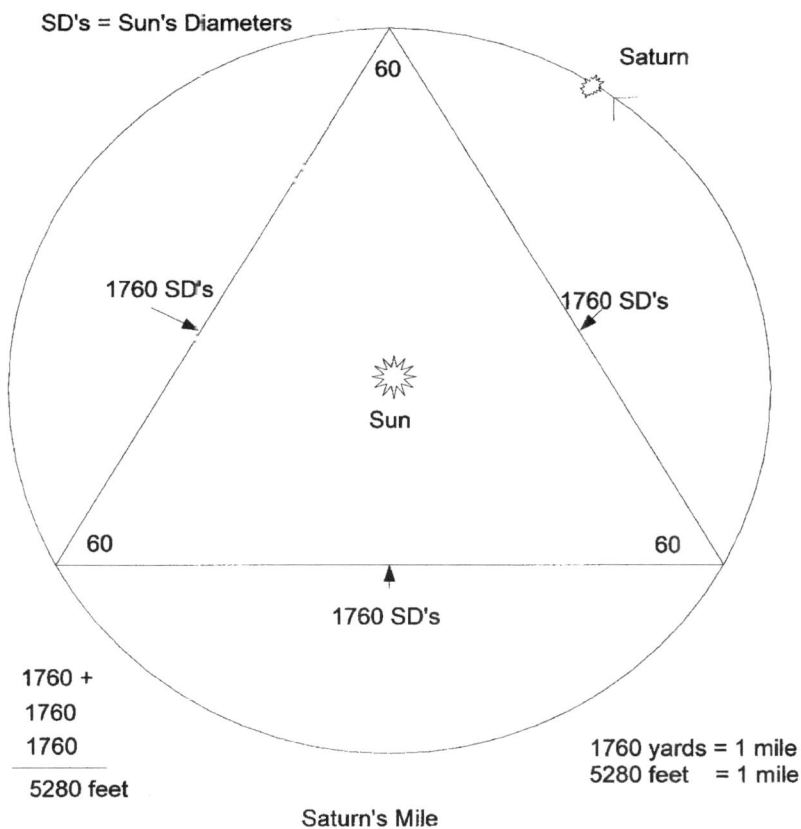

HOW WE WERE MADE

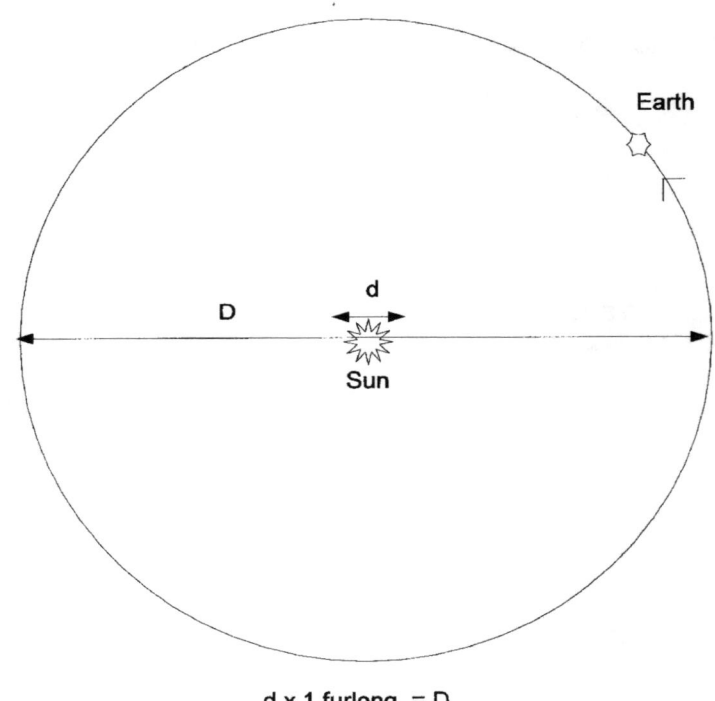

d x 1 furlong = D

Earth's Furlong

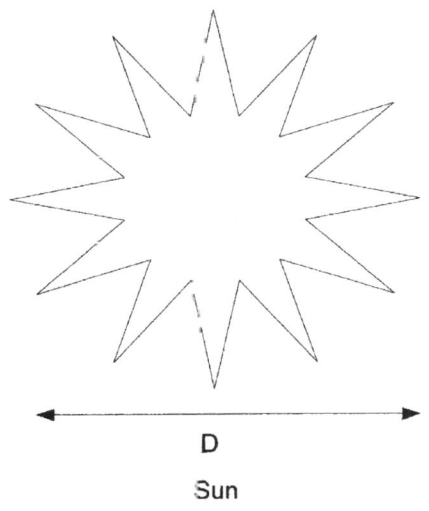

D
Sun

6th magnitude star

D = 2160 x d

Sun and Stars

HOW WE WERE MADE

For the second observation:

The mean surface to surface distance from the sun to Saturn is 882,039,910 miles, and by a piece of trigonometry (which I shall not detail here), the sides of an equilateral triangle contained within Saturn's orbit, can be calculated to be 1,527,693,100 miles. Now the sun's diameter of 865,000 times 1,760 is 1,522,400,000, giving a tolerance of 0.37% - again very very low.

Furthermore, the planets also have numbers about them associated, or derived from, these number strings. Working outwards we have the following: .

	Average distance from the Sun in Million miles	Orbital Velocity miles/hour
Mercury	36	108,000 (216,000/2)
Venus	66.6 (quoted as 67.1, so tiny error of 0.74% here)	77760 (2160 x 6 x 6) (Also 1296 miles per min, and 21.6 per sec Quoted speed is 21.8 so small error of 0.9% here)
Earth	93 (18.6 x 5) (186 encodes speed of light)	66,660

Mars	142.6 (21.6 x 66)	54,000 (108,000/2) (216,000/4)
Ceres, *et al* (The exploded planet)	279.9 (12.96 x 21.6)	no data
Jupiter	482 (25.92 x 18.6) (186 encodes speed of light)	29,160 (2,160 x 13.5)
Saturn	907 (129.6 x 7)	21,600 (also 6 miles per sec, and 360 miles/min)
Uranus	1,800 (60 x 30)	15,120 (2,160 x 7)
Neptune	2799 (21.6 x 12.96) (note the same number string as Ceres)	1228 (66 x 18.6) (186 encodes speed of light)

NB. Speed of light usually given around 186,281 depending on the reference book.

Pluto is not included as it is no longer considered to be a planet, and it also fails Bode's law for planetary positions, which confirms that view. It is about half the size of our moon.

Bode's law was formulated in 1778 and it helped in the discovery of

HOW WE WERE MADE

unknown planets, since astronomers knew where to look for them, as predicted by this law. The law is a rather strange series of numbers, based on 12, where the first two are taken as 0 and 3; after these two each number is then doubled, so we get:

0, 3, 6, 12, 24, 48, 96, 192, 384. Each number is a multiple, or sub-multiple, of 12.

4 is then added to each number to give:

4, (4+3), (4+6) , (4+12) , (4+24) , (4+48) , (4+96) , (4+192) , (4+384)

This series might also be presented as a function of 12, as all of the above figures may be rearranged to show them as factors of 12.

Whichever way the series is shown, these are the resulting numbers:

4   7   10   16   28   52   100   196   388

The distances from the Sun in Astronomical Units (Earth = 1), x 10, are as follows:

3.9	7.2	10	15.2	27	52	95.4	192	301
Mercury	Venus	Earth	Mars	Ceres	Jupiter	Saturn	Uranus	Neptune

From which it can be seen that there is a pretty good correlation, except for Neptune. So, not only are our highly repetitive number strings locked into the planets' distances and velocities, but also the relative positions are based on the number 12, which is of course twice 6.

I note with some satisfaction that the accuracies of the figures which I have quoted throughout this book are far higher than those exposed in Bode's Law.

It is at this point that I must return to the business of the cube, for the cube was Saturn's figure, as shown by Kepler, in his *Mysterium Cosmographicum*. Ref 1, p 222 says, "this is the reason for the insistence on cubic stones and cubic arks. Everywhere, the power who warns "Noah" and urges him to build his ark is Saturn, as Jehova, as Enki, as Tane etc".

Ref 18, p 113 has this to say about geometry and Kepler and the planets:

> And one day, during a class, the reason came to him. He was teaching the last book of Euclid, which contains the demonstration that there are only five possible regular solids. If these shapes should fit between the spheres of the six planets, that would be an arrangement satisfactory to his geometrician's mind. He hastily assigned his pupils a difficult construction, and busied himself with his own calculations. As if a spirit were dictating the solutions to him, there came out the following propositions:
>
> Place the cube between Saturn and Jupiter. The cube will limit the orbit of Jupiter.
>
> Place the tetrahedron between Jupiter and Mars. The tetrahedron will limit the orbit of Mars.
>
> Place the dodecahedron between Mars and Earth. The dodecahedron will limit the orbit of the Earth.
>
> Place the icosahedron between Earth and Venus. The icosahedron will limit the orbit of Venus.
>
> Place the octahedron between Venus and Mercury. The Octahedron will limit the orbit of Mercury
>
> And there resulted the distances between the orbits in the Copernican system. Re-examination confirmed this curious discovery. The Lord God had revealed his Euclidean intentions; the

HOW WE WERE MADE

mystery of the structure of the universe was disclosed. And the insignificant schoolmaster of Graz became famous at one blow. 'And yet', he wrote, 'I began this investigation only for my own amusement'.

I know just how he felt!

It is clear from the first reference above however that there was knowledge of Saturn and its cube before Kepler discovered it, and, in the ancient past. The attached illustration shows Kepler's geometric solar system, the cube of Saturn is visible.

KEPLER'S GEOMETRIC SOLAR SYSTEM

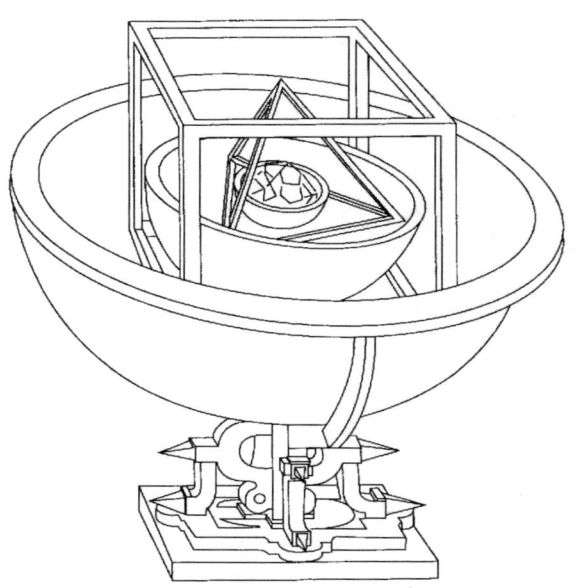

X
THE PENTAGON
and others

The Greeks had a profound belief in numbers and their almost magical qualities, and, that numbers were also represented by geometrical shapes; for example that a point equals 1, a straight line is 2, a triangle is 3 and a square is 4, and so on. But they also believed that the world was a dodecahedron, whose twelve faces stood for the 12 signs of the zodiac, and whose measures were that of the year. Kepler, as outlined above, was to observe 2000 years later that the dodecahedron "would limit the orbit of the Earth", Ref 1, p 187 contains a statement by Plutarch, who had it from Plato:

> Is their opinion true who think he ascribed a dodecahedron to the globe, when he says that God made use of its bases and the obtuseness of its angles, avoiding all rectitude, it is flexible, and by circumtension, like globes made of twelve skins, it becomes circular and comprehensive. For it has twenty solid angles, each of which is contained by three obtuse plains, and each of these contains one and a fifth part of a right angle. Now it is made up of twelve equilateral and equiangular quinquangles (or [regular] pentagons), each of which consists of thirty of the first scalene triangles. Therefore it seems to resemble both the Zodiac and the year, it being divided into the same number of parts as these. [From: *Quaestiones Platonica* 5.1, 1003c R Brown trans.), in *Plutarch's Morals,* ed. W. W. Goodwin (1870), vol. 5, p. 433.]

The authors carry on to say "In other words it *is* steriometrically the number 12, also the number 30, the number 360 ("the elements which are produced when each pentagon is divided into 5 isosceles triangles and each of the

HOW WE WERE MADE

latter into 6 scalene triangles") - the golden section itself. This is what it means to think like a Pythagorean".

The word 'regular' used above in 'regular pentagon', means that this pentagon is completely symmetrical – all angles are the same and all lines are the same length, and so the areas of each pentagon are identical. There is an infinite number of irregular pentagons, wherein angles and lines are of differing sizes, and these may also be referred to as polygons.

But there is more, much more, hidden in this wonderful structure, and which also measures so much of our structured environment.

These arcane facts are due to four more extremely important numbers buried in this solid, which are identical with the number strings we have already seen elsewhere, and which the authors of the above have missed, because the four extra numbers are not mentioned in their book. And clearly, Plutarch did not know of them either, or, he did not wish to reveal the even stronger connection between the dodecahedron and the world. The key to the first number lies in the words 'solid angles, each of which contains one and the fifth part of a right angle' (a solid angle is that which is between the surfaces at the point where the three surfaces meet). A right angle is 90^0, and a fifth part of it is 18^0; accordingly the total angle is 108^0, that is, $90^0 + 18^0$. This is a number string we have met many times before (for example it is the radius of the moon – 1080 statute miles). 108^0 is also the angle between two sides of a pentagon. But, incredibly, because there are 20 of these solid angles in the dodecahedron (count the points in the figure), there are then, 20 x 108^0 degrees in total; yes, there are 2160^0 in all. The very familiar
6 x 6 x 6 = 216.

The third number is 72^0, which is the crest angle of the scalene triangles, and the fourth is the 54^0 which sits in the other two corners of the scalenes.

It is these four numbers, 108^0, 2160^0, 72^0, and 54^0, which go unnoticed by Plato, by Plutarch, and by professors de Santillana and von Detchend, the authors of Ref 1. The dodecahedron is shown in the illustration.

THE DODECAHEDRON
TIME, EARTH, MAN, THE STARS. ALL ARE HERE.

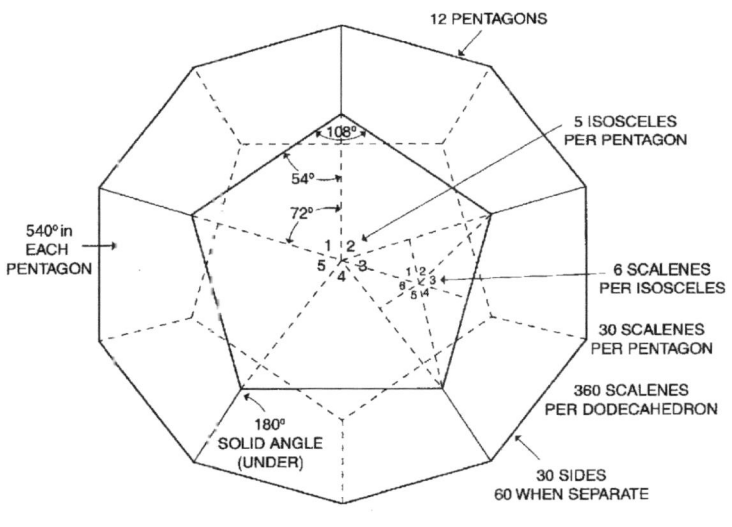

HOW WE WERE MADE

There are 12 pentagons, which can easily be confirmed by counting them on the figure.

Each pentagon can be divided into 5 isosceles triangles (isosceles means that two sides of the triangle are the same), and then each of these may be divided into 6 scalene triangles (a scalene is one that has no sides or angles which are the same). There are then 30 (5 x 6) scalene triangles per pentagon; I have not attempted to draw the 30 scalene triangles inside one of the pentagons as it would be rather confusing. But obviously there are 30 of them.

Because there are 12 pentagons and 30 triangles in each, it follows that there are 360 triangles on the surface of the dodecahedron.

If the 12 pentagons are considered separately then there is a total of 60 sides in all (5 x 12), and if they are counted while connected together as the dodecahedron, then there are 30.

Each pentagon has a total of 540^0, this is 5 x 108^0.

All of the numbers are here; 6 and 60 (the number base of Sumer), 12 (hours, months, phalanges etc), 20 (one third of 60), 30 (the number of days in the ancient month), 54, and 540 (one quarter of 216, and others which I will come to), 72 (the time in years for one degree of movement of the Precessional Cycle, and twice 36), 360 (the number of days in the ancient year). But, most exciting of all – 108 and 2160 (666). It was also, as Kepler discovered, the shape which limits the orbit of the Earth. As we have seen thus far, all of these numbers crop up in a myriad of important places involving the Earth, space, time and mankind itself. It does appear that the Greeks were given knowledge of this strange solid which contains all of the important encoding numbers in its construction.

Plutarch's comment (above) regarding twelve skins, and flexibility, is interesting as it indicates that such a shape could be inflated to form a smooth sphere where the lines of the pentagons would be bent to accommodate the curvature the Earth's surface. Such a construction can be seen in a modern football, except that the makers have made the ball's surface from a mixture of 12 regular pentagons and 20 regular hexagons (six sided polygons). They could equally have made the ball from regular pentagons only.

We shall be coming back to the dodecahedron when I discuss the foundations of life itself.

I have pointed out that some of the trigonometrical functions also connect together various of these sacred numbers; these are (again):

$$\text{Cosine } 216^0 = \text{Cosine } 36^0 = 0.81$$
(1/81 is the ratio of Earth-moon mass & 2160 the moon's diameter)

and
$$\text{Sine } 21^0 \ 6' = 0.36$$

also
$$\text{Sine } 6^0 \ 12" = 0.108$$
(in this one the numbers 6, 12 and half of 216 are joined)

plus
$$\text{Tangent } 12^0 \ 12" = 0.216$$

Additionally
$$\text{Sine } 54^0 = 0.81$$

It will be recalled that 54 is one quarter of 216, and is the number of statues at Angkor Wot, and the orbital velocity of Mars in (thousands of) miles per hour. It is also the 'inverse' of 36 in a right angle triangle, in that 90 − 54 = 36 (54^0 is called the 'complement' of 36^0); accordingly, 54 is thereby linked to the other sacred numbers. But, remarkably, 54 is related to 90 in another capacity, for the ratio 54:90 is also the ratio 6:10; we have met this one before in the form 216:360. It is the ratio of the gods' number base of 6, to man's decimal number base of 10. But the surprises continue, for the ratio

HOW WE WERE MADE

36:54 is none other than our old friend 0.666! Its ratio to 66, that is, 54:66 (where 6 x 6 is the coded form of 360), is the *sine of itself* repeated forever – 0.818181818181, (sine $54^0 = 0.81$, while $54/66 = 0.818181$), hammering home the message over and over again, to the end of the page, and beyond. With its connection to 0.81, and the ratio of the Earth's mass to that of the moon – 1/81, it can be seen that 54 is indeed an integral part of the scheme of sacred number strings.

The number 90^0, which also represents a quarter of the Model Year - 90 days, is related to the number base of Sumer (60) in the ratio 60:90, which is also 0.666.

These number strings are also connected via right-angle triangular ratios, and these are shown in the two illustrations.

Running through them one at a time, it can be seen that the three triangles with 60 and 30 degrees link 72 to 36, 216 to 108, and 2.592 to 1.296, and, as we saw above, the ratio of 60 to 90 is 0.666. These 'half', or 'double' ratios are beguiling in themselves, they do keep cropping up all over the place, including in music in the concept of the 'octave'. An octave is the most elemental relationship between frequencies, used in music, throughout history. When a string, or pipe, for example, are vibrated by plucking or blowing them, then they will vibrate at some specific resonant frequency f. When the string or pipe is halved in length, for instance by placing a finger half way along the string (called a node, or still point), then both halves will now resonate with a new frequency which is double that of the original – 2f. This new frequency – 2f, is called an octave. It used to be divided up into 8 parts which is why it is called an octave, but around the year 1700 this was changed to our old friend 12, so an octave now has 12 'intervals', as they are called. Musicians recognise that the most natural frequency relationship exists when the string is divided with two still points instead of one, that is, dividing the string into three parts not two, so the ratio between the original frequency and the two-thirds length of string is 2:3, or 0.666. In other words the frequency of the two-thirds part of the string will be 1.5 times (1/0.666) the original full-length frequency. Harmony indeed. With the others of the number based systems we have come across so far, a complete symphony is

TRIANGULAR CONNECTIONS

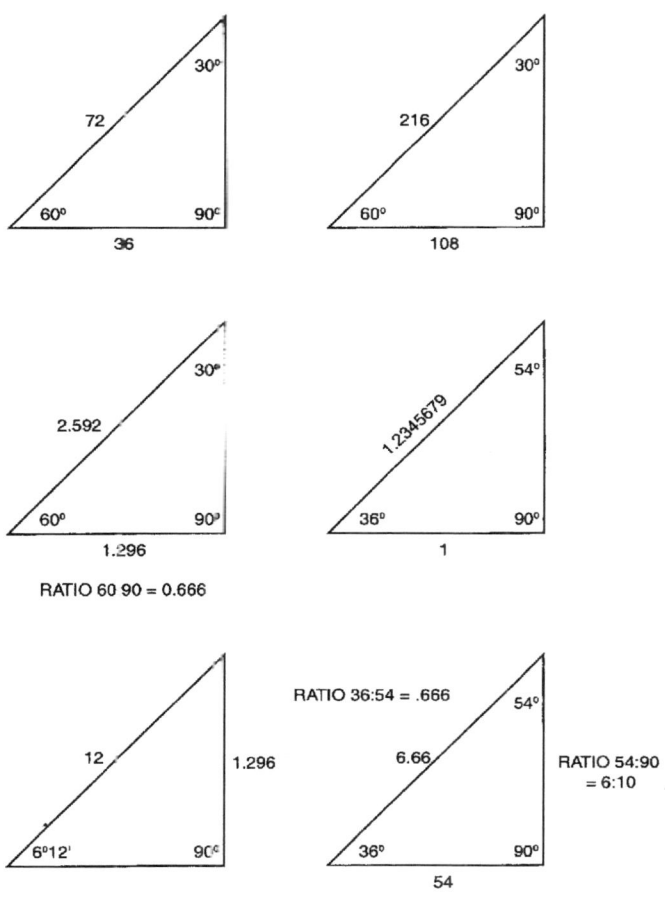

HOW WE WERE MADE

TRIANGULAR CONNECTIONS

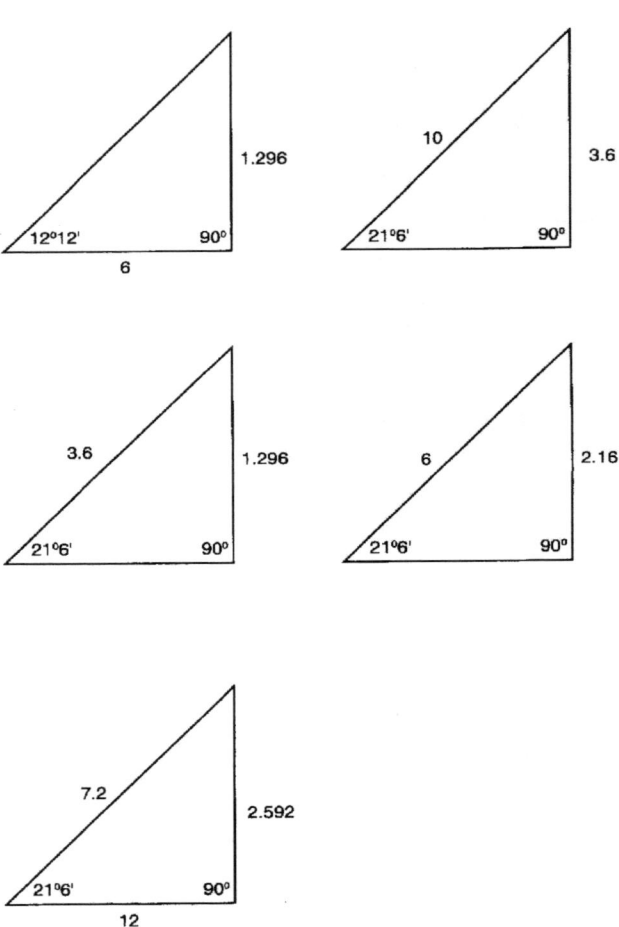

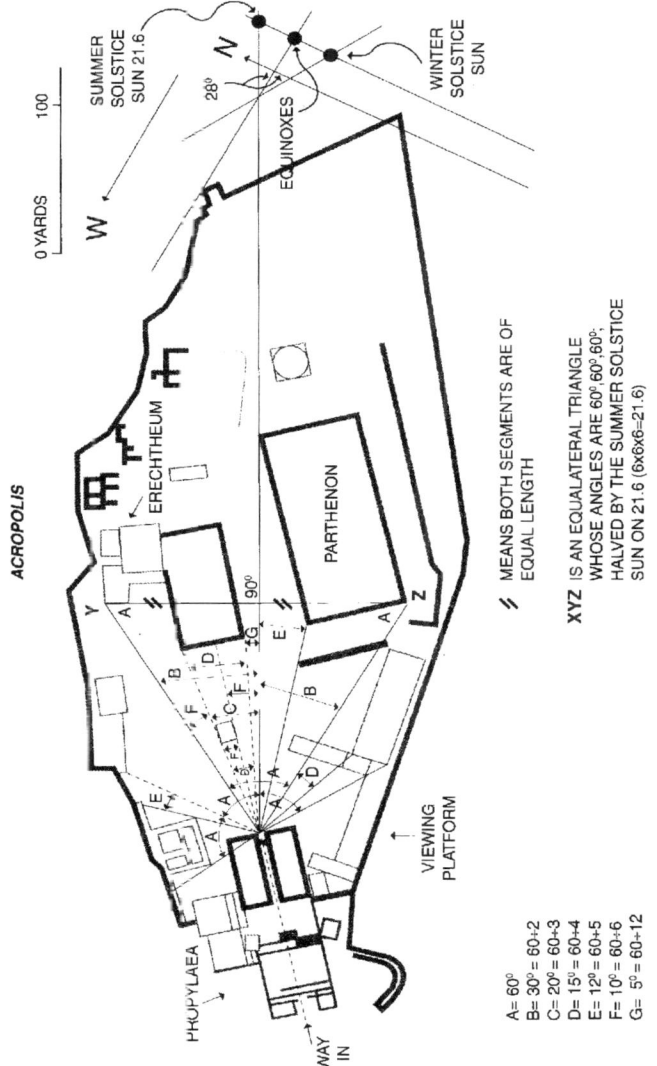

HOW WE WERE MADE

in evidence.

The angles of 36 and 54 produce a side of unity matched with the string 1.2345679, the strange inverse of 0.81; this triangle also couples a side of 54 against a hypotenuse of 6.66.

An angle of $6°$ 12" has a side of 1.296 with a slope of 12.

While $12°$ 12' puts 6 against 1.296.

$21°$ 6' is particularly productive: 10 against 3.6, 3.6 against 1.296, 6 against 2.16, and 7.2 against 2.592.

Also, remember from page 95, the angle of the north face of The Great Pyramid is $51.84°$ (which is twice the Precessional Cycle (PC) of 25,920 years - with the comma and the zero altered), and which has these attributes: cosine $51.84° = 0.618 = 1/\Phi$; sine $51.84° = 0.786 = \pi/4$; tangent $51.84° = 1.272 = \Phi^{1/2} = e - 1$. This is a unique angle.
The PC, the pyramid, Stonehenge and the 3 universal constants Φ, π and e, all stated in one angle.

While discussing angles, I have produced a plan of the Acropolis in Athens in the illustration, which shows quite clearly that the whole incredible edifice was laid out according to the number 60.

The famous Parthenon used to contain a gigantic golden statue of of the goddess Athena, whose 'number' was 60. This is the same number as the god Anu who ruled at Sumer millennia before, and the name of the building called the Erechtheum is clearly named after the city of Erech in Sumer. It looks like the gods moved west from Sumer to Greece.

The entrance to the Acropolis was (is) via the Propylaea, which looks uncannily like the barrel of a cannon pointing at the other buildings on the site, and, on reaching the mouth of this 'cannon', the viewer is presented with a panorama of structures whose corners are related to the viewer by angles of 60^0, and sub-multiples of 60, – 30, 20, 15, 12, 10, and 5 degrees. But the most impressive is that seen on the summer solstice (21.6), when the viewer, the top corner of the Parthenon, and the rising sun form a straight line. On that day an equilateral triangle is formed, with its three corners positioned at the viewer, the top corner of the Erechtheum, and the third at the bottom corner of the Parthenon. The three angles of this triangle are 60, 60 and 60. It is split down the middle by the sun's rays which form an angle of 90 degrees with its 'base' (that is, the line from the Parthenon to the Erechtheum). This produces two triangles whose angles are 30, 60 and 90 degrees, and, as we saw from above, these make for some very meaningful ratios between the sides of the triangles. Like the pyramids, and other massive buildings from the ancient world across the globe, the Acropolis is built from megalithic blocks of stone (here marble) which fit together with impossible precision. The columns of the Parthenon for example are made from blocks weighing 10 tons whose joints are one fifth of the thickness of a human hair -- and there is no mortar. The whole of the Acropolis was built, and is still standing, without the aid of a single daub of adhesive material such as cement. The entire construction is so well machined and flat-faced that all surfaces sit with one hundred per cent contact between their faces, thus ensuring absolute efficiency and stability – rendering the use of mortar irrelevant. And all done by a man with a mallet and a chisel? I think not.

There are also relationships between our number strings when expressed in a circle. It will be recalled that we are still using the circle of 360 degrees from ancient times, and I showed at the beginning that the Model Year in the past was 360 days too. What is more, the point already made about half and double ratios also applies to circles, in that the radius is half of the diameter or vice versa. Some of these circular connections are shown in the illustration below.

In discovering these ratios I have used the value of Perfect Pi for the calculation, which was the actual value of pi as used by the ancient civilisations, and so they too would have arrived at the same numbers as those shown here. They had these numbers whether we like it or not; we

HOW WE WERE MADE

might not like it, but that is just because we now know that real pi is not exactly three.

A sphere with a radius of the god's 60 (diameter 120) produces a circumference of 360, but, even more interesting is its surface area of 43,200 square units. These are four very important number strings.

A radius of 2160 (diameter 4320) produces a circumference of 12,960.

A radius of 360 (diameter 720) produces a circumference of 2160.

A diameter of 360 produces a circumference of 1080.

A radius of 4320 years produces the circumference of the Precessional Cycle of 25,920 years, which, when divided up like a clock face into 12 sections, renders each section equal to 2160 years.

A radius of 10 has a circumference of 60. We have met this relationship several times already.

A radius of of 720 produces a circumference of 4320.

A radius of unity makes a circumference of 6.

A radius of 12 has a circumference of 72.

There are others. A number of these circles may be joined as a mechanical set of cogwheels whose radii are years. These cogs, mounted as a gear train, with each having a Radius of Time, therefore also have a number of teeth around their circumference equal to a certain number of years. They are the Wheels of Time. But here, since the Wheels of Time are acting together as a rack and are, therefore, rotating in synchronism, there is a third variable. That third parameter is the speed of revolution of each Wheel of Time. The rate of turn is measured as Revolutions per Eon, where an eon is 1 Precessional Cycle of 25,920 years, as shown in the following image.

It can be seen that the Revs/Eon readouts are also part of the number string patterns, which feature so prominently in the mathematics of the ancients.

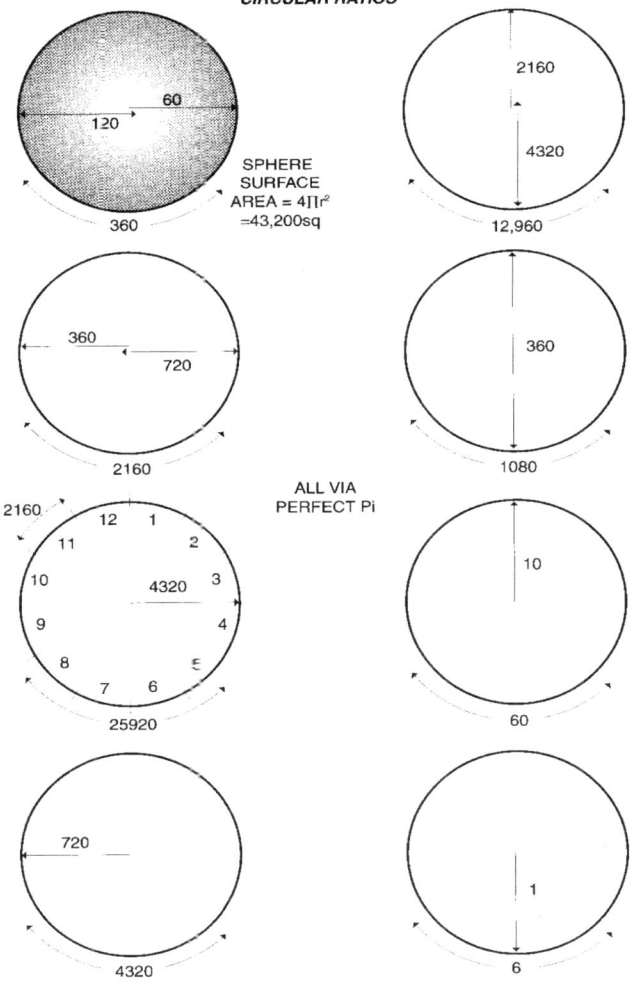

187

HOW WE WERE MADE

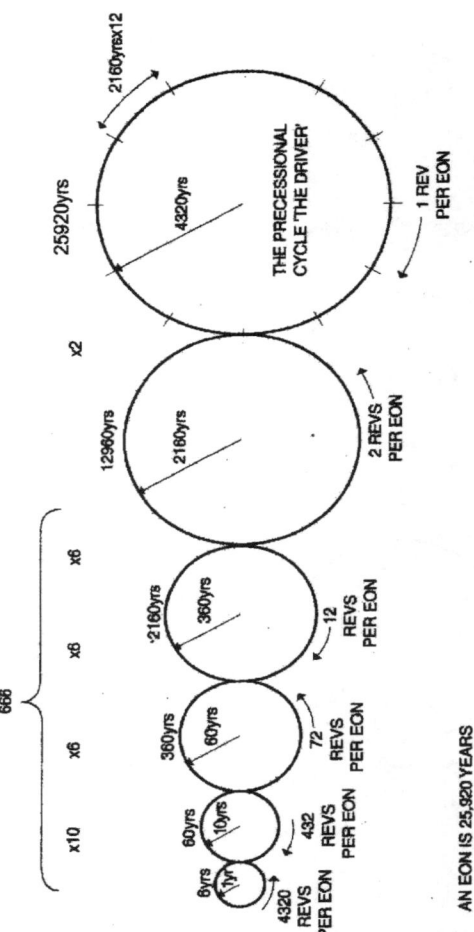

XI

CONSTANTS

We frequently read that we, and the Earth, are a carbon based life form, and doubtlessly this is the case. Without the element of carbon, life as we know it it would not exist. Carbon provides the structure for all fibres of plants and animals. These tissues are built of elements grouped around chains or rings made of carbon atoms. Carbon forms more compounds than all other elements combined. In 1961 the isotope carbon–12 was selected to replace oxygen as the standard relative to which the atomic weights of all other elements are measured. There are various types of carbon, but the most important and the most basic is the carbon atom that is called C-12, because it has 6 protons and 6 neutrons, and is symbolised as 12/6C. Here we see a direct statement that the origin of life itself is based on 6. Applying the principles that have been used throughout this book it can be seen that the neutrons and protons represent 6 x 6, which multiplies out to 36; that is, each proton can be matched against each neutron in 36 different ways (like a pair of dice, there are 36 combinations, just as there are 36 divisions on a roulette wheel, and just as there were 36 divisions on the spinning discs which sat atop of the omphalos (navel) stones at the ancient Greek oracle centres. And recall that all of the numbers from 1 to 36 add up to 666).
6 x 12 is another old favourite, 72.

There is a rather strange development associated with the ability of carbon to form other compounds, for in three cases, at least, it formed such compounds with itself. Until 1990 only two forms of pure carbon were known – diamond and graphite. The first being the hardest substance on Earth, while graphite is one of the softest! But then another was confirmed in 1990, it is carbon – 60. Actually it belongs to a class called fullurenes

HOW WE WERE MADE

which are hollow carbon compounds made up of 12 pentagonal and differing numbers of hexagonal faces. Fullerene consists of even numbers of carbon atoms with a range up to 600 atoms per molecule. The best known and studied of these fullerenes is carbon – 60, also called the Buckminsterfullerene or Buckyball. It was given that name after the eponymous architect who designed buildings in geodesic shapes like a football, and, as the C_{60} molecule looks exactly like a football, the two names were joined in 'Buckyball'. As Fuller was merely imitating the design of a football's construction, it does appear to me somewhat unfair that the designer of the football was not located so that C_{60} could be named after him, and not someone who had plagiarised his work.

C_{60} has a stunning assemblage of sixes, 60 atoms, with 6 neutrons and 6 protons per atom. This is a line-up of 666, which is quite explicitly displayed. The total number of neutrons per molecule is therefore 360, as is the number protons also 360, and their total, is then, 720. The structure of C_{60} consists of 12 pentagonal (5 sided) and 20 hexagonal (6 sided) faces. It is interesting to see that the number of atoms, at 60, is the number of points on the 12 pentagons (5 x 12), which is the same as those on the dodecahedron – if its pentagons are counted as if they were separate from the others, as I pointed out when commenting upon that shape. In addition, others which crop up are 120, 720, 108, and 540. This structure is shown in the illustration.

On Earth C_{60} occurs naturally in ancient rocks and in some soots, but it is now possible to manufacture it in mass quantities, and it is proving to be an extremely useful compound which has found a place in lubricants, in superconductors, as a radioactive shield, as a hard coating, in batteries and ball bearings. It is such a friend that they will go on finding many more uses for it, and so they should, considering its 'number' is 60, the number of the god Anu and the goddess Athena.

CARBON 60 (C60)

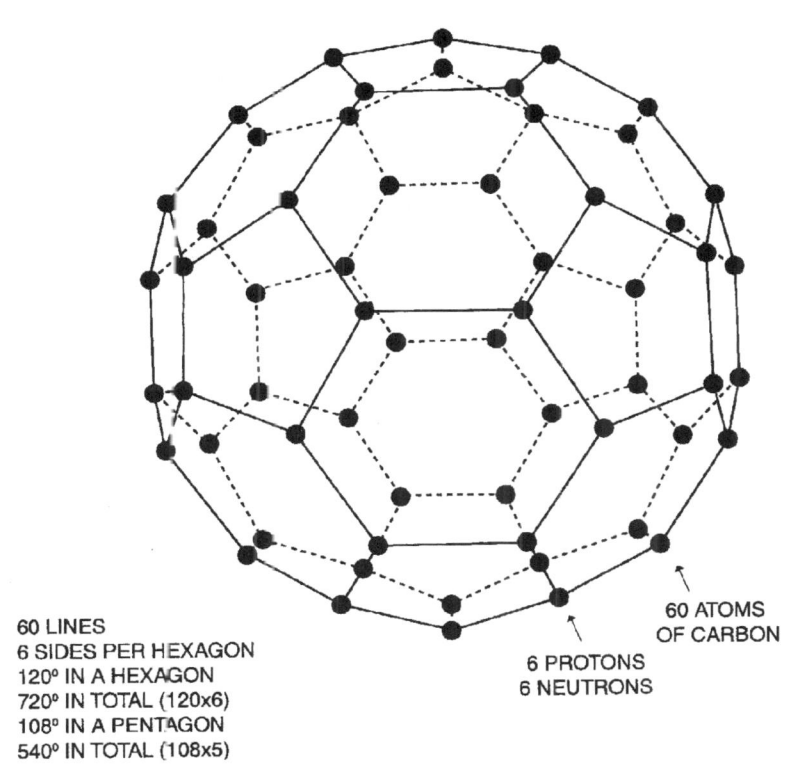

60 LINES
6 SIDES PER HEXAGON
120° IN A HEXAGON
720° IN TOTAL (120x6)
108° IN A PENTAGON
540° IN TOTAL (108x5)

6 PROTONS
6 NEUTRONS

60 ATOMS
OF CARBON

HOW WE WERE MADE

There are certain measures which have been with us since time immemorial, and others which we have invented in recent times to measure entities that have been discovered, and need a standard to gauge them by.

The four standards I have covered so far are:

Time (seconds, days etc)
Length (feet, inches etc)
Geometry (degrees, minutes, sines etc)
Plain numbers (for counting entities)

I had supposed that other parameters would have been given a rather random assignment of scales, created by discoverers and inventors so that they could allocate calibration to the variables in their newly created systems. I was then, once again, a little taken aback to learn that the scale created by Daniel Gabriel Fahrenheit in the 1700's, to measure the degree of warmth, or temperature, was not at all a random one plucked out of the air, but was in fact based on 360 degrees, 30 degrees ($1/12^{th}$ of 360 or ½ of 60), and 90 degrees – the right angle. His original plan was to take his zero point as the temperature of an equal mixture of ice and salt; he then s*elected* the freezing point of drinking water to be 30^0, and again *selected* the normal body temperature to be 90^0 (both were later revised upwards to 32^0 and 98.6^0). The next point on his scale was the boiling point of the same water, which he *selected* to be half of 360^0 away from the freezing point, ie 180^0, thereby giving it a value of 210^0 (later revised to 212). The scale could then be calibrated according to these divisions, whereby the unit of temperature is $1/180^{th}$ of the difference between the freezing and boiling points of water, which it still is today.

This meaningful scale is also being killed off by the dreaded desire for everything to be on a metric scale, in this case the centigrade (or Celsius) degree, which is far too crude to be useful. However, in some fields of engineering another temperature scale, called the Rankine is used as an absolute zero scale (favoured over the degree Kelvin, where one Kelvin is the same as one degree Celsius). One degree Rankine is equal to one degree Fahrenheit, but the absolute zero of Rankine is minus 459.67^0 F. It is favoured because Fahrenheit is a much wider scale than Celsius, and can therefore indicate to a finer degree of accuracy.

Fahrenheit's thermometer was filled with mercury which is a metal that responds well to temperature changes. Curiously, this same liquid metal was used to construct the first barometer. In the mercury barometer atmospheric pressure balances a column of mercury. Normal atmospheric pressure is about 14.7 pounds per square inch, which is equivalent to 30 inches of a mercury column. Yes, 30 inches, just as 30^0 (later 32) was to be the freezing point of water in another mercury instrument. Water, as we shall see shortly, features considerably in the divine system of number strings. Both thermometer and barometer scales are shown in the sketch.

Quartz has been a revered mineral from the dawn of time, right through to today where it is still an essential part of our lives. It is one of the most abundant on Earth, and is commonly seen as sand; each grain of sand is a piece of quartz, which is made of silicon and oxygen. It comes in many colours, but the clear transparent variety was particularly prized, it is called rock crystal. Ref 3 describes how, in the ancient past, it was used to make optical lenses, and is usually found in very small lumps, or even as crystals, and has been mistaken for diamonds; in fact this colourless pure variety is used as a gemstone. Strangely, it was, in addition, the material of the mysterious crystal skulls. As well as the clear variety there are also other colours of quartz which have different names, and most of which are classed as precious or semi-precious stones, but the most common is the milky white opaque variety called milky quartz. One type of quartz is amethyst whose transparent colours vary from deep purple to pale blue, and which Bishops wear as a ring. Others are: smoky quartz, from grey-brown to almost black; citrine, a yellow stone sometimes sold as topaz; aventurine, green-reddish; chrysoprase, light green; plasma, dark green; morion, deep brown to black; and rose quartz, a large chunk of which I bought recently for £1 in the gift shop of The University Museum in Oxford.

HOW WE WERE MADE

FAHRENHEIT'S ORIGINAL SCALE

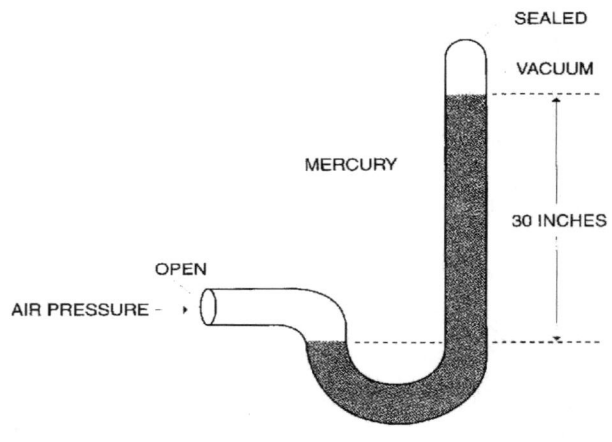

BAROMETER

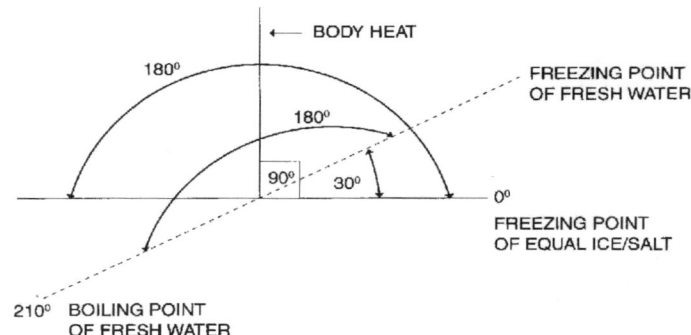

Quartz is a very hard mineral, it is number 7 on the Mohs Hardness Scale, where talc is 1 and diamond is 10. There are only a few minerals harder than quartz, and these are usually rare gems such as topaz, emerald, garnet, beryl, sapphire, the abrasive corundum, and of course diamond. This means that it is very difficult to work without the use of modern tools, particularly as it is prone to splintering. It is then difficult to understand how objects made from this mineral could possibly have been wrought to such beautiful exactness, and polish, as is evidenced from the objects they have left behind. In their book, 'The Mystery of the Crystal Skulls', Chris Morton and Ceri Louise Thomas devote considerable time and space to investigating the provenance, age and possible manufacture of several of these crystal skulls, including scientific examination of the structure of the crystal.

The most wonderful of the skulls is the 'Mitchell-Hedges' skull, found by the eponymous lady, with her father, in a Mayan pyramid in Belize in 1924. This skull is life size, including the removable lower jaw, and is made from a single piece of absolutely pure rock crystal. That such a chunk of that purity should have been available is in itself an astonishing find, but when it is realised that any sculptor today requires a block of about three times the intended volume before he starts, then it is even more confounding. This skull is not only incomparable, it is also polished to a high faultless shine – this on a very hard material, and, under a microscope, there are no signs of tool marks. Even with finely powdered quartz which, it might be argued, could have been used, there is no way that the fine indentations which mark out the teeth and other features, could have been internally so polished. The teeth, according to the above book, have an 'X' cross section and are not human.

The polishing of very hard materials is not confined to quartz, for in Egypt there are countless objects of polished granite, some of megalithic proportions, while others are of fine stone vases such as the pre-dynastic ones found by William Flinders-Petrie in the 1880's. Granite is a stone, not a mineral, and as such is a composite of several different minerals, but the major component is quartz granules; sandstone is very similar. They are therefore not given an overall hardness figure on the Mohs' scale, but any cutting and polishing would have to contend with the hardness of its matrix

HOW WE WERE MADE

of quartz.

A couple of years ago I watched a television documentary which was concerned with investigating granite statues in central America. Part of the team consisted of an English sculptor who had taken with him his kit of hardened and sharpened steel chisels for the very specific purpose of testing the local stone. They established a base camp near to where there were a number of carved granite statues, and then selected a large untouched granite boulder lying nearby. It was then agreed that he would carve this boulder into a copy of the original, while the others went off into the interior to explore for a couple of weeks before returning. This was supposed to demonstrate the methodology in the same way that modern flint knappers can copy ancient flint artefacts. After much hammering, we witnessed the sight of the steel chisels simply bouncing off the boulder without making much impact. His attempts to carve out a roundel for even one eye socket were unsuccessful, and at the end he commented that he did not know how 'they' had done it, particularly as they did not have metal tools – but, as we saw, even these had no impact. Clearly a technology at work here that we still do not comprehend. It bears repeating that granite and sandstone are mainly composed of quartz which makes them very hard stones to work, yet these are the materials of the pyramids, Stonehenge, the huge Ethiopian monuments, the colossal slabs of Baalbek, and so on all around the world.

There are, in the scheme of things, some special qualities about quartz which I need to bring out. Firstly, it is a six sided crystal, as shown in the drawing All crystals have 'axes of symmetry' passing through their structure, and quartz has 6 of these, each at 60^0 to each other. There is another axis which is perpendicular to the others. The 6 axes mean that the crystal may be rotated around the perpendicular axis in 6 different positions yet appear to look the same in all 6.

These qualities make quartz a very special material in this search for an underlying uniformity. In the time of ancient Greece quartz was given the name krystallos, which also meant ice and water, because they look the same. They believed that quartz was just another form of water which had turned to ice, and then passed through another stage to remain perpetually

QUARTZ AND ICE

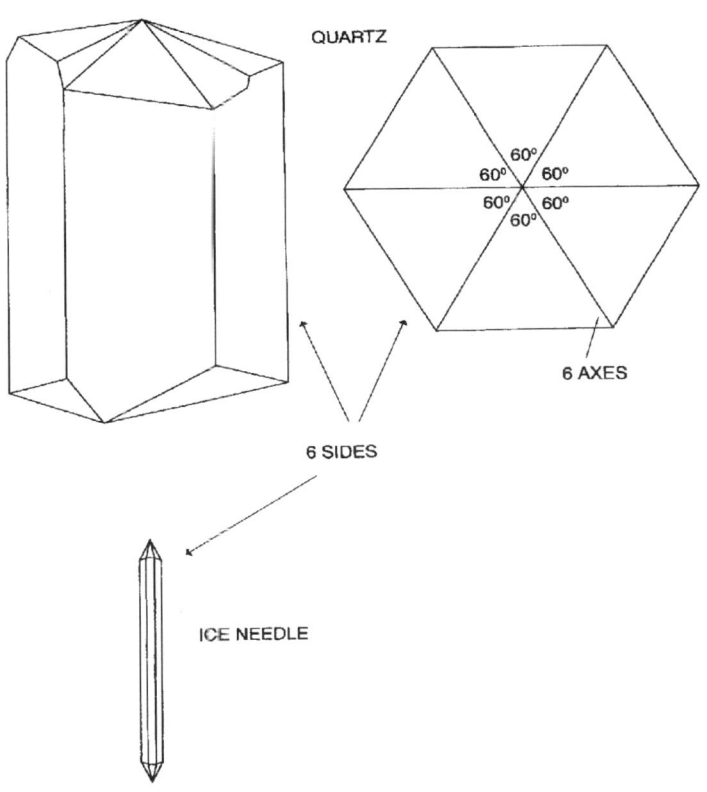

HOW WE WERE MADE

hard. But there is more to this than meets the eye, and it begs the question - were they able to study ice and water under a microscope, using perhaps quartz as lenses? The reason for this query is that water, as it begins to change into ice, goes through an initial phase whereby objects called 'ice needles' begin to form. It is only when the process goes further that these ice needles start to adhere to each other that we begin to observe what we understand to be true ice. But here is the rub, the ice needles are identical in every way to the structure of real quartz. They form 6 sided crystals because of the natural arrangement of oxygen and hydrogen atoms in the crystal. If ice starts to form in humid air, then the crystals tend to accrue speedily, to develop fronds, accumulate together and build into snowflakes. How could the Greeks have made such a connection between quartz and ice without also having the technology to observe at the microscopic level?

The snowflake is a phenomenal model of things 6, and I only mention it here for that reason, and its connection to ice and hence quartz. All of the branches come out of the centre at 60^0, and there are always 6 branches to each snowflake. All snowflakes have this identical symmetry, but all are also different from each other in more subtle ways. Furthermore, the branches or twigs, which emanate from the main ones are also at 60^0. This goes on ad infinitum, down to the minutest examination, it is always 60^0. At the centre of every snowflake are 3 concentric hexagons (6 sided figures), giving a total of 36 sides; as these are inside each other they line up as 666, as shown. The internal angles of each hexagon are split into 60^0 resulting in 12 of these per hexagon. Each hexagon has a total of 720^0 inside it, thus giving a total of 2160^0 for all three. All of the sacred number strings are here in this exquisite creation.

When a snowflake falls onto water it screams a high pitched scream. The scream comes from air pockets trapped inside the snowflake which vibrate as it crashes. But guess what? The pitch, or frequency, of the noise, is $12\ (\times 10^5)$ cycles per minute.

This is an excellent example of the concept of the fractal, discovered by Mandelbrot, which I touched upon at the beginning; in fact he based his researches on the work of the constructs contained in 'Von Koch's snowflake'. Interestingly, Von Koch's snowflake starts life as an equilateral triangle, whose three angles are 60^0, 60^0, 60^0. When this triangle is inverted and re-imposed upon itself it forms the 'Star of David'. Each point of the star, which is itself an equilateral, is then again treated in the same way. This procedure is repeatedly applied to each smaller and smaller triangle – a very simple process, but the end result is a proper snowflake, whose every tiny angle is 60^0, and which has 6 branches, just like quartz. These are shown in the the two illustrations. Three vast von Koch's snowflakes have been laid down in crops in England (to my knowledge). These were: 25 July 1997 at Silbury Hill; 8 August 1997 at Milk Hill; 16 August 1998 at Hackpen hill;. All in Wiltshire near to Avebury stone circle and large white horses cut into the chalk hills.

Quartz has also played other parts in human existence, for example it was the mystic 'crystal ball' which was used to seek out future events and personal destinies, but, like the crystal skulls it is a mystery as to how rock crystal could not only be shaped into a perfect sphere, but also polished to a high sheen. It is a material, which, like glass, is extremely hard and also brittle and inclined to shatter. With today's modern tooling equipment these works are now fairly straightforward. Robert Temple discusses crystal balls at some length in Ref 3. From his researches we learn that these objects have been found in prehistoric burial mounds in England, in the tomb of King Chalderic ll of France, and also once formed part of the Crown Jewels of England. He comments "... do not make the mistake I did of a special trip to the Tower to see the crystal-tipped sceptre, as it disappeared 350 years ago". This is a reference to the revolting Cromwell (in that he was in revolt) who did so much to destroy England, and certainly destroyed the jewels (or stole and sold them? no one knows). Temple says that there are many museums with collections of crystal balls and lenses, some of which are not recognisd as such by ignorant archaeologists, and end up instead in the geological sections. They were also well known in Greek and Roman times as he quotes several ancient references to them, but in all cases the balls and lenses already exist when discussed by the classical historians; there is never any explanation as to how they came into being.

Without quartz it is difficult to imagine how our modern world could

HOW WE WERE MADE

A TYPICAL SNOWFLAKE

SECRETS OF THE SNOWFLAKE

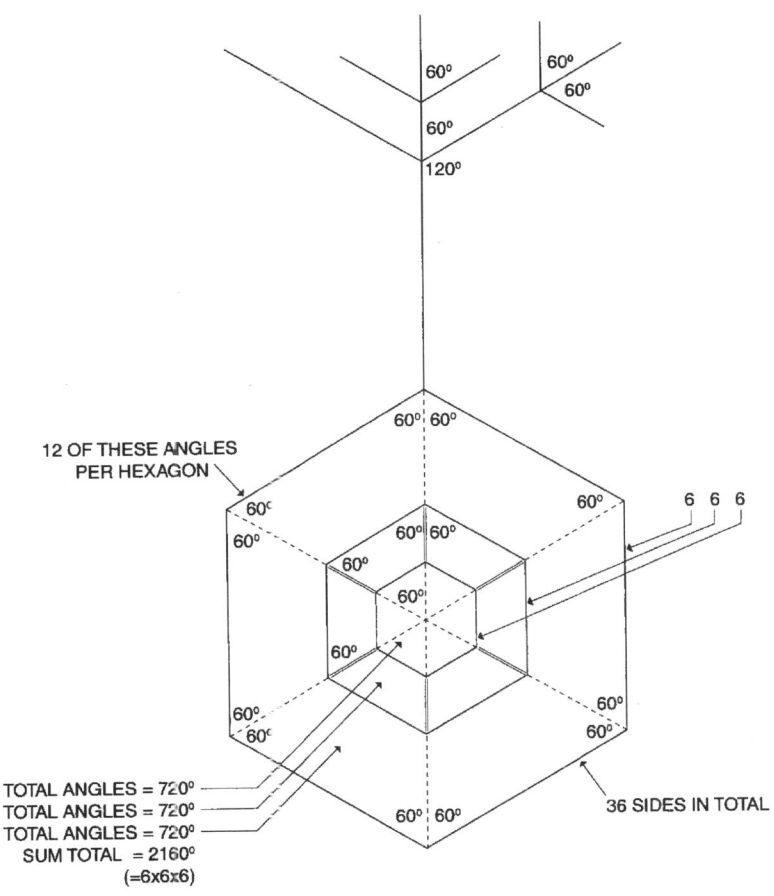

HOW WE WERE MADE

exist, for this mineral is also called sand. Without sand we would have no buildings since they require sand to make mortar to stick the bricks and stones together. The very bricks are made from a combination of clay and quartz, and some other materials as well, and, if the base of the house is one of concrete, then this too is a quartz foundation. But, just as important, is that in living inside buildings we need light to see by. Of course, today we have artificial light and so in theory could do without the sunlight inside the home, but anyone who has lived through a dark grey British winter, with the house lights on at midday, will confirm that this can be very depressing, hence the hordes of Brits who jet off to Spain or Florida every winter.

However, lacking quartz, the inside of our houses would have been in complete darkness (apart from artificial lights), for quartz is also glass, which can be made into sheets which can then provide windows to let the sunshine in, and keep the cold out. Glass is made by melting sand (quartz) and then cooling it quickly before it has time to form itself back into crystals. It is so popular with those builders of monstrous office blocks which have come to ruin the vistas of our cities, that whole buildings can be formed of glass on their exteriors, these then present colossal slabs of sheet glass to the viewer so that the whole sky appears to be walls of quartz.

So, the very fabric of our shelters is quartz; the mortar, the bricks, the concrete and the glass, allow us to construct solid, safe, and bright places in which to dwell. But quartz, as glass, is abundant: in thermometers, barometers, pressure gauges, drinking glasses, mirrors, spectacles, binoculars, microscopes, cameras, TV screens, computer screens, radio valves, light bulbs, film projectors, car headlights, and bottles. Toilet pans, WC cisterns, baths and hand basins are all coated with glass. Framed pictures may be behind glass. Power transmission lines use huge ceramic insulators. The use of glass in the laboratory is everywhere, as it is in the kitchen as cooking bowls, cups, and plates. Shop windows may display crystal chandeliers, and sell crystal bowls. As hard as quartz is, we use it on our holidays to lie in its soft warm embrace on the beach, but, when stuck to paper, it becomes a hard abrasive – sandpaper. We even use it to produce food in the form of massive greenhouses stretching over many acres.

But quartz performs an even more important function nowadays, because it governs our world through the control of time itself. Quartz possesses a phenomenon known as the *piezoelectric* effect, something that was discovered in 1880 by the Curie brothers but which remained nothing more than a curiosity (hope you got the pun) for decades. This effect is such that when a piece of quartz is subjected to physical pressure, or force, it produces electricity during the change in pressure. Conversely, if electricity is applied to its ends then it will change its physical shape. If an alternating voltage is applied then it will vibrate physically, or, if it is vibrated physically then it will produce an alternating voltage. This in itself is a quite remarkable finding, but even more so is the fact that these vibrations, either electrical or physical, are consistently *stable* – this is very important. In the field of electronics an important circuit is that of the *oscillator*, a device which is designed to produce an alternating current of a particular and fixed frequency; unfortunately, these were liable to 'wander' off the desired frequency and it was difficult to make one stable enough to meet the specified requirements. The introduction of a quartz crystal into the circuit however changed all of that, because, with its great stability it was able make the required frequency stay very close to the desired state, even though this would be different from that of the crystal. The description of how that is done in a 'negative-feedback oscillator' is far too complex to describe here, but I have shown a simple block diagram of the set-up in the sketch, along with the equivalent electrical circuit of a quartz crystal, for completeness. These, I should point out, have been in use for perhaps 50 or 60 years.

The circuits are used to control virtually all electrical equipment; television, radio, computers, mobiles, the telecoms networks and hence the Internet, video, aircraft, radar, cars, missiles, rockets, and satellites. And of course, if you glance at your wristwatch, you will probably see the word 'Quartz' on its face, unless it is an old fashioned mechanical version such as a Rolex. In a science fiction scenario, an alien race or a James Bond villain, could disable the world by causing quartz crystals to malfunction, such is its ubiquity. Quartz is also a form of silicon which is used to make transistors and integrated circuits, and so, even the circuit which the vibrating quartz crystal is controlling, is itself a form of very pure quartz.

HOW WE WERE MADE

QUARTZ AS AN ELECTRICAL COMPONENT

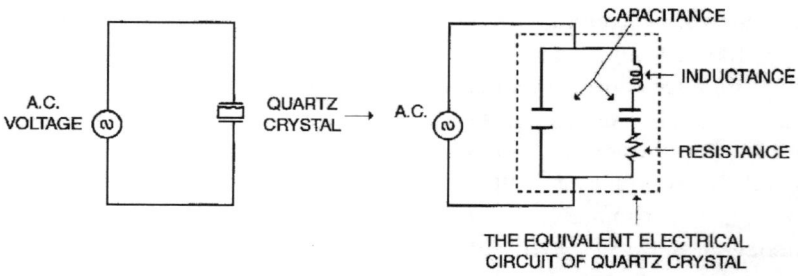

THE EQUIVALENT ELECTRICAL CIRCUIT OF QUARTZ CRYSTAL

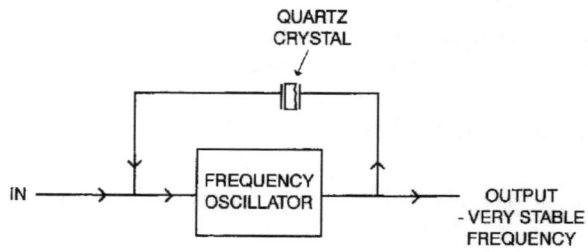

But, I have kept the best till last, for when quartz is subjected to an alternating electric field it produces a fixed oscillation at a frequency of 6 (x 10^6) cycles per 60 seconds, which is also 360 (x 10^6) cycles per 3600 seconds. So here we have a material which was once used in an hour-glass to measure the passage of time, and here it is again measuring time electronically. When used in wristwatches this frequency is reduced through integrated circuits to produce a frequency of 1 cycle per second to drive the watch, that is, 60 pulses per 60 seconds. How synchronous is that? The watch measures time in units of 60 and is controlled by a substance which is itself moving in units of 6, and the watch face is also a mirror of the Precessional Cycle's zodiacal circle in space, which I dealt with earlier.

Also, and here I was almost persuaded to believe in coincidences, is yet another bizarre thing about quartz, it melts at 3600^0 F. It may be recalled that I was surprised to find that this temperature scale was also based on the number 6, via the circle of 360^0 (6^2), in the first place. Not only the structure of quartz is based on 6, but also its vibration, and its melting temperature; and it shelters us in our homes and controls our lives via electronics.

Lastly, it will be recalled from the discussion on the PHM, that the resting pulse in a healthy individual is 60 heartbeats per 60 seconds; this is in absolute harmony with the watch on the wrist so that the quartz crystal and the heart are beating together as one. When the PHM looks at his watch he views the hands through a quartz cover.

Can anyone nominate another substance upon which we depend so much (apart from air and water)?

I have touched upon ice crystals and their 6-based construction, but ice is very special in another way too, for, in its solid form, ice is less dense (less heavy) than when it is liquid, so that when it is placed in water it floats. This is such a commonplace occurrence, even in the pub with an ice cube floating in the drink, that it is taken totally for granted. But it should not be, for water is virtually unique in the world in having this property; 99.9% of other materials do not have this facility, in that their solid form is heavier than

HOW WE WERE MADE

their liquid, so, if a lump of solid metal was to be placed in a bath of the same molten metal, then it would sink to the bottom. In technical terms water reduces its 'specific gravity' when it freezes from 1 to 91.7% of its original weight. In doing so it expands its volume, and this expansion is irresistible, which is why pipes will burst if the water inside freezes. Tests have shown that putting water into a sealed tank whose sides are of iron several inches thick, and then freezing the water, will cause the tank to be split open such is the force exerted by the ice. It expands from from 1 to 1.09 times its original volume on freezing. Conversely, water can not be compressed (although it can be pressurised).

If ice did not float then life would be very different indeed, for if ice sank then ponds and rivers would freeze from the bottom upwards, ultimately freezing the whole body of water and thus killing all life forms in the water. But, since the ice forms, and stays, on the top, this insulates the water below and prevents further heat loss through evaporation, thereby protecting the living organisms from death by freezing. This is a planned outcome, not only does the phenomenon not kill off life, it also does the opposite and saves it.

A further peculiarity about water is that its area covers a huge part of the planet's surface, and its composition is such that it is susceptible to rapid evaporation, leading to vast quantities of water vapour circulating in the air which then become dense enough to form clouds. These are then blown over dry land, and if temperature and moisture conditions are right, precipitation (rain or snow) occurs. This wets the land and provides us with drinking water, and plant life can grow. Without this circulation the land would be dry dead desert and we could not survive, but this process is in itself an astonishing accomplishment. Just think about it – a vast body of undrinkable, almost poisonous, sea water, is lifted up into the air (thus purifying it), it is then carted over to the land where it is dumped on us to keep us alive. And then it drains back into the sea. Water, as I mentioned earlier, also forms 66.6% of humans and mammals. Each cell of every mammal including humans is 66.6% water. All beautifully designed, by 'them'.

Water, although it appears to be a very simple substance, is not well understood by science and it acts in ways which defy scientific theories which are designed to predict how it should behave when subject to changes, such as those due to temperature changes. One theoretical prediction for the reaction of water to heat, is that it should boil at $360°$ F *below* the actual boiling point of $212°$ F, and this is $180°$ F above its freezing point (and note the 360 here).

Water is composed of 3 atoms (6/2), these are made up of 2 of hydrogen and 1 of oxygen. But the oxygen atom has 6 electrons in its outer shell, which, strangely, can hold 8, but which are empty unless bonded to another atom. Hydrogen has 1 electron, and so when two hydrogen atoms come upon an oxygen atom, their 2 individual electrons can bond into the 2 empty spaces in the shell of the oxygen atom, which produces a molecule of water. The bond is immensely strong, and one of the holy grails of cheap energy is trying to find an efficient way of separating these two atoms, so that we could have plentiful supplies of hydrogen gas, since there are enormous stocks of water on Earth. Like carbon, water is yet another fundamental substance essential to us, and all kinds of living forms, which is based on 6. Needless to say, there are also large quantities of oxygen present in air too. Hardly surprising then that all things 6 is the favourite number of the gods.

We have already seen how the number string 186 features in several ways, including as the speed of light, so let us now have a look at the speed of sound.

The speed of sound in air is 736.3636 miles per hour at $32°$ F, which is a pretty meaningless number apart from the collection of 36's in there; but on converting it to other units we see some familiar strings, for this is also 360 yards per second, or 21,600 yards per minute, or 1,296,000 yards per hour, or 1,080 feet per second, or 12,960 inches per second. All very well-known numbers. Incredible.

If the temperature of the air is raised to $36°$ F, then the speed of sound increases to 738.9 miles per hour. The square root of this number is 27.1828, a number string which may be remembered from an earlier encounter, for it is the universal constant 'e' – 2.71828. So, the roots of both the speeds of

HOW WE WERE MADE

light and sound have meaningful number strings.

Having discussed water in terms of its function and structure, allow me now to consider the speed of sound through it. This is usually quoted for a range of temperatures, so I have chosen to analyse it at 98.6^0 F, body temperature. At this heat the velocity is given as 3,049 miles per hour, and notice how much faster sound travels in water than in air. Once again this is a string that does not jump out and cry for attention, but on converting it to other units there are more surprises. It is 1,666.666 yards per second, or 100,000 yards per minute, or 6,000,000 yards per hour. Also 300,000 feet per minute, or 60,000 inches per second, or 3,600,000 inches per minute, or 216×10^6 inches per hour. Here again, the same old number strings.

Bringing quartz back into the picture we may also ask if there is any significance here too. Well, this one is quite spectacular. The speed of sound through quartz is 13,636.36136 miles per hour (note the plethora of 36's again) which is even faster than in water; this converts to 6666.666 yards per second. How incredible is that, bearing in mind what I said above, about quartz and the number 6. Cast your mind back to the speed of the planet, which is this figure in miles per hour. The speed also converts to 1,200,000 feet per minute, or 72,000,000 feet per hour, or 14,400,000 (12^2) inches per minute.

The relative of quartz – granite, a rock which I have commented on many times, and which had some unknown, but special, meaning to the ancients, also comes in for some special numbering.

The velocity of sound in granite is 8836.38 miles per hour, which translates to 4320 yards per second, this is twice 6 x 6 x 6; or 25,920 yards per minute (the length of the Precessional Cycle in years), or 12,960 feet per second, which is half of the cycle. It is evident that quartz on its own has one set of sacred number strings, and even when formed into a conglomerate rock like granite it is re-tuned to a different, but equally special, set of number strings, thus retaining its integrity as a carrier of the secret encoding. I have to wonder whether this speed of sound, whilst traversing through granite, is connected in any way to a possible method of working it into shapes in a manner that such a speed would facilitate. If it is subjected to a physical sound or physical vibration (not an electrical one) of 6 megahertz (MHz) (or 6×10^6 cycles per second) which travels through the granite at 12,960 feet per second, then, from the equation for wavelength (L) = speed/frequency, we obtain an L of 0.025920 inches (Precession of the Equinoxes), which is about $1/39^{th}$ of an inch, the distance between the centres of the specks of quartz which make up the granite. I do not possess the equipment necessary to find out what would happen to the granite if this was to be done, but I suspect something wonderful would take place.

The first metal that mankind was given was copper, and it was that metal from which the axe of the frozen mummy of the Alps was made; he was found in the early 1990's and dated to circa 5,000 years ago. The speed of sound through copper is 7,359.8616 miles per hour when the copper is at the boiling point of water. This rate translates to 3,600 yards per second, or 216,000 yards per minute, or 12,960,00 yards per hour, or 10,800 feet per second, or 129,600 inches per second. These figures are precisely 10 times those for air. The first three numbers here encode the number strings 6^2, 6^3, and 6^4.

Lastly, one of the greatest gifts to mankind, and one which enabled him to move out of the stone age proper, was the creation of iron, one use of which was the making of a plough that meant settled living instead of a nomadic hunter-gatherer existence. This metal too has special numbers coming out of the speed of sound through it, which is 11363.635 miles per hour. Converting again we get 333,333.33 yards per minute, or 20,000,000 yards per hour, or 16,666.66 feet per second, or 10,000,000 feet per second, or 60,000,000 feet per hour, or 20,000,000 inches per second, or 1.2×10^9 inches per minute, or 7.2×10^{10} inches per hour. Quite impressive.

I shall continue to search for those camouflaged number string secrets which have been programmed into the most essential of places. In this short presentation I have located, calculated and documented some of the areas of

HOW WE WERE MADE

time and substance which have clearly been deliberately designed with their measures hidden from sight, but which nevertheless are produced to a specific set of numbers over and over again, once they are analysed further. There must be a lot more.

Fortunately, some of the ancient measuring systems are extant, and this has allowed me to seek out and detect those which are still measured as they were in the olden days. But there must be some, such as the measuring of weight and the size of liquid volume, which were once stated in some forgotten units aligned to sacred numbers, alas now lost and an area of research in itself.

I would be grateful for any others that you may know of, or discover as a result of reading this book, and could send them to me via email at wneil@iee.org

Full recognition will be given should they be used in any future publication.

The final chapter consists of bringing together all of the number strings discovered and discussed in this book, with the reminder, once again, that we are not concerned with the decimal point or the size of the string, this is all about set patterns of number strings.

And so, what does it all mean? The only explanation which I can attach to these findings is that we, and our environment, have indeed been manufactured, in the same way that we might make a goldfish bowl and stock it with plants, water, air, food etc and then insert the goldfish. The Romans invented the Coliseum, where poor humanity (and innocent animals) was dragged from afar and made to stand there in the arena while they were tortured and butchered, with the floor awash with their blood. And the purpose of this insane behaviour? ..... erm ... entertainment! Doing on a smaller scale what the 'gods' are still doing -- to us. The ancient Greeks used to believe that we are only the playthings of the gods; here for their amusement and manipulation, an entertainment. Perhaps they walk visibly beside us, but we do not recognise them for who they are; or invisibly, due to our limited vision, existing in another part of the spectrum. We transmit radio and television pictures which are all around us and through us yet we cannot see them unless we have the right kind of receiver – a TV set, in order to decode the signals. We are receivers but are not made to see those signals. There are very many other images surrounding us but we are ignorant of them because they are invisible, due to our existence in a narrow sector of the frequency spectrum. A dog's sense of smell is 44 times greater than a human's. An eagle can see a mouse from 150 feet up. How puny we are!

Whether they are visible but unrecognised, or invisible, they are, in either case, able to influence and direct our actions. Perhaps they play games amongst themselves, with us as the game-pieces, challenging each other via human wars, human love, human invention.

Maybe Shakespeare (or whoever wrote 'his' plays) was close when he wrote, or was told to write, "All the world's a stage, and all the men and women merely players". One of their games is to give us bits of the truth, but then sit back amused by our inability to see that what we have just been told, or seen, is actually the truth, such as the line above.

HOW WE WERE MADE

XII
CONCORDANCE

	Number String & Code	Assigned to
1	$6/6$ or 6^0	Unity At moon's equator 1 nautical mile = pi ($\times 10^{-1}$) statute miles
1,111		Miles per minute, speed of Earth around Sun
10	60/5	Decimal system, human hand & feet Days per decan – Egypt Days per decan star " Sarsen trilithons at Stonehenge On the moon, ratio of circumference in nautical miles to the diameter in statute miles Minutes of longitude at the equator of the moon is pi statute miles - exactly Radius whose circumf is 60 by Perfect Pi
100		Feet, length of one second of longitude at equator Feet, " " " latitude

HOW WE WERE MADE

		Thousand feet, length of one degree of longitude at the moon's equator
		Thousand yards per minute, speed of sound through water
108	(6 x 6 x 6) x 5	
	or (6 x 6 x 6)/2	
		Square feet, area of sphere of PHM, mansphere
		Statues per road at Angkor Wat
		Degrees in the solid angles of a dodecahedron
		0.108 = sine 6^0 12" (note the 2 numbers)
1,080		Radius of moon in statute miles
		Mayan number '3 tuns', note the 3
		Circumf whose diameter is 360 by Perfect Pi
		Feet per second, speed of sound in air
10,800		Sumerian number 'sar es'
		Heraclitus's 'great year' of the Aion
		Number of stanzas in the Rigveda
		Number of bricks in the Indian fire altar

		Feet per second, speed of sound in copper
108,000		Sumerian number 'sar u es' Miles per hour, orbital velocity of Mercury
1,080,000		Sumerian number 'sargal-ia'
10,800,000		" " 'sargal-u-ia'
12	6 x 2	Years of Jupiter's revolution Phalanges in fingers (not thumbs) Inches from head to centre (see diagram) Length of shod foot Stone in weight Ribs per side On a jury Inches per foot Lunar cycles Months per year Menstrual cycles per year Signs of the zodiac Hours per day Hours per night Numerals on a clock face Pence per shilling Units per dozen Dozen per gross Fruits on the tree of life Disciples Knights of Round Table (initially) Eggs per carton

HOW WE WERE MADE

	/	Gates in the Holy City
	1	Angels per gate
All in the	1	Tribes
Holy City	1	foundations
	1	Names of the apostles
	\	Thousand stadia, its measure

Sun's speed towards Vega in miles per second

Base of Bode's law series for planetary distances

Pentagons in a dodecahedron (Greek model of the Universe)

Minutes in the equality Sin 6^0 12" = 0.108, unites all 3

Degrees & minutes in Tan 12^0 12" = 0.216, highly symbolic

Intervals in an octave

In several triangles, unites more number strings (see diagram)

As carbon – 12, the basis of life, called 12/6 C

Pentagons in carbon – 60, the fullerene

Times 10^6 Hertz, the scream of a crashing snowflake

Sothic cycles of 1,460 yrs in pre-dynastic Egypt

Times 10, days per season – Egypt

stone weight of the PHM

Jesus can call up 12 legions of angels (legion of 6000)

Radius whose circumf is 72 by Perfect Pi

Number of protons & neutrons in Carbon 12

		Times 108 , inches per minute, speed of sound in iron
120		Life of man, as per Genesis 6 Gilgamesh to cut this many poles for an ark
12^2		Mayan number '1 baktun' Hours, is 518,400 seconds – 20 Precessional Cycles in years Times 10,000 inches per minute, speed of sound in quartz Hours in 6 days, to create the world Times ten, minutes in one day
1,200		Hindu number 'kaliyuga' , divine years Inches per second of latitude
120,000		Yards per degree of latitude
1,200,000		Feet per minute, speed of sound in quartz
1228	(66 x 18.6) (186,281 is the speed of light)	Miles per hour, orbital velocity of Neptune

HOW WE WERE MADE

1,296	(6 x 6 x 6) x 6	
		Perimeter of square of PHM multiplied out, mansquare
		Miles per minute, orbital velocity of Venus
		Divided by 2^4, gives 81, the Earth's mass is 81 times that of moon. Further, $1/81 = 0.012345679012345679$ recurring
12,960		One half of the Precessional Cycle
		Feet in 4320 yards, see this number below
		In miles, circumference of Earth's core, by Perfect Pi
		Inches per second, speed of sound in air
		Feet per second, speed of sound in granite
129,000		Inches per second, speed of sound in copper
1,296,000		Sumerian number 'sargal-as'
		Mayan number '9 baktuns'
		" " '36 tuns'
		Hindu number 'tretayuga', human years
		Number of seconds in a circle
		50 Precessional cycles in years

		Yards per hour, speed of sound in air
12,960,000		Sumerian number 'sargal-su-nu-tag'
		Mayan number '3,600 tuns', note this number
		Hindu number '10 tretayugas', also 36,000 divine years
		500 Precessional Cycles in years
		Yards per hour, speed of sound in copper
129,600,000		Feet, the polar circumference of Earth
		10 'sargal-su-nu-tags'
		5000 Precessional Cycles in years
142.6	(6 x 6 x 6) x 66	Millions of miles, distance from Sun of Mars
15,120	(6 x 6 x 6) x 70	Miles per hour, orbital velocity of Uranus
1,728	(6 x 6 x 6) x 8	Cubic inches in one cubic foot
17,280		66.6% of the Precessional Cycle of 25,920 years

HOW WE WERE MADE

1,728,000		Hindu number 'kritayuga', human years – the golden age and 4,800 god years
17,280,000		6 Pictuns (Mayan)
1.728×10^{12}		Cubic stadia in the Holy City (note the 10 & 12 here)
180	(6 x 6 x 6) x 5/6	Millions of miles, distance from the Sun of Uranus
216	(6 x 6 x 6)	The key
21. 6		21st June, Midsummer's day, the summer solstice
		Time in minutes for the PHM to walk exactly 1 mile
		In degrees, the tilt of earth's axis
		In degrees, the tropic of Cancer
		In degrees, the tropic of Capricorn
		In degrees, the arctic circle down from pole
		In degrees, the antarctic circle up from the pole (the 5 above are during the 'ice age')
		As degrees, is also 21^0 36' and 21^0 2160", note number strings
		As degrees, lat., distance between Stonehenge & Giza pyramid
		Miles per second, orbital velocity of Venus

21 - 6	21st of each month, 6 months apart, for solstices & equinoxes
216	Square feet, area of cube of PHM, mancube
	Bones in a human
	Inch circle of the PHM, with Perfect Pi, mancircle
	Cubic feet in one cubic fathom
	Million years for the sun to revolve around the galaxy
	Cosine 216^0 = cosine 36^0 = 0.81 (1/81 is ratio of earth-moon)
	Sine 21^0 6' = 0.36
	0.216 = tangent 12^0 12"
	Million inches per hour, speed of sound in water
2,160	Diameter of moon in statute miles
	Years for sign of zodiac to change
	Mayan number '6 tuns', note the 6
	2,160 BC, carbon dating of Stonehenge Silbury Hill, and the dawning of the age of Aries the Ram
	The duration of the Christian era in years, under Pisces
	AD, the dawning of the Age of Aquarius
	In miles, radius of Earth's core
	Seconds is 6 hours – half a day
	Degrees in total of solid angles in a dodecahedron
	Radius (diameter 4,320), with circumf. 12,960 by Perfect Pi
	Circumf of circle of radius 360 by

HOW WE WERE MADE

	Perfect Pi
	Degrees total in hexagons in every snowflake (see sketch)
	In ratio to gravity shell of 3,600 miles, gives 60:10
21,600	Sumerian number 'sar as'
	Minutes in a full circle
	Area in square fathoms of Utnapishtim's cube - Sumeria
	Circumference of Earth in nautical miles
	In miles, circm. of Earth-moon gravity system by Perfect Pi
	Circumference of the moon in nautical miles
	Miles per hour, orbital velocity of Saturn
	Yards per minute, speed of sound in air
	In ratio to the Precessional Cycle of 25,920 years, gives 10:12
216,000	Sumerian number 'sargal'
	Volume in cubic fathoms of Utnapishtim's cube – Sumeria
	Miles, the nearest s to s distance moon to Earth
	Yards per minute, speed of sound in copper
2,160,000	Sumerian number 'sargal-u-ia'

24	(6 x 6 x 6)/9	
		Hours in full day
2,400		Hindu number 'dvaparayuga', divine years
2,592	(6 x 6 x 6) x 12	
		Million months for the Sun to revolve around the galaxy in a Cosmic Year
25,920		Length of Precessional Cycle in years

One quarter of this in miles, is exactly the circumference of the moon in statute miles by Perfect Pi
Circumf whose radius is 4,320 by Perfect Pi
Yards per minute, speed of sound in granite
Multiplied by e and π, distance c to c Earth to moon at perigee
In ratio to 21,600, gives 10:12
Twenty of these is 518,000 years, which is the number of
seconds it took 'to create the earth', 6 days, and the number of minutes in the Model Year

HOW WE WERE MADE

279.936	(6 x 6 x 6) x (6 x 6 x 6) x 6) /1000	Millions of miles, distance from Sun of exploded planet Ceres
2,799	" /100	Millions of miles, distance from Sun of Neptune
	This number string is also 216 x 1296 & very special indeed	
29,160	(6 x 6 x 6) x 135	Miles per hour, orbital velocity of Jupiter
3	6/2	The ancients' Perfect Pi
Weeks per month – Egypt
Seasons per year   "
Feet per yard
Feet radius of sphere of PHM, with Perfect Pi, mansphere
Three headed dogs guarding Gymir's home
Atoms in water molecule
30		Demigods, to start of dynastic Egypt
Days per month – Egypt
X holes at Stonehenge
Y holes at Stonehenge
Upright sarsen trilithons at Stonehenge
Degrees, occupied by each zodiac

		sign
		Number of scalene triangles per pentagon
		30^0 Fahrenheit, originally assigned freezing point of water
		30 inches of mercury in a barometer
300,000		Feet per minute, speed of sound in water
36	(6 x 6 x 6)/6	Sum of numbers 1 to 36 = 666
		Highest number of factors, & a square root, for any 2 digit number
		Decans per year – Egypt
		Constellations to match the decans
		Sumerian number 'es u'
		Inches in one yard
		Post holes in second circle at Woodhenge (4 missing)
		Inch stride of the PHM
		Inch reach of the arms of the PHM
		Inch waist of the PHM
		Inch division of the body of the PHM into two
		Million miles, Mercury from Sun
		Cosine 36^0 = cosine 216^0 = 0.81 (1/81 is Earth -moon ratio)
		0.36 = sine 21^0 6'
		36^0 is same string as 360
		Combinations of a pair of dice
		Divisions on a roulette wheel

HOW WE WERE MADE

360   Divisions on omphalos wheels at the Greek oracles
Days in the Model year
Degrees in a circle
Daylight hours per decan – Egypt
Nighttime hours per decan   "
Sumerian number 'ges as'
Mayan number '1 tun'
Hindu number for human years equal to 1 divine year
Feet – the sides of Utnapishtim's cube, Sumeria
Degrees longitude
Degrees latitude
Miles per minute, orbital velocity of Saturn
Number of scalene triangles per dodecahedron
Circumference of sphere whose radius is 60, by Perfect Pi
Diameter whose circumf is 1080 by Perfect Pi
Number of protons per molecule in carbon-60
   "   neutrons "   "
Million cycles per hour, the frequency of quartz
Yards per second, speed of sound in air
$1/360^{th}$ is width of one degree of longitude at equator, actual width is 365.22 (x 10^3) feet – the year

3,600		Seconds per hour
		Sumerian number 'sar'
		Heartbeats per hour in a healthy PHM
		Hindu number 'tretayuga', divine years
		Seconds in a circle
		Seconds in an hour
		Years, for conjunctions of Jupiter & Saturn to repeat exactly
		In miles, radius of Earth-moon gravity system
		In nautical miles, radius of Earth by Perfect Pi
		Degrees Fahrenheit, the melting point of quartz
		Yards per second, speed of sound in copper
		In ratio to 2,160 gives 60:10
36,000		Sumerian number 'sar u'
		Hindu number '10 tretayugas', divine years
360,000		Feet per degree of latitude
3,600,000		Inches per minute, speed of sound in water
432	(6 x 6 x 6) x 2	Square root of the speed of light (186,281 miles/sec)

HOW WE WERE MADE

4,320	As yards, 12,960 feet
	Radius whose circumf is 25,920 by Perfect Pi
	Circumf whose radius is 720 by Perfect Pi
	Yards per second, speed of sound in granite
43,200	In years, time to move from max to min of earth's tilt
	Heartbeats per 12 hours in a healthy PHM
	In days, Mayan number 6 katuns, note the 6
	1:43,200 is ratio of height & perimeter of Giza pyramid to radius and circumference of Earth
	Surface area of sphere whose radius is 60, by Perfect pi
	Miles per hour, Sun's speed towards star Vega
	Seconds in a 12 hour day
432,000	Sumerian number 'sargal-min'
	Hindu number 'kaliyuga', human years
	Berossus' 'great year'
	Number of Einherie, the valiant dead, in Valhalla
	Number of syllables in Rigveda

4,320,000		Sumerian number 'sargal-u-min' Hindu number 'mahayuga', human years Inches, per degree of latitude
43,200,000		Yards, polar circumference of Earth
4,320,000,000		Hindu number 'kalpa' Age of the Earth in years
482	(6 x 6 x 6) x 12 x 18.6 (speed of light is 186,281)	Millions of miles, distance from Sun of Jupiter
5	60/12	
0.5		Multiplied by the Precessional Cycle, gives 12,960 (see above)
500		As 500 million inches, the polar diameter of Earth Precessional Cycles, giving 12,960,000 years – the Sumer number 'sargal-su-nu-tag'-
5000		Precessional Cycles, giving 129,600,000 Sumer number of 10 'sargal-su-nu-tags'
54	(6 x 6 x 6)/4	One quarter of 6 x 6 x 6 Statues on each side of the roads at Angkor Wat Thousand miles per hour, orbital

HOW WE WERE MADE

		velocity of Mars
		Degrees in 2 angles of the scalene triangles of a dodecahedron
		In a right angle triangle, the complement of 36^0
		Sine $54^0 = 0.81$ (1/81 is ratio of Earth-moon mass)
		The ratio 54:66 = 0.8181818181
		The ratio 54:90 (degrees) is the ratios 6:10 & 216:360
		The ratio 36:54 (degrees) is 0.666
540		Gates in Valhalla
		Statues in total in the roads at Angkor Wat
		Degrees, internal, of a pentagon
6	6	A Perfect Number (see text)
		A triangular number, whose 3 angles are 60, 60, 60 degrees
		The number base of Sumer, called 'as'
		Kings die inc. Eric Bloodaxe at Stainmore
		Rings of wooden circles at Woodhenge
		Rings at Mount Pleasant, another treehenge
		Feet, height of the Paradigm Human male
		Parts of humans, 2 legs, 2 arms, 1 trunk, 1 head
		Openings in the head, 2 ears, 2 eyes, 1 mouth, 1 nose
		Bones in both arms

Feet cube enclosing PHM, mancube
Feet per fathom
Decks in Utnapishtim's ark
Thousand feet, width of one minute of longitude at equator
Thousand feet, "   " of latitude
Earth's gravity is 6 times the moon's
Minutes is 360 seconds
Hours is 2160 seconds
Days is 12^2 hours
Miles per second, orbital velocity of Saturn
Protons & 6 neutrons in Carbon 12, 12/6C, 'the basis of life on Earth'
Ditto, for carbon-60
Spots on a die
Sides to a quartz crystal
Axis "   "   "
Sides to an ice needle
Branches to every snowflake
Sided hexagons, 3 of at centre of every snowflake
Million cycles per minute, the frequency of quartz
Electrons in outer shell of oxygen atom
Million yards per hour, speed of sound in water
Days, is 518,400 seconds = 20 Precessional Cycles in years

HOW WE WERE MADE

60
    Also the number of Sumer, called 'ges'
    The 'number' of the god Anu, chief in Sumer
    The 'number' of Athena, goddess in Athens
    Heartbeats per 60 seconds in a healthy PHM
    Seconds per minute
    Minutes per hour
    Minutes per second
    Seconds per degree
    Dogs' heads guarding Gymir's home
    Years conjunction of Saturn and Jupiter
    Aubrey Holes at Stonehenge (only 56 located)
    Bluestones at Stonehenge
    Stones in the Rollright stone circle
    Post holes in outer circle at Woodhenge
    Plethora of 60's in the Black Sea 'Stonehenge'
    Year sigui period of the Dogon people
    Bones in both legs
    Fathoms cubed in the ark (cube) of Utnapishtim -Sumeria
    Nautical miles, width of 1 degree latitude
    Times the radius of Earth, is mean distance to moon, c to c
    Percent of the moon's surface can be seen from Earth

Gilgamesh to cut poles of this
length in cubits for a boat
Degrees, the Acropolis is laid out
in sub multiples of 60^0
Radius of sphere, producing
circumference of 360, & surface
area of 43,200 square units, by
Perfect Pi
Circumf whose radius is 10 by
Perfect Pi
Carbon-60, the fullerene, with 60
atoms per molecule, 6 protons & 6
neutrons
Millions of miles, distance from
Sun of Jupiter
Degrees to the 6 axes of a quartz
crystal
Degrees to the 6 branches of every
snowflake
3 60^0 angles in equilateral triangle
& the basis of 'von Koch's
snowflake'
Thousand inches per second, speed
of sound in water
Million feet per hour, speed of
sound in iron

66   66

66 feet x 660 feet is one acre
Length of cricket pitch in feet
As 6.6, the miles per hour a PHM
can comfortably jog
The number of feet used to
measure the USA, by T Jefferson
Times 10^{-2}, miles per second,

HOW WE WERE MADE

660,000		speed of moon around the Earth
		In inches per hour, rotation of moon on its axis
666	666	
		The Key to 216
		The sum of all the numbers between 1 & 36
		Line up of hexagons in centre of every snowflake (see illustration)
66.6		As a percent, the weight of water in the PHM
		As a percent, the area of water on Earth during the 'ice age'
		Million miles, Venus from Sun
0.666		Gilgamesh is two thirds god
		The ratio 36:54 degrees, complements of each other in triangle
		The ratio 60:90 (Sumer number base to 90^0)
		Natural frequency relationship in music (see text)
		As a fraction of the Precessional Cycle of 25,920 yrs, it is 17,280. The Holy City is 1.728×10^{12} cubic stadia
66,660		Miles per hour, orbital velocity of Earth
6666.666		Yards per second, speed of sound in quartz

66,666,666		Precessional Cycles of 25,920 years, which is 1.728×10^{12} cubic stadia in the Holy City. 1,728 cubic inches in 1 foot
72	(6 x 6 x 6) x 1/3	Inches, the height of the PHM Inches per fathom Years to move one degree of the Precessional Cycle Degrees in crest angles of scalene triangles in a dodecahedron Circumf whose radius is 12 by Perfect Pi Times 10^9 inches per hour, speed of sound in iron
720		Miles per minute, Sun's speed towards star Vega Radius whose circumf is 4,320 by Perfect Pi Number of neutrons & protons per molecule in carbon-60 Degrees per hexagon in every snowflake
7,200		Mayan number '1 katun'
72,000		Inches per minute of latitude Jesus can call up this many angels
72,000,000		Feet per hour, speed of sound in quartz
77760	(6 x 6 x 6) x 360	Miles per hour, orbital velocity of Venus

HOW WE WERE MADE

864	(6 x 6 x 6) x 4	
8640		Hours in the Model Year
86,400		Seconds in a day
864,000		Hindu number 'dvaparayuga', in human years
86,400,000,000		Hindu number 'mahakalpa', & possible age of our galaxy
9	(6 x 6 x 6) /24	Stones of water in the PHM Months in the womb Times does Skirnir ride around Gymir's home Each row at Angkor Wat has a 9 headed serpent
90		Days between each equinox and solstice in the Model Year Degrees per right angle The ratio 60:90 is 0.666 (Sumer number base:90^0) 90^0 Fahrenheit, originally assigned to body temperature
907	((6 x 6 x 6) x 42)/10	Millions of miles, distance from Sun of Saturn

The escape velocity from Earth is 24,979 miles per hour, compared to Earth's circumference of 24,902 miles, a difference of only 0.31%.

The polar diameter of Earth is 500 million inches.

One degree of longitude at the equator is 365.22 feet (x 10^3), which encodes the length of the year of 365.25 days. As this is $1/360^{th}$ of the circumference of Earth it also encodes the length of the Model Year; that is, one degree of longitude encodes both the actual year and the Model Year simultaneously.

The ratio of the circumferences of Earth/moon is also 365.7 (x 10^{-2}).

The square root of the speed of sound, in air at 36^0 F - 738.9 miles per hour is 27.1828, which is 'e' times 10.

---------------- || ------------

As for the number string 186:

186,000 miles per second is the speed of light (actual quoted speed varies according to which book of reference is consulted, but is sometimes given as around 186,281, an error on 186,000 of 0.15%, which is insignificant. Take your pick as to which reference source you use).

18.6 is the 18.6 year Saros cycle of the moon.

When the above decimal point is replaced by a multiplication sign, we have 18 x 6, which is 108. This is one half of 6 x 6 x 6.

I have discovered that real pi is related to the speed of light in the equation pi = $^{6/2}\sqrt{(186,000/6)}$ ie the cube root. This equation gives pi = 3.141 (x 10^{+1}). Pi statute miles, 3.141 (x 10^{-1}), is one minute of longitude at the

HOW WE WERE MADE

moon's equator, while all of its minutes of latitude are pi miles too; and the moon has a great cycle (the Saros) of 18.6 years, which is another connection between the two number strings. One square minute at the moon's equator is pi^2 statute square miles, and the circle inscribed in this square has a circumference of pi^2 statute miles (not square miles).

The square root (the $6/3^{th}$ root) of 186,281 is 432 (to 3 significant figures) which is twice 6.6.6 .

The Sun is moving around its galactic centre at 186 miles per second.

18.6 x 5 is 93 (million) miles, the average distance of the Earth from the Sun.

186 (actually 18.52) miles per second is the orbital velocity of Earth around the Sun.

--------------- ll ------------

About $51.84°$, the slope angle of the north face of the Great Pyramid. This is tied to the Precessional Cycle of the Equinoxes as follows:

$51.84°$
51,840 years – twice the Precessional Cycle of the Equinoxes of 25,920 years

Here the decimal point and the comma are interchangeable, as are the zero and the degree sign.

Cosine $51.84°$ = 0.618 = $1/\Phi$ ($\Phi = 1.618$)

Sine $51.84°$ = 0.786 = $\pi/4$ = $\sqrt{(1/\Phi)}$ [$\pi/4$ radians = $45°$, the angle of the diagonals across the base of the pyramid!]

Tangent $51.84°$ = 1.272 = $\sqrt{\Phi}$ = $e - 1$ [$e = 2.72$]

This angle of $51.84°$ is nothing less than remarkable.

The above important equalities are my own discoveries.

--------------- || ------------

Cosine $216°$ = Cosine $36°$ = 0.81
(The moon's diameter is 2160 miles and
1/81 is the ratio of Earth-moon mass)

Don't $216°$
and 2160 miles or years
look the same?

The gods have used this device before; remember that the slope angle of the Great Pyramid is tied to the Precessional Cycle in the same way:

$51.84°$
51,840 years.

Sine $21° 6'$ = 0.36

also

Sine $6° 12''$ = 0.108
(in this one the numbers 6, 12 and half of 216 are joined)

plus

Tangent $12° 12''$ = 0.216

The connections, via geometry, of the key numbers of 6, 12, 216, 108, 36 and 81 are quite extraordinary.

HOW WE WERE MADE

Sine 6^0 12" = 0.108
(in this one the numbers 6, 12 and half of 216 are joined)

Further, from Professor Stecchini (Ref 19, p. 377), we have:

$$\sin 18^0 = \cos 72^0 = 1/2\Phi$$
$$\sec 36^0 = \csc 54^0 = 2/\Phi$$
$$\sin 54^0 = \cos 36^0 = \Phi/2$$
$$\sec 72^0 = \csc 18^0 = 2\Phi$$

Recall that:
$18 = 6.6.6/12$
$36 = 6.6.6/6$
$54 = 6.6.6/4$
$72 = 6.6.6/3$

We are looking at the design specifications of the 'gods'.

Ratio of: Earth statute miles/Earth nautical miles = 24,901.55/21,000

= 1.15

= π/e

Escape velocity from Earth = 24,979 miles/hour }
}
Equatorial circumference of Earth = 24,902 miles }

Ratio of: Moon's equator in statute miles/moon's equator in nautical miles

$$= 6785.8401/21{,}600$$

$$= 3.141592 \, (\times 10^{-1})$$

$$= \pi$$

Ratio of: Moon nautical miles/Earth nautical miles ($\times 10^{-1}$)

(when both are stated in statute miles)

$$= 0.3141/0.1153$$

$$= 2.72$$

$$= e$$

Both moon and Earth designed to universal constants!!! - And highly connected to each other. These too are my own discoveries.

HOW WE WERE MADE

TABLE OF CONCORDANCE

	6^1	6^2	6^3	6^4	6^5	6^6	6^7	66
x 1	6	36	216	1296	7776		279936	
x 2	12	72	432	2592				
x 3	18	108	648					
x 4	24	144	864					
x 5	30	180	1080					
x 6	36	216	1296					
x 7			1512	9072				
x 8	48		1728					
x 9	54							
x 12			2592					
x 18.6								1228
x 24			5184					
x 66			142.6					
x 2 x 18.6				482				
x 1/9	0.666							

242

Addendum

I came across another startling fact about the location of Stonehenge, too late to include in the main body of the book, but felt that it was too good to leave out, and so I include it here as an addendum.

This is not my finding and is known of in the ley lines community. Stonehenge is connected to two other ancient monuments in this area of England, sometimes called the 'enchanted land' because of the plethora of all kinds of buildings from the ancient past, and also because of the large number of highly intricate crop glyphs, or crop circles, which appear regularly each year. Many folk believe that there is a connection between the two. Crop glyphs always 'come down' near an ancient site, or near to one of the many whites horse figures carved into the chalk hills.

One of the sites is Old Sarum, a colossal prehistoric hill fort, later the site of a Norman castle and cathedral. These were afterwards abandoned and a new cathedral was built 2 miles down the road in Salisbury. The other point of the triangle is on Grovely Castle, another prehistoric hill fort and high point.

The connection is with an equilateral triangle which has sides that are 6 miles in length, presenting the number 666. The three angle are of course 60^0, 60^0, 60^0, A double line up of the number. The map is overleaf.

The right-hand line of the triangle is also a ley line; this is a straight line connecting Stonehenge, Old Sarum, Salisbury Cathedral, a ruined chapel to the south, Clearbury Ring and Franckenbury Camp. All ancient.

HOW WE WERE MADE

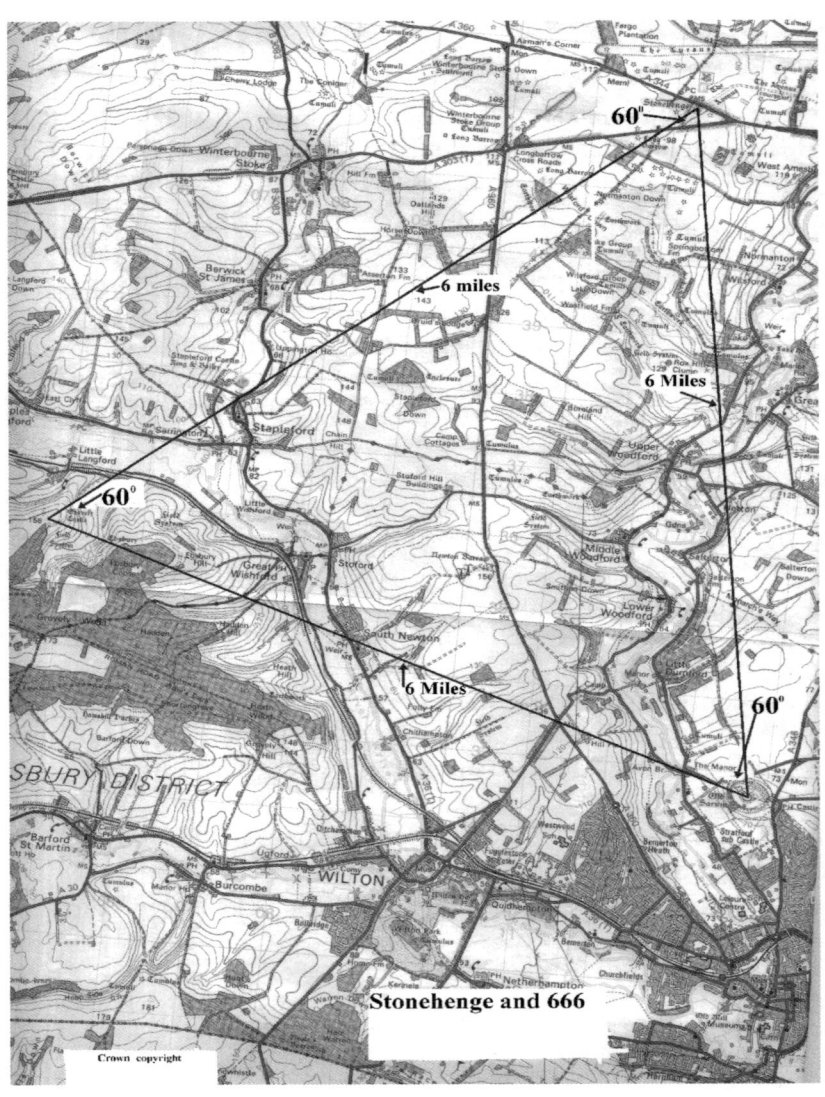

REFERENCES

1. Santillana, Professor Giorgio de, & Dechend, Professor Hertha von. *Hamlet's Mill*, David R Godine, Jaffrey, New Hampshire, 1999.
2. Rohl, David. *Legend,* Century, London, 1998.
3. Temple, Robert. *The Crystal Sun,* Century, London, 2000.
4. Aldred, Cyril. *The Egyptians*, Thames & Hudson, London, 1987.
5. Shaw, Ian, and Nicholson, Paul. *British Museum Dictionary of Ancient Egypt,* BCA, London, 1995.
6. Sitchin, Zecharia. *When Time Began*, Avon Books, New York, 1993.
7. Ifrah, Georges. *The Universal History of Numbers,* Harvill, London, 1998.
8. Temple, Robert. *The Sirius Mystery,* Arrow, London, 1999.
9. Ashe, Geoffrey. *Mythology of the British Isles*, Methuen, London, 1993.
10. Jones, Professor Gwyn. *A History of the Vikings*, OUP, Oxford, 1973.
11. Burl, Aubrey. *The Stone Circles of the British Isles,* Yale University Press, London, 1977.
12. Gimpel, Jean. *The Medieval Machine,* Pimlico, London, 1992
13. Ruduax, Lucien, and Vaucouleurs, G. De. *Larousse Encyclopedia of Astronomy,* Paul Hamlyn, London, 1966
14. Sitchin, Zecharia. *The Wars of Gods and Men*, Avon Books, New York, 1985.
15. Bauval, Robert and Hancock, Graham. *Keeper of Genesis*, Mandarin, London,1997.
16. *Encyclopedia Britannica*, Deluxe Millennium Edition, 3 CD ROM Set, 2000.
17. Hancock, Graham. *Fingerprints of the Gods*, Mandarin, London, 1996.
18. Thiel, Rudolf. *And There Was Light*, Andre Deutsch, London, 1958.
19. Stecchini, Professor Livio Catullo. In the Appendix to Tompkins, Peter. *Secrets of the Great Pyramid*, Penguin, Harmondsworth, 1978.
20. Stirling, William. *The Canon,* (1st pb. 1897), Garnstone Press Ltd, London, 1974.

HOW WE WERE MADE